KT-134-558

TOTAL QUALITY MANAGEMENT
IN THE PUBLIC SECTOR

TOTAL QUALITY MANAGEMENT IN THE PUBLIC SECTOR

An international perspective

**Colin Morgan and
Stephen Murgatroyd**

Open University Press
Buckingham · Philadelphia

Open University Press
Celtic Court
22 Ballmoor
Buckingham
MK18 1XW

and
1900 Frost Road, Suite 101
Bristol, PA 19007, USA

First Published 1994
Reprinted 1994

Copyright © Colin Morgan Associates/Murgatroyd and Associates 1994

All rights reserved. Except for the quotation of short passages for the
purposes of criticism and review, no part of this publication may be
reproduced, stored in a retrieval system, or transmitted, in any form or
by any means, electronic, mechanical, photocopying, recording or
otherwise, without the prior written permission of the publisher or a
licence from the Copyright Licensing Agency Limited. Details of such
licences (for reprographic reproduction) may be obtained from the
Copyright Licensing Agency Ltd of 90 Tottenham Court Road,
London W1P 9HE.

A catalogue record of this book is available from the British Library

ISBN 0 335 19102 9 (pb)   0 335 19103 7 (hb)

Library of Congress Cataloging-in-Publication Data
Morgan, Collin.
    Total quality management in the public sector : an international
perspective / Collin Morgan and Stephen Murgatroyd.
        p.   cm.
    Includes bibliographical references and index.
    ISBN 0–335–19103–7. — ISBN 0–335–19102–9 (pbk.)
    1. Total quality management in government.   I. Murgatroyd,
Stephen P.   II. Title.
JF 1525.T67M67   1994
350.007'8—dc20   93–24014
                                                           CIP

Typeset by Graphicraft Typesetters Ltd, Hong Kong
Printed and bound in Great Britain by
Biddles Ltd, Guildford and King's Lynn

from Colin Morgan

to the professionals in teaching and health care who have given me many insights on *quality* in recent years.

from Stephen Murgatroyd

to all civil servants, teachers, nurses, doctors – especially those with whom I have worked – and others who strive to provide quality often despite the systems created for them.

Contents

Acknowledgements

A considerable number of persons have encouraged or enabled the development of this project. They include Sarajane Aris, Chris Born, Urvashi Bramwell, Chris Chapman, Gilbert Clairbaut, John Hart, Geoffrey Samuels, Judith Jossa, Juanita Olson, Glyn Rogers, Joseph Sensenbrenner, Don Skilling, Susan Wasson, Bryan Karbonik, Mark Patterson, Shogane Cachone, George Winter, Melanie Moore, Chris McVittie, Don Murphy, Larry Lachelt, Nick Baktya of Tinsel Media, Shelley Tobo Gadereau, Faye Schmidt, Barbara Stroh, Giselle Gaboury-Smith, Patrick Diggins, John Hilsum, Pat Murgatroyd, Gerry McKinney and a number of others. Financial assistance for the work of this project was provided by Athabasca University's Faculty of Administrative Studies, The Open University and PSQ International Inc.

We would also like to acknowledge the continued support of Open University Press, who also published our text *Total Quality Management and the School* in 1993. They have been considerate, helpful and skilful in their support of this work.

While many people have been involved, sole responsibility for this text and its accuracy rests with the authors. We have made every effort to confirm our sources and to verify our observations, but accept responsibility for that which is presented here.

Introduction

TQM (Total Quality Management) is the acronym and term used for a body of management beliefs and practices which is making the headlines in the 1990s. In fact, TQM is not 'just another management approach', it is no less than a paradigm shift, a new management (philosophy, set of concepts, and tools) which has come from the world of manufacturing but which is now being applied across all types of organization.

In the industrial world, the application of TQM has dramatically transformed the quality of the product and reduced waste and costs beyond limits previously hardly thought possible. Moreover, TQM has also radically altered the way in which all members of the organization work and contribute to total performance. Those manufacturing and service companies which have embraced its philosophy to change their organizational design and empower their workers at all levels have achieved remarkable levels of performance and a clear competitive edge over their rivals. At the end of the day, they have achieved this competitive edge by the acclaim which their customers have given to their products or services; they have achieved the test of quality set by the customer and have profited accordingly.

This book essentially addresses the following question: Can TQM be widely applied in a non-manufacturing context, so that its management practices can work with similar good effects in public sector provisions? The aim of the book is therefore to evaluate the extent to which the ideas and approaches of TQM are relevant to the public sector, i.e. non-profit provisions such as government, health, education and social services. Also, we want the book to enlarge the knowledge base of those working in the public sector who have already had some introduction to TQM. Our fieldwork in a range of public sector situations to date has suggested that though the acronym of TQM and some of its ideas are known by a range of public sector managers, the awareness of what TQM is really all about is often superficial, and people have a relatively poor understanding of both the origins of TQM and the range of its different concepts and tools.

Because TQM is not simply a set of techniques – a purely mechanistic approach to the production of artifacts – but a wholly new management approach to organization, with a work ethic which aims to make use of brain power, creativity and work experience of the entire workforce, it clearly sets a challenge for all types of organizations, in all countries. Many exponents believe that TQM has a generic validity, so that it has come to be applied outside of manufacturing to service industries and, more recently, to the non-profit and public sector activities. As a consequence, more general managers in the public sector either must know about TQM, because it has been 'legislated' by higher authority as the management approach that should be adopted, or because they want to because of what they have heard about its potential. This book, then, is also aimed at those coming to TQM for the first time. It is understandable that 'new-to-TQM' readers should want a critical appraisal of TQM before they take what they see as the 'risk' of trying it out, hence the approach we have adopted of evaluating the central concepts and practices of TQM against the cultural traditions of public sector work practices, and of illustrating TQM applications in actual public sector situations.

TQM is associated in many minds with Japan, for it was there that the ideas and practices which have now come together under the acronym TQM were first comprehensively applied, even though its theoretical fathers and teachers were principally American. TQM has therefore come in the first place both from a particular occupational culture (manufacturing) and national culture (Japan). The once held idea that it is 'culture bound' for both these reasons has now been rejected, for it is increasingly being applied in both North America and Europe, including the UK. Such has been its impact that in the 1990s it is on the agenda for all national cultures and all occupational activities.

We intend that the whole approach of this book should convey that TQM is not a set of ideas of the quick-fix variety, but a demanding philosophy and set of concepts. TQM is not something which can be introduced lightly into an organization – whether public sector or manufacturing – for in its entirety it implies total culture change from the top to the bottom of the organization. We have therefore organized the book into two parts. Part 1 is essentially theoretical, all about TQM itself. It is intended that the material presented in Part 1 should introduce or extend the ideas of TQM to public sector managers, as well as discuss issues regarding the applicability of TQM approaches to the public sector itself.

Chapter 1 describes and discusses the full range of TQM concepts, beliefs and practices. In Chapter 2, we give an account of the intellectual origins and founding fathers of TQM, for we believe that all practising managers who are using, or considering using, what is a new management paradigm should know about its origins. Chapter 3 considers particular issues and objections to TQM in the public sector, and from the analysis suggests that TQM needs to be seen within a framework which can span all organizational settings. We see this framework as an important point of departure for all public sector managers considering evaluating and applying TQM, because it advocates an approach which avoids an evaluation of TQM for the public sector on an 'all or nothing' basis. We intend that the book should bring out exactly what in TQM is immediately valid for the public sector and the types of TQM approaches which are being made to work at the present time.

In Part 2, the book considers in turn the four public sector areas of health, education, government and social services. For each of these public sectors, material is presented either to illustrate the ways in which the TQM pioneers are introducing and applying TQM concepts and practices at the present time in a number of English-speaking countries, or to demonstrate the issues and constraints connected with potential TQM start-up and implementation.

It is our intention that the issues explored, the case materials presented, and the tools and applications illustrated in Part 2, should have a general applicability across the public sectors so that all the case studies independent of occupational setting should be intelligible and useful to all public sector professionals. We intend, therefore, that the reader should study each of these sections – health, education, government and social services – irrespective of their own professional area. By so doing, we would hope that our readers will appreciate the scope for what we categorize in Chapter 3 as the core, adaptive and the more problematic opportunities of TQM in public sector contexts. Also, that from reading the case applications of TQM in the other public sectors, managers will derive ideas on how to apply the concepts or techniques to their own sector. In the concluding chapter, we attempt an overall evaluation of TQM for the public sector by assessing its achievements to date and taking a position on the TQM concepts and practices which are most applicable to its culture. In so doing, we also reflect on the viability of TQM applications within the context of constraints posed by democratic control.

This book, then, is aimed at all those who have a management responsibility in the public sector provisions of health, local government, education and social services. In using the term 'management responsibility', we are definitely not restricting its application to 'the management', 'general management', 'section leaders', etc., or to anyone else whose title implies a distinctive management role. We intend it to be embraced by every role-holder who has a responsibility for delivering to the patient, student, client or ratepayer some service or product. Everyone involved in these professional areas of the public sector – from the front-line social worker, class teacher, ward nurse or office receptionist in a local government office, to the general managers of functional areas – contribute to the quality of the service as experienced by the consumer. In terms of the canons of TQM, all role-holders have a 'management responsibility' to ensure that the supplier–customer relationship works optimally; hence, both the formally designated managers in these public sector provisions, and the rank-and-file should equally evaluate the appropriateness and fit of TQM to their situation. Better still, this evaluation should include experimenting with some of the key ideas of TQM.

This book represents an early evaluation of TQM for the public services, and it is important to realize that it is very early days in the application of TQM in these contexts. The case materials we have presented really reflect the work of some TQM pioneers in the UK, Canada and the USA in the public sector. These early adapters of TQM from its manufacturing roots will attempt to develop and customize the philosophy and practices of TQM to the public service sector in the coming years and believe they will be able to produce results that go beyond those we illustrate here. If this book achieves the purpose we set for it, it will have helped readers from the public sector to adopt and adapt TQM to their own working environments.

PART
1

The nature of TQM in the public sector

1

Total Quality Management

In this chapter, we examine and explain the definitions of Total Quality Management (TQM), and set out that which we see to be its main concepts, beliefs and practices as they are generally understood by most TQM practitioners across the world. Before outlining the details, however, let us first set the tone of our approach to TQM. Total Quality Management is a general philosophy and set of ideas which has paradigm wholeness – an entity of related concepts, beliefs and working practices that have come together from different authors and cultural directions over a period of some thirty-five years. This paradigm rests on a set of common assumptions about how to achieve quality of performance for products or services within and between organizations. The particular mix and emphasis given to the range of TQM assumptions can of course differ from author to author and practitioner to practitioner, but nevertheless there is a common perspective.

While there is no single 'agreed' formulation of TQM, the range of important works about how to achieve quality do address similar targets and raise common issues. There are certain core ideas as well as specific principles of TQM which go across the whole range of contributions to theory and practice about the achievement of quality, and these synthesize into the coherent framework now recognized as, and called, TQM. Perhaps the key idea of well-established TQM is to synchronize strategy, vision and operations. This is what, according to Weir (1992), is the really radical aspect of the TQM approach. It means working at three levels:

- Corporate mission and vision.
- Strategic organization and targeting.
- Operational description, codification and control.

We have used the word 'paradigm' in connection with the core ideas and practices of TQM. A paradigm is a set of integrated ideas which stand together to define a territory of understanding. Paradigms represent frameworks for action. Paradigms have their own integrity, values and assumptions. Here we should recall that Kuhn (1970) defined a *paradigm shift* as a new conceptual tradition, a radical change in interpretation, whereby science takes a wholly new and changed perspective towards an area of knowledge and activity. This notion of paradigm shift can legitimately be applied to TQM because the core assumptions which the 'quality authors' – the parents of TQM – have advanced and practised, have been wholly subversive of many long-held assumptions regarding the management and work practices of people, whether in the manufacturing or service industries. There is no doubt that TQM has created a paradigm shift in management thinking in the manufacturing industry, and the results in terms of the quality of the products and the acclaim given to them by the end-user have been nothing short of revolutionary. If we think only of the motor car, this product now has a life-expectancy several times that which it previously enjoyed and each single car is produced by a fraction of the people and at a fraction of the cost once thought possible. TQM is bringing about similar enhancements in the service industries (e.g. banking, travel, legal and professional services) and the new paradigm has challenged managers in the public sector to ask: 'Can TQM bring equivalent benefit in quality performance in health, education, social services or government provisions generally? Can the assumptions and practices of TQM be made to fit types of service provisions which have their own unique defining features? Can effective TQM practices be applied to services which have wider community or political control to their management – something which Toyota cars or McDonald hamburgers do not have?'

It is these key questions which this book attempts to address by analysing those issues which must be confronted when applying TQM in the public sector and by describing applications of TQM which are currently being made in public sector, non-profit provisions in the UK and North America. The first step, though, is to consider what exactly is meant by TQM?

Defining Total Quality Management

The following are assertions or statements about TQM. Some are our own summaries of what we have heard others say about TQM; others are our paraphrases of TQM definition statements from texts on quality and the management of quality. When you read through them, note both the range of assumptions they cover and the key ideas which recur:

- TQM involves everything an organization, a society, or a community does, which in the eyes of others determines its reputation on a comparative basis with the best alternatives.
- TQM – A total system of quality improvement with decision-making based on facts – data collection – not opinion or impression.
- Total quality embraces not only the quality of the specific product or service which the end-user or the customer purchases or receives but everything an organization does internally to achieve continuing performance improvement.
- TQM assumes that quality is the outcome of all activities that take place within an organization; that all functions and all employees have to participate in the improvement process; that organizations need both quality systems and a quality culture.
- TQM is a way of managing an organization so that every job, every process, is carried out right, first time and every time. It affects everyone.

The key features of these five statements seem clear enough: TQM is total in the sense that it must involve everyone in the organization, and that this total management approach is about both systems and a culture which impinges on all the internal detail of working in the organization, i.e. all of the internal processes. There is also the important assumption that decision-making in respect of all the detail should be based on data.

At first glance, these statements do not appear to be radical or revolutionary, but if we think about them in contrast to the conventional assumptions about management and quality which have dominated for so long, they really represent a radical shift. Previously, only those at the top of organizations were charged with the general responsibility for quality – the arch definers of quality were the named quality controllers who came into action when the product or process was virtually completed. In the old paradigm, quality was effected by screening production processes, products or warranty costs, or reviewing services after the processes had been completed, whereas the whole thrust of these statements about TQM is that quality has to be built in from the beginning and that the achievement of quality standards is the responsibility of everyone.

A second important assumption embedded in these statements is that quality is the result of every single step or job process being seen as an opportunity to eliminate error or waste and that *everyone* should take responsibility for and participate in this. This assumption also has radical implications for change. In the old paradigm, the rank-and-file workers were not seen as the people who should concern themselves with improving their part of the whole operation. At its worst, the operatives were seen to be linked to the processes they were involved in, almost like automatons; there was no invitation for them to analyse and control their own work processes in order to eradicate error or waste, or design for themselves a wholly new process, and thus play their part in enhancing the quality of the component product. Management was seen as best able to define both *what* was needed and *how* best the needs of the organization could be met. Taylorism (Taylor 1947) gave rise to these assumptions and practices. In the TQM approach, all processes must be subject to the utmost scrutiny by those directly associated with them, and what is more the workers at all levels must be empowered to enhance these processes. The crucial assumption here is that, if quality is enhanced incrementally by those closest to the processes of the whole endeavour, the total effect of all process enhancements on the complete end-product or service is an enormous gain in quality.

The second statement in the list on page 5 reveals another very important shared assumption in the new paradigm of TQM thinking, namely that discussion and decisions regarding quality improvements for the microprocesses of activity, must be based on hard data and not on impressions or an expressed opinion justified in terms of kudos of wide or long previous experience. In the new paradigm of TQM, all strategy and improvement decisions should be research-based: they must be supported by data which are collected scientifically on all aspects of the operation, even those internal processes which everyone in the old way of doing things believes they know so intimately. Also in the new paradigm the collection and analysis of systematically collected data are not to be the prerogative of 'boffins' in white coats, but should be the responsibility of all grades of worker. Indeed, an important responsibility of senior management in TQM is to educate and train the rank-and-file worker to obtain and use data to drive quality improvement.

Here are some assertions about TQM which convey further important assumptions, concepts and beliefs:

- The core of TQM must be the customer–supplier interfaces, both internally and externally, and the fact that, at each interface, there are processes which convert inputs into outputs. Clearly, there must be commitment to building in quality through management of the outputs.
- TQM is user-driven, it cannot be imposed from outside the organization, as perhaps a quality standard or statistical process control can. TQM is concerned chiefly with changing attitudes and skills so that the culture of the organization becomes one of preventing failure – doing the right things, right first time, every time.
- TQM refers to the systematic management of an organization's customer–supplier relationships in such a way as to ensure sustainable, steep-slope improvements in quality performance.
- A philosophy and culture of never ending improvement, TQM leads first to customer satisfaction and then to customer delight.

These four statements contain some further important concepts and assumptions about TQM. The first of these is that TQM has a focus on the *customer*, and that the concept of the customer has several expressions. First, there is the customer in the end-user or purchaser sense – the external customer, the person who enjoys the finished product or receives the contracted service. One of the statements – TQM is user-driven – sums up the importance of the end-user/purchaser or customer. In the new paradigm of TQM, it is held that only the customer can legitimately define for him or herself what is quality; hence data from customers are vital in quality decision-making and management. The TQM approach therefore puts the customer at the other end of the spectrum of value from that accorded them by Henry Ford, when he said his customers could have a car in any colour they wanted, as long as it was black!

TQM does not, however, only give primacy to the *external customer* who buys the product and service. It also conceives there to be a whole range of *internal customers* within the organization, whatever its type. The TQM perspective considers that all the people working within the organization – whether manufacturing, commercial service, or public sector provision – are linked in a network or *chain of customer–supplier relationships*. Hence, the intent of TQM is that all internal customers are to be equally well satisfied with the service or product they are supplied with as are the external or end-user customers to be.

Also, embedded in the statements above is the key assumption that improving the performance of all the processes which take place between internal customers and suppliers will cumulatively have a dramatic effect on the quality of the overall finished product or service. This standpoint is frequently expressed in terms of a total commitment to the elimination of error and rework – all processes, whether they are major or minor, should be right first time. There is also the related commitment to constant improvement by integrating customer feedback into refining the design.

Although as we said earlier there is no one formulation of TQM that is universally accepted, the TQM assumptions we have been describing above are those which give TQM its coherent form as a management approach. In fact, there is one official definition of TQM which embraces most of the assumptions we have discussed above and which can serve very well as an initiating or baseline definition of what TQM is all about:

> . . . a total organizational approach for meeting customer needs and expectations that involves all managers and employees in using quantitative methods to improve continuously the organization's processes, products, and services.
>
> (American Federal Office of Management and
> Budget Circular 1990, cited in Milakovich 1990b: 209)

There are a whole range of concepts and applications associated with TQM which we will be presenting below as well as elaborating further the assumptions introduced so far, but we find this definition useful as a key point of departure to the full understanding of TQM because it stresses the aspect of organizational or management wholeness to the approach. Where TQM is properly expressed, it is an overall or total management application of the concepts as a coordinated whole and committed overall management philosophy. TQM is therefore essentially a management concept, a total approach to the application of a range of 'quality' assumptions and practices, each of which has been demonstrated in some context or other to have enhanced both quality and organizational performance. There are often claims that this or that company or department is using TQM, but on closer examination it is usually found that what the managers are applying are some of the well-known quality concepts but without adopting the total management approach which coordinates the full range of assumptions about quality. Total Quality Management assumes that quality is the outcome of *all* activities that take place within an organization; that all functions and *all* employees have to participate in the improvement process; that organizations need both quality systems and a quality culture and that these are the responsibility of management. If 'quality' is the centrepiece of this total management approach though, what in fact do we mean by 'quality'?

What is quality?

Before we look further at the specific concepts and practices of TQM in more detail, it is essential that we consider here whether there are any useful overarching definitions of quality. By 'overarching' we mean views of quality which can unite under the TQM umbrella the full range of organizational activities, whether they are concerned with manufacturing or service provisions, or whether they are in the commercial or public sectors.

The definition of 'quality' chosen by the European Organization for Quality Control (EOQC) and the American Society for Quality Control is:

> Quality: the totality of features of a product or service that bears on its ability to satisfy given needs.

This is essentially a transcendental view of quality, implying a sense of excellence – something which, in its completeness, is more felt than measured. It does not, however, convey what the determinants of the excellence are, and is therefore a good example of why the definition of quality can be extremely difficult to pin down.

In discussion, people use the word to carry their own emphasis behind a concept of excellence or TQM, but the particular nature of the emphasis is concealed behind the word. We therefore need to consider what these different emphases can be. We shall find that the emphases imparted to the word 'quality' do vary, and that the emphasis given in service contexts can be different from that usually used in manufacturing contexts.

From the manufacturing viewpoint, it has been suggested that there are several views or emphases to a definition of quality (Open University 1987):

1. *Product-based emphasis*: quality is related to the content of the product, i.e. the range of features or the quantity and type of the ingredients.

This is an economics-based view that essentially refers to what some call *grade*.

2. *Manufacturing emphasis*: this is conformance to specification of the product. While the specifications of Rolls Royce and Mini are different, both can attain an equal test of quality in terms of the consistency of their conformance to the required specification. For some, this particular emphasis is the totality of the definition: 'Quality is conformance to requirements – nothing more, nothing less' (Crosby 1979).
3. *Customer/user-based emphasis*: this is the 'fitness for purpose view' in the eyes of the user or customer.
4. *Value-based emphasis*: this is the composite of the manufacturing and user emphases, i.e. what the customer wants at an acceptable price and conformance to specification at an acceptable cost. Quality improvements are therefore to be seen as increases in the conformance of a product or service or specifications which enhance the capability of a product or service to meet customer expectations.

The above emphases do not, however, entirely get to grips with the implications of what some hold to be an important distinction between manufacturing and services. In manufacturing, goods are made first and then sold and consumed so that the customer becomes significant during the final stage of the overall process. In the service industry, services are sold or contracted first and then produced and consumed with production and consumption possibly being simultaneous. For manufacturing, the implication of this distinction is that quality is essentially about conformance to product specification, whereas for the service industry, quality is essentially about the customer/user focus because this customer dimension is embedded in the whole transaction from initiation to completion in the service context. Following from this kind of distinction, some TQM writers have drawn a distinction between what they see as essentially 'industrial' and 'social' models of TQM.

Quality in the service context

In this book, we consider the applicability of TQM to the public sector. Overwhelmingly, the public sector is concerned to provide services rather than manufactured products, so that the issue of what are the additional or distinctive features of quality in the service context is relevant to our evaluation of TQM. We are unable to find a general model of service quality for the public sector alone, but many have delineated the generic features of quality in services generally on the grounds that knowledge about the quality of goods is insufficient to understand service quality. There are also those writers who have carried out an in-depth analysis of the nature of service quality in specific service fields. The health sector in particular has received extensive treatment (Marzalek-Gaucher and Coffey 1990), and we shall consider this in Chapter 4 where we introduce and present case studies of TQM in health. Here we present the accepted features of service quality.

According to Parasuraman *et al.* (1985), Haywood-Farmer (1988) and others, there are three well-documented characteristics of services – intangibility, heterogeneity and inseparability – which must be acknowledged for a full understanding of service quality. First, services are intangible because they are performances rather than objects; most services cannot be counted, measured, inventoried, tested or verified in advance of delivery to ensure quality. The main implication of intangibility is that generally one cannot store a service, thus removing the final quality check commonly found in the manufacturing sector.

Second, services have customers with very heterogeneous needs. Consumers of the same services do not all have the same priorities. Consider, for example, airline passengers. Different passengers may have different priorities, e.g. schedules, schedule reliability, booking arrangements, seat alignments, on-board meals, choice of film, friendliness of flight attendants, etc. An analogy may be drawn in the public sector. Within any classroom in a school, the particular learning needs of individual students will be different – some will be more numerate or literate than others, and some will have different ambitions for applying the particular knowledge being taught to them. Similarly, in the health sector, some patients crave their own room on hospitalization, whereas others do not want to be on their own.

Third, services have 'inseparability', by which is meant that the production and consumption of services are not separate as they are in manufacturing. As a consequence, in the service industry, quality is not engineered into the product at the manufacturing plant and then delivered intact to the consumer. Rather, quality occurs during the delivery of the service, usually during the interaction between the client and the key contact person from the service provider. In these situations, the consumer's input becomes critical to the quality of service performance. Indeed, in many service contexts, the customer wishes to participate in creating the service. This is certainly true for health, education and social service encounters between professionals and clients, as well as for some aspects of government provision. Regarding government provision, whether at the local, provincial or central level, the customer or stakeholder is sometimes intimately involved in the process, for example in planning decisions for housing or industrial development if quality (lack of disagreement) is to be achieved.

It is for these reasons that writers on service quality have defined service as a 'deed', a 'performance' or an 'effort', thus highlighting the inherent importance of the consumer of the service having an active involvement in the production or completion of the service process itself.

Following from these features of intangibility, heterogeneity and inseparability, the nature of how quality is evaluated for services is conceived to have a different emphasis from that of manufacturing where quality judgements are essentially responses to tangibles. Service quality judgements

Table 1 Determinants of customers' perceptions of quality in service provisions

---

1. *Reliability*, e.g. performing the service at the designated time
2. *Responsiveness*, e.g. willingness to provide the service
3. *Competence*, e.g. possession of the required skills and knowledge to perform the service
4. *Access*, e.g. approachability and ease of contact with the providing institution, etc.
5. *Courtesy*, e.g. politeness, respect and friendliness of contact
6. *Communication*, e.g. keeping customers informed in language they understand; also listening to them; it means explaining the service; explaining any options or costs; assuring the customer that a problem will be handled
7. *Credibility*, e.g. belief that they have the customer's best interests at heart, trustworthiness, honesty, etc.
8. *Security*, e.g. freedom from danger, risk or doubt
9. *Understanding/knowing the customer*, e.g. making the effort to understand the customer's needs by providing individualized attention
10. *Appearance/presentation*, e.g. the physical facilities, the appearance of personnel, tools or equipment used, etc.

---

are considered to be driven by a comparison of consumer expectations with their perceptions of the actual service quality received. Also, this premise of service quality assumes that the judgement of the service received will have combined both the evaluation of the outcome of the service and the evaluation of the processes of the service delivery. Hence, for services there is a strong interactive component to the whole aspect of quality, and some have sought to arrive at a general model of the determinants of customers' perceptions of service quality (Table 1).

The determinants of service quality given above (based on Parasuraman *et al.* 1985) demonstrate the weight of interactive components in judgements of service quality. It is these interactive properties which have led some to label the nature of quality in the service sector as *preferential*, so distinguishing it from the *objective quality* of the manufacturing sector, where quality is in the main associated with the properties of an object which can be measured and demonstrated in a tangible sense. In contrast, quality in the preferential sense is identical not with the properties of an object but rather with the capacity of the properties to achieve a goal, this goal being a state of affairs which is preferred to other states.

What are the categories of properties to achieve a goal? Are there components of any service which generate the types of perceptions of service quality set out in Table 1? In Fig. 1 we propose what we call the 'Triangle of Service Quality', which we have based both on models of service quality proposed for the commercial sector, such as that suggested by Lewis (1987), and on analyses of service quality in the service sector, such as that proposed

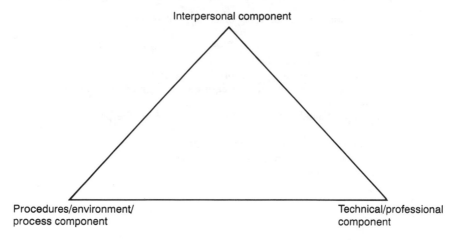

Figure 1   The triangle of balance in service quality

by Donabedian (1980) for health service provision (which is mostly associated with the public sector, except perhaps in the USA).

The triangle is equilateral with the apices concerned with: the interpersonal component of the service; the physical context and procedures surrounding the service; and the technical or professional service component itself. The model assumes a balance between the three types of component for the production of a good service. For example, too great an emphasis on procedures/processes and the message to the customer becomes: 'You are a number and we are here to process you using our procedures'. Too great an emphasis on the interpersonal can give a strong impression: 'We love you and we try hard but we don't necessarily know what we are doing'. Finally, too great an emphasis on the professional and technical judgemental aspects of the service can give the following message to the client: 'We know exactly what we can do and how to do it, but we don't care about you much as an individual'.

Both from our own experience and the available literature, we suggest that this simple model of what defines service quality fits all service contexts, whether a mundane commercial domestic service such as an on-site carpet cleaning service, or a highly specialized professional service such as that of a medical specialist or teacher. Donabedian (1980), an American and the original guru of quality in the health services, sees quality in health service provision as a product of technical, interpersonal and amenity factors, and it is just this definition of quality which is promoted in British National Health Service (NHS) policy statements at the present time. For example, the policy document *A Quality Health Service for Wales* (Welsh Office 1990: 4) defines quality as:

the quality of technical care, which links directly to its effectiveness or ability to achieve improvements in health (health gain); the quality of inter-personal relationships with all 'customers' needing to be treated with sensitivity; and the quality of amenities, that is convenience, creature comforts, and the quality of the environment in which the care is given.

In education, we found that school children we interviewed used different vocabularies to describe their perceptions of teaching quality, which in essence fell into these same three categories. Three aspects of quality recur in students' accounts of why they learn more with some teachers than others: 'they are willing to help you individually' (interpersonal), 'they really know their subject' (technical) and 'there is control, you know what you are supposed to do' (procedures/environment).

Having established what we feel to be a good operational view of quality in the service context, something we see as wholly relevant to public sector provision, it is important to note that some writers believe that attitudes to quality vary with culture, in particular, a distinction is drawn between the Western and Japanese views of quality. Weir (1992: 3–4) has written:

> Part of the reason for Japanese success is their concept of quality. Quality is seen as a comparative and relative factor as compared to the absolutist and essentialist ideas of quality which are still current in many western organizations. In Japanese organizations quality is seen as something to be achieved and as an ever receding standard which once approached provides a benchmark for the next attempt. In western organizations it is seen as a norm with relative fixed attributes, as an ascribed value.

In essence, this is the TQM attitude towards quality. Earlier, we teased out some of the bedrock assumptions regarding what TQM is all about. We now return to look at these assumptions, their associated concepts, beliefs and practices in some detail, before discussing the intellectual origins and founding fathers of TQM principles and practice. This order is deliberate, because we do not wish to present TQM as a set of ideas fragmented between various personalities in an analogous way to religious denominations. There is to a degree some denominationalism among TQM practitioners, but to focus on this rather than on the core of what TQM is about, would be to avoid a full understanding of the central tenets of the philosophy.

TQM concepts and beliefs regarding management and organizational context

Corporate quality planning

Quality is a strategic issue for corporate management. It requires the production of a medium- to long-term organization-wide or corporate plan which specifies the quality dimensions of future strategy by way of a vision statement, goals, objectives and action plans which have *explicit quality orientation*. The quality policy will be wholly anchored to a generic strategy which has been chosen to obtain best competitive positioning within the particular marketplace.

A corporate vision

By a corporate vision we mean the overarching concept or guiding force to which the organization is working in its marketplace or environment, and which finds expression in an economical published vision statement. The vision concept and statement should be seen to embody two components: a guiding philosophy and a tangible image (Collins and Porras 1991). The corporate vision is therefore a shared image of fundamental purpose to which all are to be committed; the vision itself is very simple.

What is important is that the vision statement embraces the hopes and aspirations of all those associated with the organization. The Japanese for such vision statements is *Kaisha Hoshin*, which means basic challenge, which is similar to the definition of fundamental purpose offered above. Others have used the similar notions of 'compelling guiding force' or 'the spark'. The organization's vision statement should become the basic challenge – the force which shapes and energizes all its members. It should, according to Murgatroyd and Morgan (1993), be:

- *Challenging*: always in sight but not out of reach.
- *Clear*: not open to conflicting interpretations by any group or individual.
- *Memorable*: a statement that is no longer than 20–25 words is ideal.
- *Involving*: a statement that enables and empowers *all*.
- *Values-driven*: there should be a strong tie to the values desired.
- *Visual*: it should be something that can be represented or pictured visually.
- *Mobilizing*: it should demand a response from all.
- *A guideline*: it should be something by which *all* engaged within organizations can measure their actions against daily.
- *Linked to the needs of customers*: the ultimate test of a vision will relate to the actions and achievements of customers.

Total commitment of senior management

The commitment of all senior staff towards culture change based on continuous quality improvement is seen to be essential. This factor has been demonstrated to be the most important determinant of a successful TQM implementation, and its absence the reason why quality circles almost wholly failed in many western countries and a prime reason why TQM fails. It is the single-minded obsession of the chief executive and other senior managers with issues of quality which must bring about total organizational change.

Commitment to a changed culture of control in the organization

The commitment is not only to total quality improvement of all aspects of production or the service process, to changing the nature of organizational design and working practices in respect of authority relationships and responsibility as we have already indicated, but to total cultural change in terms of 'control' values. TQM requires the institutionalization of participation on a permanent basis, so that traditional stratification and protocol disappear. In the TQM environment, responsibility is decentralized downwards with the aim of utilizing every ounce of intelligence and ingenuity of the rank-and-file worker. This is, of course, the opposite priority to that which characterized the segmentation-of-task approach of the mass production methods which held sway for much of this century. Under the working methods best characterized by those applied by Henry Ford and 'Fordism', the rank-and-file worker was not supposed to think or concern himself with any other task than his own. Questions of policy for, or improvement of, quality were matters for higher authority. The very restricted status of the rank-and-file worker was not of course confined to manufacturing, for even in the highly professionalized public sector service provisions such as health or education, stratification was prominent and 'front-line' professionals were not expected to question higher status authority figures such as consultants in hospitals or headmasters in schools. In the pre-TQM 'Fordism' managerial culture, it was the management's job to do the thinking about quality, and the job of the rank-and-file to do the doing without asking questions. This 'authority' – some might say authoritarian environment – contained even stronger 'walls against participation and communication', where it was also overlaid by significant social class differences (particularly, perhaps, in the UK), with their extra social distancing features deriving from modes of speech, contrasting scholastic backgrounds, and assumptions of authority deriving from inherited power linked to historic conquest and control. Cultural practices regarding authority, participation and individual responsibilities can be very subtle and all pervading in organizations, so that they require very deliberate proactive effort to change them.

The TQM 'post-Fordism' or 'post-modernism' context calls for a management environment where human dignity and independence of the individual worker are respected; total quality cannot be achieved without it. The fundamental difference of TQM as a management approach, therefore, is that it is more democratic. This does not mean that management abdicates control, far from it, but that the type of control and leadership is very different. TQM is decidedly people-centred and might equally be called 'Total People Management', even though it is often erroneously seen as an approach characterized by 'high-tech'. In TQM, technology represents but tools in the hands of human actors; they alone can command the ultimate benefits to be achieved in terms of quality products and services.

The organizational culture – the implicit rules, assumptions and values which bind an organization together (Ott 1989; Mills and Murgatroyd 1991) – must radically alter to accommodate TQM. A successful TQM organization is one which has created a culture in which: (1) innovation is valued highly; (2) status is secondary to performance and contribution; (3) leadership is a function of action, not position; (4) rewards are shared through the work of teams; (5) development, learning and training are seen as critical paths to sustainability; (6) empowerment to achieve challenging goals supported by continued development and success provide a climate for self-motivation. This TQM culture minimizes the control role of those in leadership positions and maximizes the power of the employees nearest to the customer. It gains energy from achievement and a sense of ownership of the problems and future of the organization. It is post-modern in the sense that it takes us beyond organizational designs we now consider 'modern' into a new age of organization.

TQM control conceived as an inverted pyramid

In the traditional view of organizational authority and status patterns of control, 'the management' is seen to be at the apex of a triangle with the rank-and-file forming the base. In this pattern of management control, it is the apex which is seen as being closest to the customers in terms of knowing about their needs and how to achieve a quality product. In this model, the 'workers' are seen as supporters of what the management is striving for. The TQM philosophy of management inverts this pyramid of control, by putting the rank-and-file closest to the customers as only they can improve the processes which will enhance the quality of the product or service. Hence in the inverted pyramid model, it is the job of management to support the 'front-line' workers by understanding the detail of their internal supplier–customer working practices and problems, by analysing the obstacles to improvement, and listening carefully to the rank-and-file workers' ideas on improving quality for their customers (see Fig. 2).

This TQM inverted pyramid model embraces, therefore, the notions of minimum hierarchy, democratization and the key component of *empowerment* for all individuals and work teams. The abandonment of the traditional pyramid of control is therefore essential to TQM, and it may even be that even the concept of the inverted pyramid is not wholly suited to some service organizations. Perhaps under TQM some service organizations should best be conceived as a network of units that are free to act while retaining their links with one another, but with some central units to shape overall direction.

Empowerment

The linked principle of delegated control means that responsibility should be decentralized downwards. People who have the ability to make quality

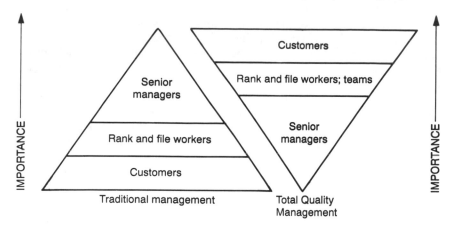

Figure 2   TQM: The inverted pyramid of control

improvements should be given the authority to make them. This process leads to semi-autonomous work groups and greater self-control for individual rank-and-file workers, so that they become involved in issues which were previously the prerogative of management. The term 'empowerment' is now widely used to refer to this delegation of control, enabling teams working together to manage their own processes in such a way as to achieve the high levels of performance expected of them by the organization.

Our definition of empowerment sees it as the ability of an individual or a team to work in their own way within agreed time-lines and with agreed resources to achieve a goal set by the leadership of the organization, but it is not an unfettered freedom to determine what goals the team has for the organization as a whole, or how they would like the organization to be. Basic empowerment springs from the vision and goals that have already been set by the organization's leaders. What a team or an individual is empowered to do is to turn the vision and strategy into reality through achieving the challenging overarching goals set for them by the leaders or senior management. Individuals are therefore being empowered in terms of how they can achieve the goals set, not in terms of what the goals might be.

The centrality of processes and measurement in TQM

A central belief of TQM is that enhancement in the quality of outcomes – and continuous advancement at that – is achieved through improving each of the many processes which take place in all types of organizations. Certainly, this belief has been dramatically empirically validated in manufacturing organizations as we can all attest as consumers of products. More recently, parallel evidence has become available for commercial service organizations and there are a growing number of case studies which we will refer to in the occupational sectors of this book which show that similar gains can be achieved in the public sector context.

However, what *is* a process? A process is the mechanism by which inputs are converted into outputs. Outputs include products, services, materials, procedures, information, skills, etc., so that the product differs from the inputs. All work is carried out by a process and the outputs of all processes serve as inputs to other processes, so that all work relates to tasks which encompass input–output relationships that are linked together both within the organization and between the external and internal spheres of organizational activity. The very foundation of TQM is to treat every task as a process so that task management under TQM becomes a need to define the process, to monitor its performance and to forecast the required inputs and the desired outputs.

Processes can only be monitored and brought under control by gathering and using data; hence the key concept in TQM of measurement, especially Statistical Process Control (SPC: Oakland and Followell 1992). This refers to measurements of the performance of the process and the feedback required for corrective action, where necessary. SPC methods, backed by management commitment and good organization, provide *objective* means of controlling quality in any transformation process, whether used in the manufacture of artifacts, the provision of services, or the transfer of information. SPC within TQM is not just concerned with measuring conformance – that is, where the process is not producing the particular standard set for it – it is also intended to act upon those processes which are meeting the specification intended at the present time so as to disclose where variability can further be reduced so as to gain further enhancements. The whole TQM approach to processes and their measurement is therefore characterized by:

- No process without data collection.
- No data without analysis.
- No analysis without decision.

The prime purpose of SPC is to divert attention from *ad hoc* individual pieces of data and focus on the process as a whole using a systematic approach. While data collection and analysis can often be undertaken by individuals, the tasks of identifying and eliminating troublesome assignable events as well as identifying and reducing random causes of variation are much more effective in a group-working environment. Interdepartmental experience within teams can be used to maximize problem-solving success.

In SPC, two kinds of data are recognized:

1. *Variable data*: everything that varies in measurable units such as on a digital or analogue scale, such as waiting time in a hospital, school attendance, delivery to a correct address.
2. *Attribute or countable data*: including all dichotomous states such as right/wrong, good/bad, etc.

The majority of problems have been found to relate to attribute data, and this kind of data is simply plotted using frequency diagrams. In organizations where the philosophy and practices of TQM are at their maximum, all levels of worker are taught to use statistical techniques in a demystified way.

Detection and measuring devices are therefore of prime importance in the management of quality. When objective recording and reporting systems are in place, significant deviations from the standard of product and service intended will be made evident and so can be examined for their improvement. If there is no reporting and recording scheme, there is no sound basis for saying anything about the nature and number of defects or about the processes by which they are created, detected and removed. TQM is therefore assertively a management philosophy based on facts from rigorous data collection, an approach which ignores opinion, anecdote and impression.

Process owner

All work units can be conceived as locations where a range of processes take place, where inputs are transformed in the process into outputs for a 'customer'. Certain prime people are responsible for the process which transforms the particular inputs into outputs, and these are the process owners. Whatever supplies, training or other resources are made available to the process owners, only they can significantly enhance the effectiveness of the process.

Specific process concepts used in TQM

The following are process concepts which have within the TQM approach been widely used in manufacturing and which are available for translation into practice in the service and public sectors:

- *Zero defects*: not making mistakes in the way any process or activity is conducted and ensuring that all benchmarked performance criteria are met. A conceptual model of the factors leading to defects is given in Table 2 (Course PMT605, Open University, p. 21).
- *Defections*: not losing a customer, patient, student, client, etc., to a competitor provider.
- *Cycle time*: working systematically to reduce the time it takes to complete any or all of the activities in, for instance, a school (e.g. the time taken to register a student, the time taken to successfully teach a particular curriculum, the time taken to complete the school photographs, etc.).
- *On-time performance*: to work systematically to ensure that all scheduled deadlines are met 100 per cent of the time by everyone.
- *Labour content of work*: to work systematically and intelligently to reduce the labour content of work for a given level of achievement while enhancing job satisfaction, and to do this without any loss of staff so that

Table 2 Causes of defects in processes

Cause of failure	Factor
Failure of control	Inadequate management, planning, control procedures and control staff; inadequate or inappropriate tools
Mechanical	Devices inadequately set up, inadequate maintenance, poor error detection and poor error reporting
	Staff stress, isolation, uncomfortable and/or inconvenient environment, lack of support, lack of feedback, poor training, poor error detection
Excessive complexity	New processes, new languages, new representations, new applications, new products, or new users, poor design, poor communication, inappropriate size or performance constraints, lack of simplifying models
Inconvenience	Lack of forethought, lack of interest/capacity in man–machine interface, ergonomics or work study, lack of consultation, lack of evaluation and observation
Unfamiliarity	Lack of training, lack of support, isolation, lack of simplifying models, lack of forethought

more staff are available more of the time for tasks and activities deemed essential.
- *Plan to action time reduction (P ≫ A)*: reducing the time taken between the development, planning and testing of a new service and its full implementation.
- *Space reduction*: reducing the reliance on expensive capital space for the performance of the tasks of the organization.
- *Customer satisfaction*: making significant differences to the levels of satisfaction with the product or service expressed by all customers, both internal and external.

In TQM, then, SPC concepts are made to permeate all levels of the organization from managing director to the shop floor.

The TQM concept of the customer

In TQM philosophy and practice, the concept of the customer has been refined and extended to include customers external to, and within, the organization. Within the organization, all workers are to be seen as both customers and suppliers; hence in TQM practice, the customer can also be an internal colleague, not just the external receiver of the end-product or service.

In the TQM approach within the organization, for each worker, the next person with whom they interact in terms of supplying a part of a product or a service is a customer, so that the organization internally can be viewed as a complex of customer/supplier roles.

In the sense in which this extended concept is to be fully applied, all workers – whether in manufacturing, commercial or professional services – need to see themselves in their own activities as being 'processors' in the sense that they make or do something which involves an input to them and an output from them. Hence, in the eyes of the supplier they will be seen as a 'customer', and in the eyes of the customer as a supplier. All workers in any organization will therefore be simultaneously 'supplier', 'processor' and 'customer'. Under TQM, the key questions for each individual then become: Do I meet the needs of my customer or user? Have I discussed my needs with my suppliers so that they can appreciate my situation?

Because everyone has a wide range of suppliers and customers, the task of answering these questions is an onerous one, which is good reason in itself to look upon TQM as a very demanding management philosophy. However, the Pareto principle (after an eighteenth-century mathematician) states that about 20 per cent of process interactions will be critical in that they create 80 per cent of the problems, and if at the very least this 20 per cent of processes can be identified and worked upon, major improvements can be achieved for a relatively small amount of effort.

Mortiboys and Oakland (1991) have suggested that each person in the quality chain within the organization should interrogate every interface as follows:

Customers

• Who are my internal customers?
• What are their true requirements?
• How do I find out what their requirements are?
• Do I have the necessary capability to meet those requirements? If not, what must I do about it?
• Do I continually meet the requirements? If not, what are the reasons?
• How do I monitor changes in requirements?

Suppliers

• Who are my internal suppliers?
• What are my true requirements?
• How do I communicate my requirements?
• Do my suppliers have the capability to measure and meet the requirements?
• How do I inform them of changes in the requirements?

There is, then, within the 'redefinition of the customer' aspect of TQM, a central focus on the internal supplier–customer chains. However, this is not to suggest that an equivalent importance is not placed on the end-user or end-receiver customer who is external to the organization. How the external customer perceives the product or service for his needs, or indeed views the types of new product or service which should be provided, are central and all pervading concerns. TQM thinking holds that the quality of a customer's experience of a product or service will be mediated by 'moments of truth', when the quality of a product or experience is immediately available to a participant, that is when the truth about the quality of a reality is revealed by culture, values and acts experienced by customers.

The moment of truth in the customer's view of the world is a sense of discrepancy between what is expected or desired and what is occurring or being received. Moments of truth affect the way we think about a great many experiences. Consider your experience of the ground crew at an airport being unable to locate your luggage, or of a restaurant being unable to accommodate your reservation, or of a plumber not arriving to repair a leaking pipe when he said he would. These all lead us to talk vociferously about these experiences to others. Our experience of quality as customers is an important reality definer whether we are in the internal or external customer chain. TQM is about managing these customers' experiences in the widest possible sense. It is at 'moments of truth' that the quality of the service or product as an *experience* is mediated to customers (whether internal or external), so the task of effective management is to manage the moments of truth.

The commitment to a constant string of small improvements as well as the setting of outrageous goals

In the TQM approach, there are no quick fixes but a belief that high-quality change and improvement is the product of 1–2 per cent of improvements achieved over a wide range of processes on a continuing basis. Minimizing inefficiencies, particularly those concerned with waste and rework, are important constituents of this. A fundamental stance of TQM, then, is the elimination of defects. Defects can be either errors or faults. Errors differ from faults in that they are blemishes in products or services and are the more simple and preventable elements in incremental quality enhancement. Faults are conceptual or analytical mistakes. A project-by-project improvement strategy in which small incremental improvements are continually achieved is central to TQM. Whereas all organizations may improve at a normal evolutionary rate by using these TQM approaches, it is held that TQM organizations improve at an extraordinary or steep slope rate. Hence the aim in the TQM organization is to maximize the number of projects or processes being improved.

However, the TQM approach also allows for the setting of what at first may appear to be outrageous improvement goals, i.e. radical and massive leaps forward. Such 'Hoshin' goals are elaborated upon later in this chapter.

The concept of quality costs and cost of non-conformance

Quality-related costs are all those costs and activities that do not add value. The two classes of these costs are: (1) costs related to a deficiency in the predicted performance of a prescribed system or operation; (2) costs incurred because the system or operation itself is less than adequate. For both, there are direct and consequential costs.

If we take direct and consequential costs together, the costs associated with poor quality can be placed in one of three main categories (Hutchins 1992):

1. *Failure and consequential costs* (both internal and external): the internal ones are the cost of doing again what has already been done, i.e. re-work, or repairing or modifying the result of an activity together with the loss of use of existing resources. In manufacturing, these problems do appear on the inventory, but in service organizations the equivalents are hidden in direct costs. External failure costs such as product recall or withdrawal, or adverse criticism in the media or excessive after-delivery service or maintenance support, can be categorized as chronic or sporadic.
2. *Appraisal costs*: poor-quality appraisal or monitoring, or the fact that these functions are carried out because failures are known to exist.
3. *Prevention costs*: these cover field testing or developmental testing, i.e. the investments for improvement.

Quality costs are optimum at the level of the best performer in a given market, as perceived by the customer end-user who has a choice between providers. Customers are not homogeneous nor are their expectations static. Some customers will 'increase' their expectations when they perceive the standards set by the best performers in the marketplace. This axiom raises the issue of 'what is the marketplace?' in the case of public sector provisions. We discuss this in Chapter 3.

For service organizations more generally, there are a whole range of apparently minor but significant quality-related cost elements: unclear data, wrong label, wrong instructions, unclear handwriting, documents incomplete, wrong code, misunderstood information, poor delivery, mistake, missed operation, forgetfulness, lost forms, misfiling, keyboard errors, untidy work, wrong priorities, poor communications. Some writers have suggested that the opportunity costs of these quality elements can be as much as 40 per cent of total costs.

The importance of teams in TQM

For a number of reasons, TQM views teams as central to a commitment to learning and the changes for quality improvement which this produces. TQM requires that the organization regards itself as a learning entity for all of its members. That is, it is critically important that all workers are systematically seeking to learn about and continuously improve their work. If this does not take place – if there is no search for continuous improvement (what the Japanese call *kaizen*) – then workers at all levels in the organization are in danger of replicating existing performance levels rather than aiming for significant and substantial shifts in the level of 'value added' achieved.

Teams are more powerful learning entities than individuals seeking to learn on their own. Teams provide an environment in which learning can be articulated, tested, refined and examined against the needs of the organization and within the context of the learning of others. To be effective, team-based learning activity needs to cover: the needs of the team, the needs of the individuals within the team, and the needs of the organization. By articulating these three sets of needs within the team, it has frequently been demonstrated that real progress and development can take place within an organization (Liswood 1990).

Moreover, the type of team used for learning and change is crucial in TQM. Most quality improvement opportunities lie not within the natural work group but outside, that is across departments, so that the TQM approach calls for the maximization of inter-departmentalism. Departmentalism is widely experienced to lead to compartmentalization – where each department works for itself and does not understand the needs of other departments. TQM, therefore, searches for new arrangements for 'horizontal' coordination within the organization to the extent that 'cross-functional management' is seen to be one of its essential features.

What this TQM approach recognizes, therefore, is that when it comes to quality, organizational sub-units have both joint interests and separate interests. Traditional management approaches have to some extent reified and underlined the structural authority of the separate interests related to the functional specialities expressed in departments. This can lead to departments focusing on consolidating and strengthening their own position in relation to other units, and giving scant regard to the needs of their interdependence. This phenomenon can squander, fragment and fritter away human energies in ongoing struggles. TQM-generated cross-functional teams, on the other hand, optimize interdependence. TQM aims, then, at an organizational vitality which is a balanced articulation of both interdependence and autonomy. It wants both cross-functional teams and departmental teams who are given real authority.

This TQM cross-functional team practice gives middle managers an important place on the teams and a distinct place in quality improvement as they stand at the crossroads of the vertical and horizontal planes. They are responsible for the quality improvement activities that take place among rank-and-file employees, so with TQM their role is significantly enhanced in overall management and their importance as team leaders cannot be underestimated.

Another key feature of the TQM approach to teams, whether departmental or cross-functional, is that in effective organizations they are self-managing. This means that they are able to determine their own procedures, sub-goals, objectives and ways of working providing that the goals they set are commensurate with the strategic goals of the organization as a whole. Putting this another way, within the parameters of the challenges faced by

Table 3 Items in a team empowerment contract

1. What is the focus to the work of this team?
2. What is our membership and what are our roles?
3. What are the values/principles which this team wishes to work to?
4. What are the specific challenges of the work focus?
5. What are the (specific, measurable) goals of the team?
6. What support and training needs do the team have?
7. What support will the team need from top management?
8. What milestones can we identify for the team's work?
9. What acknowledgement and rewards do the team suggest would be helpful?
10. What commitments are the team declaring?

the organization and set by the organization's strategic goal process, teams are free to work in their own way to achieve these goals within an agreed budget and an agreed schedule. Self-managing teams are empowered to achieve the outrageous goals of the organization. These latter conditions would present a particular challenge to those organizations where the TQM principle of devolution of power and resource to work teams has yet to replace the ingrained tradition of top-down control over the detail of work practices.

Another important argument for teams is a pragmatic one. For TQM to achieve sustainable quality improvement over time, it has to be independent of any particular individual; it has to belong to the whole organization and to groups within it. Many excellent initiatives die when the individuals who championed them leave for other positions; innovations which are team-owned and team-sustained are far less likely to be dependent on an individual champion. By working through self-managing teams and by insisting on the development of teams within the organization, the momentum for TQM can be assured along with its sustainability.

High-performing organizations are collections of high-performing teams. Whether it is Boeing's teams working on the design and construction of the Boeing 777 or Ford's teams working on the design and development of its 2000 series cars and trucks, or teams working in the British Columbia or Alberta Governments focused on service quality improvements, or a school team working on reducing the time taken to achieve certain literacy standards in primary schools – teams are the key vehicles for meeting challenging and demanding goals and sustaining their performance over time. In consultancy work, we have recommended that teams operate under an 'empowerment contract' with management which can cover the sort of items shown in Table 3.

Teams, then, are the building blocks of the TQM organization. Whether they are departmental or cross-functional teams, they need to be autonomous in such a way that they can respond quickly to the market, whether internal or external; they should have their own 'profit' responsibility, and be as self-supporting as possible by giving them control over a large part of their earnings (Mastenbroek 1991). The extent to which this desideratum can be made to fit the public sector context looks a very challenging proposition for those who are advocating major change in public sector provisions.

TQM and the use of tools

The importance of data collection has already been stressed above, and there are a range of typical TQM 'tools' which are generally applied in the evaluation of processes. The occupational case studies in Part 2 of this book will illustrate the application of some of these. Quality, though, as we have already said, is also concerned with the analysis of data and the formulation of strategy, hence a whole range of other tools are used. Table 4, taken from Murgatroyd and Morgan (1993), shows the range of tools that are available.

The TQM-run organization will have a range of processes under investigation and a number of project teams working in quality improvements, so that tools are required to record what is going on, to set objectives for project teams, and to ensure that the records are practical and used to feed-back to the members what is happening. Recording and managing TQM changes are therefore essential activities of the management team, and focus on the following aspects of the organization's work:

• Agreed upon indicators of performance in relation to the goals set.
• As milestones are reached on the way to achieving a goal, the processes used to achieve these milestones are written up so that all can use them. This is called standardizing knowledge or codifying best practice.
• As achievements are made, processes which link to these achievements are systematically examined with a view to 'fine-tuning' the improvements.

In organizations that have adopted TQM as their basis for working, it is not unusual to see walls covered in performance charts and achievement boards. It is also not unusual to see flow-charts of processes with red lines and marks indicating areas where changes have been made. Nor is it unusual to see members of the organization carrying data on performance indicators in their diaries – the idea of systematic measurement permeates the organization.

But there is another point here. By insisting on measurable gains and the frequent use of indicators and 'success' charts, people in the organization are being asked to make decisions and judgements on the basis of facts and data rather than anecdote, guesses, instinct or rumour. As W. Edwards Deming, a major figure in the quality movement, has cited: 'In God we trust – all others must use data!' How many times have decisions been made on the basis of very little (if any) information, guesses about consequences and no data about the history of the problem being tackled? How

Table 4 Thinking and measuring tools and their uses in TQM

Tool	Collect information	Convert to measures	Analyse process	Improve process	Set standards	Manage performance
Archetypes of systems (Senge)	✓		✓	✓		
Affinity diagram (Walton)	✓		✓	✓		
Arrow diagram (Mizuno)	✓		✓	✓		
Benchmarking (Camp)	✓	✓			✓	✓
Brainstorming (de Bono)	✓		✓			
Cause–effect diagram (Walton)	✓	✓	✓	✓		
Charts and graphs (Walton)	✓		✓	✓	✓	✓
Check sheets (Walton)	✓		✓			✓
Control charts (Oakland)	✓		✓		✓	✓
Cost–benefit analysis (Oakland)	✓		✓	✓		
Five whys (Murgatroyd/Morgan)	✓		✓	✓		
Force field analysis	✓		✓	✓		
Histograms (Walton/Oakland)	✓	✓	✓	✓	✓	✓
House of quality (Murgatroyd/Morgan)	✓	✓	✓	✓	✓	✓
Mental mapping (Senge)	✓	✓		✓		
Pareto charts (Walton)	✓	✓	✓	✓		✓
Process decision programme charts (PDPC) (Mizuno)	✓	✓		✓		
Process mapping (Murgatroyd/Morgan)	✓	✓	✓	✓	✓	✓
Run charts (Walton)	✓	✓	✓	✓	✓	✓
Sampling (Oakland)	✓	✓	✓	✓	✓	✓
Scatter diagrams (Walton)	✓		✓	✓	✓	
Six thinking hats (de Bono)	✓		✓	✓		
Six action shoes (de Bono)	✓		✓	✓		
Systematic diagram (Mizuno)	✓		✓	✓	✓	
Three MUs (Murgatroyd/Morgan)	✓	✓	✓	✓		

many attempts are made to collect systematic data about a problem before action is taken to 'fix' it? How many 'fixes' backfire because the assumption on which the fix was based turns out to be false?

Systematic data on achievement need to be subjected to critical analysis on a systematic basis. New analytical and thinking tools include: systems archetypes from systems thinking or deBono-like thinking and problem-solving skills, coupled with systematic data analysis tools such as Pareto charts, run charts, and matrix analysis and statistical process control charts (SPCCs). What these tools do is to enhance the understanding of the dynamics of a problem and at the same time build stronger, better informed and more knowledgeable teams. Without these tools being used daily by teams, problems will be poorly understood and incorrectly adjusted. When this occurs, the 'fixes' used will be unlikely to produce sustainable quality improvements which have long-term benefits and no unintended side-effects.

Other TQM concepts and practices

Benchmarking

According to Camp (1989) and others, benchmarking 'is the continuous process of measuring products, services, and practices against the toughest competitors or those companies recognized as industry leaders'. There are in fact four common types of benchmark:

1. *Internal benchmarking*: comparing similar processes performed in different parts of the organization. For example, speed of travel, expense claim payout between one department and another.
2. *Competitive benchmarking*: comparing the performance of one organization to that of a competitor on specific measurable terms. For example, the reliability of postal services against courier services or next-day delivery criteria.
3. *Functional benchmarking*: comparison of performance on the same function for all those in an industry or sector. For example, comparing bad debt ratios for each company providing electricity worldwide.
4. *Generic benchmarking*: comparing organizations on a basic practice (e.g. speed of telephone response, accuracy of payroll, time taken to order and receive an item) that is the same regardless of the industry.

Increasingly successful organizations are using benchmarking to sustain their quality improvement efforts and to focus the energies of teams on becoming industry leaders in their core processes. The parallel most frequently used is the idea of Olympic performance in athletics. Everyone knows (1) the existing 'best in class', and (2) the relative position of all competitors to both their own performance and the best in the world. Competition thus becomes defined as continually improving one's own performance so as to get nearer to 'best in class'. Benchmarking is the name given to this process.

The service standard

This can be variously defined, but most definitions convey the core notion that a service standard is a customer-driven and agreed level of performance appropriate to the type of service and population being addressed, which is observable, achievable, measurable and desirable.

Service guarantee

The following are some examples of service guarantees. Delta Hotels of Canada guarantee a one-minute check-in for executive customers, or 'you don't pay for your stay'. Canadian Pacific Hotels guarantee to provide a business lunch from seating to payment in forty-five minutes 'or you don't pay'. Sheraton Hotels in New York guarantee room service delivered within twenty minutes or 'your meal is on us'. A restaurant in Fort Meyers, Florida, places a stopwatch on your table after taking your order and you eat free if the meal is not served within fifteen minutes. Each of these service guarantees expresses in a contract form the commitment made to customers about specific service standards which are guaranteed. Unconditional service guarantees are especially powerful ways of demonstrating the commitment of an organization to customer services. It is thought that such guarantees cannot be offered by public sector institutions such as health, education, social services, etc. Yet it is increasingly the case that such guarantees are being offered. Fox Valley Technical college in Appleton, Wisconsin has won accolades for its TQM efforts. One feature of its strategy is a guarantee: if a graduate cannot find a job in an area related to his or her training within six months, the college guarantees to provide at no cost to the student, up to six free credits of additional instruction (two or three courses). In addition, if an employer is not satisfied with the skills of a graduate, the college will offer retraining with a new instructor at no cost to the student or employer.

Kaizen *(pronounced Khai-Zan)*

Kaizen is the Japanese for continuous improvement and has been fully evaluated as a quality strategy by Imai (1989). *Kaizen* seeks to direct the efforts of all employees by continually focusing their energies on improving their own processes. Using a systematic process such as Deming's Plan-Do-Check-Act (P-D-C-A) cycle, employees are encouraged to seek weekly improvements on a small scale which help meet the needs of customers, suppliers and themselves.

Quality circles

During the early 1980s, many organizations formed and developed quality circles based on their reading of developments taking place in Japan. Most commonly, volunteers from an intact work team met weekly to seek ways of solving problems and improving processes within their own departments. Quality circles work on specific problems. When the problem has been 'worked through', the team is disbanded or a new problem is defined. It is widely recognized that the quality circles begun in the UK and the USA in the 1980s were for the most part failures due to the lack of a quality organizational culture where they were sited and the absence of training in team and problem-solving skills (Hill 1991).

Value-added

This important concept is concerned with all activities which add value to a product or service and equally with all those activities which detract from value by adding costs. According to Drummond (1992), western systems of delivering products or services are not very productive: time in the production of a product or the delivery of a service is not being used effectively. He cites as an example a heavy vehicle manufacturer who takes fifty days from receipt of an order to delivery; during this time, eighteen hours are used to assemble the vehicle, so that the product receives value for less than 1 per cent of its time in the system. The equivalent time period for Nissan is 2 days and 19.6 hours. There are fourteen activities in organizations which tend not to add value to the core tasks. These are:

1. *Preparation time*: preparing to do something is not the same as doing it; preparation adds costs. In the public sector, preparation (drafts, preliminary meetings, pre-planning sessions, etc.) is a preoccupation of some departments.
2. *Waiting time*: chronic delays occur when one group of workers are waiting for the product of the work of another group. If delays occur, then there is a slow down in the work process and slow downs are non-value-adding.
3. *Unnecessary process steps*: Public Works of Canada conduct eight reviews of engineering design every time a design is commissioned. These reviews occur even if the commission is an exact replication of a previously executed design, and in 1993 a team was working to reduce the number of design review steps so as to reduce costs and increase value-added. Many processes in all organizations have too many steps which add no or marginal value to the final outcome.
4. *Over-production*: a common complaint from government ministers is that policy briefs and documents are excessively detailed, sometimes to the extent of obscuring the policy choices by the volume of detail. In other areas of the civil service, reports are produced in greater volume than is needed 'just in case someone needs one'. Production over-runs such as these are non-value-adding.
5. *Rejects*: when work is done that is not used it is rejected. Rejected work is non-value-adding and causes delays in the effective running of systems.

6. *Set-up times*: the time taken to establish a process – to set up a procedure, to re-start a procedure that is seasonal or to re-start a procedure which has failed – is known as set-up time. Set-up times are
non-value-adding in that they are simply another form of preparation.
When necessary, set-up times need to be kept to a minimum.

7. *Transportation/distribution*: anyone who has worked in the public
sector knows how much time is spent sending out material for comment, receiving comments back, processing those comments, and then
deciding what to do with them. A key part of these delays concerns
basic distribution problems – getting information out and back so that
work can be performed. While faxes improve speed, they may also
add cost.

8. *Process waste*: we have already said that some processes contain steps
which are non-value-adding. It is also the case that some complete
processes are non-value-adding. For example, it used to be the case in
one government department that all expense claims for travel out of
the jurisdiction required ministerial approval on a case-by-case basis.
Ending this process reduced costs, speeded process and increased
efficiency. If a process is included in an activity without a clear understanding of the value-added property of the process, then it should be
assumed to be non-value-adding.

9. *Materials waste*: for example, a large number of the records held on
paper in most public organizations are actually print-outs from computer files. Also, at the end of the year, there is often massive shred-
ding of reports and documents.

10. *Communications*: a failure to communicate effectively or accurately
can result in misunderstandings, wasted effort, loss of alignment within
the organization. The effects of poor communication are non-value-
adding.

11. *Administration/decision-making*: the core task of government in relation to individuals and groups within the community is to make decisions and administer them effectively. In many cases, the administrative
structures created over-compensate for the large volume of work in
which errors could occur by over-control, over-inspection and excessive documentation of actions taken. The value-added activity is making
the decision itself and effecting its consequences for the customer or
end-user. All other activities, while again necessary, can be minimized.

12. *Untidiness*: tidiness is the product of the systems being used, as is
untidiness. Untidy record-keeping, storage of needed equipment and
other resources causes delay and reduces effectiveness.

13. *Bottlenecks*: efficiency in a process is determined by the slowest stage
in the process. A receptionist in a mental health clinic can book as
many appointments in a day as she can make 'phone calls. The bottle-
neck is the time the therapist takes to see patients, usually fifty to sixty
minutes. While some bottlenecks are designed into systems, others just
emerge. For example, when patients were asked to determine how

long they wished to see a therapist for, the average time requested was
40 minutes, thus permitting a therapist to see up to ten clients per day
as opposed to seven. In many organizations, bottlenecks are inevitable.

14. *Timing*: bad timing causes problems. When something is not done on
time, it often means it was not done with proper timing (Shingo
1987). Though project management techniques have been in use for
over half a century, they are not used effectively in many service
organizations.

These fourteen non-value-adding areas all take time, energy and resources away from the core task of delivering services to the end-user. By
redesigning systems to eliminate these sources of value-losing activities, we
can increase value-added, lower operating costs and increase the perceived
value of service.

Just in time

This is the name applied to the company-wide TQM concept which had
its origin in the Toyota company – the approach was called Toyota Manufacturing System (Shingo 1989). Its particular emphasis was on delivering
specific results by involving all employees in problem-solving and making
customer satisfaction paramount. The philosophy behind Just in time (JIT)
is founded in the elimination of waste, which is defined as anything other
than the minimum amount of equipment, materials, parts, space and
workers' time that are absolutely essential to add value to the product.
This is the prototype or quintessential TQM in the manufacturing context.

In respect of the application of JIT, John Cammel (1992) has said:

Looking at business and observing where value is added and more
importantly where costly non-value added activities occur is a key to
understanding JIT and the elimination of waste. Usually I have found
that during the lifetime of a product, five percent of the time it is
undergoing a value added process whilst 95% of its time is picking
up costs.

The JIT approach, then, concentrates on the 95 per cent of non-value-
added resources. What are the analogues of 'adding value' and 'picking up
costs' in the public sector contexts, and would the key JIT question fit:
'Are you prepared to question every activity in your company to determine
its value adding right to exist?' (Cammel 1992: 25).

Hoshin planning

Hoshin planning refers to the setting by a participative process of extraordinary outrageous goals for quality improvement. Instead of the 'top-
down' approach of planning imposed on a workplace by the canons of the
'management-by-objectives' approach, with Hoshin planning the whole

notion of outrageous goals is shared within the organization in at least two significant ways: there should be participation by all in the determination of how to achieve these goals, and there should be the release of individual initiative and responsibility. The key idea behind the setting of outrageous goals is to challenge everyone in the organization to go beyond that which they know they are capable of achieving to that which they know they aspire to. Through the development of a learning organization (Senge 1990), organizations can achieve remarkable results.

Some typical Hoshin goals include: the achievement of a reduction from 2800 errors per million parts to 3.2 errors per million parts at Motorola; a 35 per cent reduction in cycle time for all cycles of activity at Xerox Canada; a 35 per cent reduction in the cost of quality within five years at IBM Canada.

The Deming wheel

This planning notion comes from W. Edwards Deming, whose seminal influence on TQM we shall describe in the next chapter. The Deming wheel – plan, do, check, action – is used at all levels in some TQM organizations. For example, the Bath Mental Health Trust are using an elaborated P-D-C-A to inform their TQM initiatives. Based on a proven methodology, the P-D-C-A cycle has been broken down into twelve steps:

Plan
1. Identify the product or service to be improved.
2. Identify the customers/suppliers for this product or service.
3. Identify current work practices/processes which have a direct impact on the service or product.
4. Using 1–3 above, narrow down the service quality improvement task to 'do-able' activities.
5. Establish cause and effects.
6. Develop plan for revised work process.

Do
7. Conduct small-scale tests of revised process.

Check
8. Evaluate test results.
9. Seek improvement in revised work process.

Act
10. Standardize the new process so that everyone performs the same task in the same efficient and reflective way.
11. Measure and systematically analyse customer reaction.
12. Acknowledge and recognize success.

Teams are asked to use this as a framework in their attempt to locate value-adding improvements.

One model of TQM or many

Within the TQM literature, there are those who deploy the notion of models of TQM – a Deming Model is contrasted starkly with a Crosby Model, for example. Or there is posited to be a Social Relationship Model of TQM, incorporating such values as empowerment of customers and employees, open communication and decision-making, etc., which is in contrast to a Standard Setting Model and Compliance Model characterized by analysis of requirements, the setting of standards, preferably through quantified statements, and the determination of variants on non-conformance. We are not attracted to such dichotomous views, preferring instead to see the TQM model adopted in a particular context, as contingent on the characteristics of the specific occupational environment, while embracing certain core features of all TQM models. We develop this view further in Chapter 3 and in our final chapter.

2

Leading thinkers for Total Quality Management

TQM has become inextricably linked with Japanese management in many people's minds because of the great success that that country has achieved in selling certain of its goods on the basis of quality. While it is certainly true that TQM has been widely developed and applied in certain industries in Japan, and to the extent that the terminology used to describe some key TQM ideas and applications is Japanese, the intellectual origins of TQM were actually in the USA.

During the Second World War, American engineers and statisticians made great efforts in the quality control of the manufacture of armaments. At that time, it was not only important that the troops had the best possible in design, but that they also had weapons which did not fail and which were highly accurate. There was, therefore, a war-driven drive to achieve product quality by the use of more sophisticated control methods than had hitherto been the case. It was the developments in improving quality at that time which really constitute the beginnings of what has now become Total Quality Management. In that sense, the seeds of TQM were sown in the USA, but they were to grow and be cultivated in the Far East from where the further propagation has brought TQM to be recognized as a key world management perspective for the 1990s.

When, after the Second World War, the Americans controlled Japan's reconstruction, Japan's manufacturing image was one of a producer of shoddy goods and manufacturers who had used underhand methods before the war – such as naming a town USA so that they could stamp 'Made in USA' on the shoddy products produced there to deceive purchasers.

Japan did have some quality products, but these were reckoned to be in certain textiles. This was acknowledged by John Foster Dulles, the American Foreign Secretary, when he visited there in 1950 and said: 'You will never be able to compete with the United States in technology, but you do make very good handkerchiefs and pyjamas which would sell very well in the USA, why don't you export these?' (Hutchins 1992). What Dulles had not reckoned with before making such an arrogant statement was the reception the Japanese would give to the American teachers of manufacturing methods which the US government was to send them to assist the country over wartime destruction. American teachers visiting Japan were the early advocates of quality and are now seen as the first 'TQM gurus'.

According to Professor Tony Bendell (1991), three groups of quality gurus can be identified as significant in the establishment of TQM during the period since the Second World War:

1. The early Americans who took the message of quality to the Japanese.
2. The Japanese who developed new concepts in response to the Americans' messages.
3. The new western wave of gurus who, following Japanese industrial success, have given rise to increased quality awareness in the west.

All the early Americans had begun with a focus on the technical aspects, such as statistical process control techniques of achieving quality, but later moved to the wider management issues connected with the establishment of an organization-wide quality approach.

Drawing on the work of Bendell (1991) and others, we need to note the names and understand a little of the approaches of some of these founding fathers of what has now become more widely called TQM, for they have by now rightly taken their place in the 'hall of fame' of seminal thinkers to the study of management in general.

The American founding fathers of quality

It was the Americans Deming, Juran and Fiegenbaum who laid the foundation of quality control in manufacturing and suggested its wider management context, which their Japanese students were to so skilfully exploit and take further. We set out below for each of these seminal leaders of TQM the key aspects of their approaches. They have also at later points in their careers codified the essentials of their beliefs into a set of steps or points – Deming's fourteen points, Juran's 'quality planning road map' and Fiegenbaum's ten benchmarks (these are summarized in the Appendix).

W. Edwards Deming is often seen as the number one guru, the father figure of the modern quality revolution. He was convinced that statistical sampling methods could be applied to manufacturing and non-manufacturing activities for productivity gains. His application of statistical process control techniques at the American National Bureau of the Census led to six-fold productivity improvement in some processes and his approaches were hailed by engineers after they were published in 1943. The application of his approaches to *quality* – the reduction of scrap and re-work in wartime arms production – were not taken on board by management after the Second World War. In the post-war boom, manufacturing companies in the USA and the UK could almost sell anything irrespective of quality control.

After the war, Deming was sent to Japan as an adviser and his message to the Japanese reflected his statistical background, by encouraging managers – whether in manufacturing or not – to focus on variability and understand the difference between special causes and common causes. The *special causes* of variation in a product, process or service were those which prevented it remaining constant in a statistical sense, and he demonstrated that they are assignable and can be identified by using the appropriate techniques and solved by those operating them. The *common causes* of variation, on the other hand, are not assignable to varying local conditions or the variation induced by particular humans, but are systemic in that they follow from a design or process defect which is constant in reducing the optimum quality. The distinction between special and common causes equates with the blemish and fault categories of defect we gave in Chapter 1.

Deming also demonstrated that these causes of variation were capable of being identified by those closest to the process, but he stressed that only management authority could eliminate common causes. Deming's approach as a whole encouraged the Japanese to adopt a systematic approach to problem-solving with senior managers leading the way in solving quality problems by what later became known as the Deming Wheel or P-D-C-A (Plan, Do, Check, Action) cycle.

Deming's concerns also went beyond the variation in processes and the responsibilities of management for quality, to embrace the customer in the analysis. In Japan in the 1950s, he taught that the consumer was the most important part of the production line; that it was insufficient to satisfy the customer, rather the concern should be with delighting the customer. In recognition of his contributions, the Japanese Union of Scientists and Engineers (JUSE) created the annual Deming Application Prize awarded in recognition of the systematic application of the quality principle throughout an organization.

Almost three decades would pass before Deming received recognition in his own country. A 1980 NCB documentary, 'If Japan Can . . . Why can't We?' turned the key, and during the 1980s, through a rigorous schedule of consultancies and lectures, Deming took his management method to a multitude of American business leaders. His method was expressed in his famous '14 points' for managers (see Appendix), which he saw as necessary to transform traditional practices if the west was to stay in business.

Joseph M. Juran is the quality guru perhaps most frequently linked with Deming when the American origins of TQM are discussed. He was an engineer who specialized and published in manufacturing quality control and, like Deming, went to Japan in the 1950s. In Japan, his lectures emphasized that quality control should be conducted as an integral part of management leadership and control. Central to his approach was the message that quality does not happen by accident, it must be planned for and is part of a quality trilogy: quality planning, quality control and quality improvement. Some of the key elements to Juran's approach were identifying customers and their needs, establishing optimal quality goals, creating measurements of quality, adopting planning processes which gave quality goals under operating conditions, and producing continuing results in terms of improved market share, prices and reduction of error. Juran concentrated not just on the end customer but identified other external and internal customers. His 'fitness of use' quality concept was therefore also to be applied to the interim product for all internal customers. Juran's discussion of quality in economic terms focused on costs, both those which were avoidable and those which were unavoidable. The unavoidable costs consisted of quality improvement measures, but the avoidable costs were synonymous with re-work, scrap and failure. An investment in quality improvement could remove this avoidable toll of defects and repair, and hence avoidable costs were like 'gold in the mine'. Juran also emphasizes the need for continuous awareness of the customer in all functions and this emphasis was reflected in his 'quality planning road map' of nine steps (see Appendix).

His more recent work has pointed up the uselessness of sloganism without planning action. Action, he asserts, should consist of 90 per cent substance and 10 per cent exhortation, not the reverse. He attributes the majority of quality problems to the fault of poor management rather than poor performance by the worker and believes that management controllable defects account for over 80 per cent of all quality problems. Juran believes that, as with Japanese industry, long-term training to improve quality should start at the top, but he knows that this irritates senior management, and says their instinctive belief is that upper managers already know what needs to be done and that training is for others – the workforce – so that it is time to re-examine this belief.

Armand V. Fiegenbaum, another major American guru, also came from a background of manufacturing quality control which was mainly developed in experience as head of quality at the General Electric Company and with extensive contacts with leading Japanese industrial giants. The statistical point of view is seen as having a profound effect on modern quality control and Fiegenbaum argues that statistical methods must be used whenever and wherever they may be useful to this end. However, these methods must be seen as only a part of the overall management system, they are not the system itself – 'Quality is in essence a way of managing the organisation'.

Although much concerned with technical and statistical issues, he emphasized management methods and considered human relations as the basic issue in quality control activities. His more recent work has added an emphasis on customers' perceptions of quality, and in defining quality for the 1990s he has put forward ten benchmarks for total quality success (see Appendix).

The Japanese gurus

Japanese scientists and engineers took the American gurus who visited them in the 1950s seriously in their advocacy of quality, to the extent that their own gurus were to take the development of what has now become TQM dramatically further.

Kaoru Ishikawa is best known for his commitment to get grassroots workers to understand and practise what quality was all about by way of *quality circles* and making simple statistical techniques accessible to supervisors and front-line workers for good data collection. Following the visits of the Americans, he was a key figure in the rapid development of the company-wide quality control movement in Japan – total participation in quality from top management to the lowest ranking employees. Seven tools of quality control are taught to all employees: Pareto charts, cause-and-effect diagrams, check sheets, histograms, scatter diagrams, control charts and graphs. According to Ishikawa, these seven tools can solve 95 per cent of problems. His contribution to the development of TQM has been the bringing about of greater worker involvement and motivation through: an atmosphere where employees are continuously looking to resolve problems, greater commercial awareness to the lowest operating level, and changed attitudes regarding ever-increasing goals.

Genichi Taguchi is the other best known Japanese quality guru in the west and his methodology is concerned with concepts of quality and reliability at the design stage, that is prior to manufacture. By way of experimental design methods, he has led a shift to quality of the product design from the earlier emphasis on quality in the production process. Taguchi methodology is fundamentally a prototyping method that enables the engineer to identify the optimal settings to produce a robust product that can survive manufacturing time after time, piece after piece, in order to provide the functionality required by the customer. Taguchi is a four time winner of the Deming Prize, and as a person evinces a humble and cooperative attitude which many see as embracing the very spirit of TQM.

Shigeo Shingo is not well known in Europe outside of manufacturing, where he was essentially concerned with quality on the production aspects of manufacturing, but we include reference to him here both because he is the initiator of the controversial Zero Defects concept and because his essential concepts look to have adaptive possibilities of transfer to service and public sector provisions. Shingo's essential approach was to recognize that however good statistical process control methods were, they could not of themselves reduce defects to zero. What was required was that processes should become mistake-proofed (*Poka-Yoke*) by design and control so as to completely reduce errors or defects. In the manufacturing context, this led to workers being able to stop the process whenever a defect occurred, define the cause, and prevent the recurring source of the defect, a process which is made possible by instrumenting machines with immediate feedback devices rather than relying on fallible human judgement.

The western perspective on Japanese TQM has derived from experience in the many Japanese-owned companies established in the UK, Canada and the USA in the last two decades. An occidental view of Japanese TQM as a whole might be that it perhaps has given the greatest prominence to worker empowerment and perhaps more than the west to worker education and training. The commitment to training and maximization of competence of the front-line worker is very great indeed. In Japan, it is perhaps these aspects of action which sustain such a belief of competitive confidence and which suggest even cultural superiority. For example:

> We are going to win and the industrial West is going to lose out; there's not much you can do about it because the reasons for your failure are within yourselves . . . For you the essence of management is getting the ideas out of the heads of the bosses and into the hands of labour . . . Business, we know, is now so complex and difficult, the survival of firms so hazardous in an environment increasingly unpredictable, competitive and fraught with danger, that their continued existence depends on the day to day mobilisation of every ounce of intelligence.
>
> (Konosuke Matsushita, cited in Hutchins 1992: 113)

The more recent TQM gurus

Philip Crosby, an American, is nowadays seen as a leader of the 'new wave' of quality gurus, and is the leading western advocate of zero defects, not just in manufacturing. In the Crosby scheme, there is a strong top-down approach, quality is driven by a management initiative from the top, while employees are involved in the operational difficulties affecting quality. He insists that the performance standard must be zero defects, not 'that's close enough'. He asserts that zero defects does not mean that people never make mistakes, but that the organization should not expect people to make them. Crosby points out that if people do not believe that zero defects is possible, they will never achieve that goal. Crosby's absolutes of quality management are: quality is defined as conformance to requirements, not as 'goodness' or 'elegance'; the system for causing quality is prevention not appraisal; a performance standard of zero defects; and that the true measure of quality is the price of non-conformance not indices. As with several of the other gurus already discussed, Crosby has his own checklist of components for quality – Crosby's fourteen steps to quality improvement (see Appendix).

Tom Peters is an American who has researched the secrets of the most successful companies. His contribution to TQM has been to celebrate a type of leadership and give prominence to customer orientation. In identifying leadership as central to quality improvement, he has characterized the type of leadership necessary as *leadership by walking about*, a facilitating, cheerleader role constantly in touch with customers, innovation and people, the three major areas common to excellent achievers. Peters' books are characterized by forty-five prescriptions for action and he also has produced a quality checklist – Peters' twelve attributes of a quality revolution (see Appendix).

3

Applying Total
Quality Management
in the public sector

The purpose of this chapter is to consider the extent to which TQM is applicable to the public sector. We have already described the development of TQM within manufacturing and indicated that it had become a holistic management approach by the 1990s, and one which is being signalled from near and far as relevant to all contexts. For example:

> ... we now need management style and methods based on effective leadership and Total Quality Management ... The competitive situation and the management breakthroughs required apply equally to managers in business and service organisations. It is just as important that they are taken up in Education and the National Health Service, as that they are practised in manufacturing industry or financial services.
>
> (Mortiboys and Oakland 1991)

In the above quotation, from one of a series of booklets on quality produced by the British Government's Department of Trade and Industry on managing in the 1990s, the two authors from the world of manufacturing are adopting the stance of the generic applicability of TQM.

TQM had in fact official policy standing in the early 1990s within the British National Health Service, the largest single employer in Europe. In health, education and government contexts generally in Europe and North America, TQM was being advocated almost as something self-evidently workable and suitable to the public sector because of its proven success in certain industries. Participants in these services were largely being asked to take on board the asserted virtues of TQM without debate about their appropriateness to the public sector. In general terms, there were on the ground a range of *a priori* based objections to TQM, which we ourselves heard widely expressed, and which were not being addressed.

We think it important therefore to take the whole issue of the generic validity of TQM head on, and to discuss in some detail the fit of TQM to the public sector, in order to establish its validity in contexts far from manufacturing. It is our view that the objections and issues relating to the application of TQM in the public sector can be seen to fall under one or other of the following five headings:

- The nature of TQM itself inhibits its application to the public sector.
- The nature of the public sector itself is inimical to the reception of TQM applications.
- The work cultures of the professional groups which characterize the public sector are inimical to TQM.
- In the public sector the customer is a more problematic concept.
- Public sector provisions are much more complicated than manufacturing.

We shall discuss each of these categories in turn and arrive at a view that: the core concepts of TQM are equally as valid in the public sector as elsewhere; that while there is some validity to each of the above positions, their force is not absolute with the consequence that other TQM concepts and practices can be seen to have 'adaptive' or 'problematic' status. We also indicate that the 'traditional' public sector environment is in any case undergoing significant change because government is re-inventing the nature of its provisions by adopting new strategies of control and delivery.

The nature of TQM itself inhibits its application to the public sector

The objections to the validity of TQM in public sector provisions which fall under this heading essentially revolve around the proposition that TQM has come from, and essentially belongs to, the industrial or manufacturing environment. This view equates TQM as a body of ideas and practices for the creating of success for physical products in a marketplace. The public sector provisions do not have these features; they are not centrally concerned with products but with the delivery of public services in a context where the whole notion of the market does not apply, or at least has not been applied until recently.

Public sector managers need to examine and to be able to respond to such objections. Just how valid are the points about 'product' and 'market'? Let us first scrutinize the manufacturing or 'product' aspect of the objection. In manufacturing, TQM has been a vehicle for reducing the variation in production processes to achieve consistency of quality product, a product orientation of 'doing the same thing right every time'. 'Right first time' has become something of a summarizing slogan for TQM in manufacturing – get it right first time every time, tighten up the systems, eliminate waste, reduce the need for post-production inspection, and all of this (plus, of course, the key human aspects of TQM we noted in Chapter 2) will reduce the overall cost of the product, and drastically improve its quality. 'Right first time' has been no mere slogan; it has been the dramatic and pervading reality of the most successful manufacturing companies worldwide in the last two decades.

However, doing the same thing right every time is not the prime need in the service industry, where to do the same thing correct each time would hardly be fitting for the varied needs of individual customers. Services, in our view, essentially have a concern – whether they are in the commercial or public sector – to do the right things for the *particular* customer. In services, therefore, the analogue of the manufacturer's product is not 'the same commodity every time', but rather 'the correct differentiated response every time' so as to meet each individual customer's needs. Rather than the elimination of variance so necessary in the manufacturing process to achieve quality of product, for the service sector the challenge is one of maintaining both consistency of standard and appropriateness of choice from a range of process options. Quality in services is therefore about the increasing of variance and the skill repertoires of staff so that they may more appropriately meet wide variations in demand.

This is not to say that in service provisions there are not 'right first time concerns'. There are. We all want the consistency and elimination of error that ensures that, for example, buses and trains run on time, letters arrive to schedule, customers are not kept waiting for their meals longer than a given period, patients can have hip replacements within a given period of expectation, etc. Nevertheless, it must be acknowledged that for service provisions there is overall a major concern among management with increasing variability rather than eliminating it. This distinction has led some commentators on the scope of TQM to view the issue in dichotomous terms and to conclude that the essentials of TQM therefore only apply to manufacturing and not services – or if to services, then not to the public sector. This view we feel is erroneous. It clearly confuses the important distinction between *type of product* and *process*. In manufacturing, the product of the activity (processes) needs to be of a standard and identical quality; in service provisions, the product of the activity needs to be differentiated according to the expectations of the customer. The central TQM concept which both have in common is elimination of variation in process, i.e. process control, whether that process be one to achieve standardization or one to achieve the delivery of the most desired differentiated response. The key issue then, is not that the type of variation differs for the customer of manufacturers and the customer of services, but that the *processes* which deliver either the manufactured product or the variable response to the service customer have consistent quality. In this latter sense, the slogan 'right first time' could equally be made to fit public service provisions – the processes need to be right first time to meet the context and the individual customer. It is the elimination of quality-defeating variations in the processes of activity that is all important, whether these are product processes or service processes.

The view we take, therefore, is that the original manufacturing nature of TQM does not of itself disable its application to the public sector. This might only be true if the central TQM concept of consistency of process is lost sight of. The different focuses of *variation* – diminution of variation on the one hand, and maximization of variation on the other – between product processes and service processes do, however, mean that there are issues to the transfer of TQM thinking to service and public sector provisions. In applying the total management approach, careful thought and explanation must be given to where, within the organization, the aim is the maximization of uniformity such as usually applies where a physical product is the output of the work, and where the attainment of quality variation is the goal such as in service encounters. In so much of public sector service provision, it is the meeting of unique individual needs which motivates and drives its participants, so much so that words such as 'the service' and 'service ethic' are often part of the vocabulary. As a consequence, any explanation of TQM to public sector professionals in its 'product' achievement terms will likely face a kind of 'tissue rejection response', and rightly so, for the manufacturing focus has only minor relevance to their worlds.

What we hope the above discussion has shown is that whereas some of the TQM concepts we introduced in Chapter 1 can have generic applicability across occupational sectors – such as the core concept of process control – others such as 'right first time' essentially belong to manufacturing contexts, but can be adapted to fit to other contexts such as that of the public sector. Regarding TQM, therefore, we should eschew a view of its concepts as having dichotomous validities, and see them has having 'core' or 'adaptive' relevance as the case may be, while the status of some might even be wholly problematic.

So much for the 'product' objection to the validity of TQM in the public sector, but what about the 'market' objection? It is self-evident that all of the concepts, beliefs and practices which now constitute the holistic management approach called TQM originated in an open market context where products were evaluated by customers for their quality against competitor products. In other words, for any particular product, there is a range of suppliers (i.e. a market) and TQM works to the advantage of those who apply its workplace practices because customers will choose between suppliers on grounds of quality of product or service in an open market. If there is no market, then it can be argued that TQM is irrelevant, or that the cutting edge of TQM is lost because the customer is not able to choose between suppliers and, as a consequence, cannot control quality by purchasing action. To what extent is this proposition correct?

Clearly, one has to agree that the absence of a market does eliminate the ultimate test of quality, whereby the consumer chooses between comparable provisions from different suppliers. Given that public sector provisions are traditionally supplier monopolies, to what extent is the usefulness of TQM seriously undermined? Our view is that the absence of a market does not of itself stop either a product or service provider from enhancing all processes involved in the manufacture of the product or the production of the service, so that waste is eliminated, measured efficiency is enhanced and costs are reduced. These gains from TQM could still be objectively demonstrated as could the quality of the end-product or service in the customer's eyes. Nevertheless, in the absence of a market, that ultimate test of customer acclaim (evaluation of product or service against others which they could obtain) cannot be expressed.

However, the concept of the market has been introduced into the public sector in recent years. In the early 1980s, there was a stream of government initiatives in many countries aimed at securing a paradigm shift within the public service sector generally – greater concern with value for money, devolution of responsibility to local levels, and attempts to shift from administration of inputs to accountability for managing processes and outputs. Concurrent with these moves, there have been calls for more responsiveness to consumers' views and the provision of greater choice. There has come about the concept of the *internal market*, most notably advocated for health and education provisions so far, but also to some extent also for local government. The growing concept of the internal market does express itself differently between public sector provisions; in the UK National Health Service, the internal market is expressed in contracts between 'purchasers' and 'providers'; in education by 'open enrolment and parental choice of school'. We shall have more to say about the internal market in the discussion of the different occupational provisions in the public sector in Part 2 of this book, but it is important to note here that the concept of the market is now no longer absent from the public sector. In so far as a full expression of TQM is dependent on the existence of a market, then, it can no longer be said that the public sector is different.

The nature of the public sector itself is inimical to the reception of TQM applications

From the opposite perspective, a number of arguments can be advanced which state in effect that it is not the nature of TQM which limits its application outside of the commercial sector but rather certain essential features about the public sector itself. The most frequently advanced are: the public sector is more resistant to change; the resourcing of public sector provisions is disconnected from performance; the managers in the public sector are not rewarded for performance or the attainment of certain quality measures; improving service quality without increasing costs is intrinsically more difficult; and public sector managers are not free to enact management in the way that managers in manufacturing or commercial service provisions are.

The public sector is more resistant to change

A belief for which there is empirical evidence is that attitudinally the public sector has conformed to one of the hallmarks of mature bureaucracies, namely an overcommitment to regulation and enforcement of precedent and rules breeding a resistance to change. Rosemary Stewart (1992) has presented research evidence to this effect:

> the small case studies done in both public and private sector UK organisations as part of the six-country EC study found more resistance amongst the middle managers interviewed in the public sector than amongst those in industry.

The reasons given were: the need for change was less evident in the public sector; there was a feeling that commercially oriented changes are inimical to the ideals of public service, which may have been one of the reasons why people joined the public service in the first place; many public servants see themselves as professionals and not managers; and a tradition of playing safe in order to avoid mistakes which can lead to politicians' questions.

This evidence would suggest that 'resistance to change' in the public sector is largely composed of occupational cultural factors. TQM calls for cultural change in all occupational settings, and there is already clear evidence (as we show in later chapters) that given the political sponsorship or consents, the public sector can thrive equally as well on cultural change as the commercial sector.

Public sector provisions are disconnected from performance

The seminal management writer Peter Drucker (1980, 1988) has observed that the management of performance cannot be expected of public service institutions given certain traditional conditions:

> [public] service institutions are typically paid out of a budget allocation. This means they are not paid by what the taxpayer and customer mean by results and performance. Their revenue flow from a general revenue stream that depends not on what they are doing but on some sort of tax.

Drucker has also graphically pointed out that the typical public service institution also has traditionally had monopoly powers so that the intended beneficiaries have had no choice. The public sector has therefore enjoyed power beyond that which the most monopolistic businesses have enjoyed:

> ... if I am dissatisfied with the service of the local [commercial] power or of the telephone service, I have no other place to go for

electric power or telephone service. But if I choose to do without power or telephone service I do not have to pay for it.

This option is not, observes Drucker, available to customers dissatisfied with public service institutions; the customers must pay whether they want to use the service or not.

In discussing above the aspects of monopoly and lack of market to the public sector, we indicated that local and national governments have now responded and are actively modifying the powers of public sector institutions to modify monopoly power and introduce some element of choice and consumer influence. But the issue of performance needs further comment. To cite Drucker (1988) again:

> Being paid out of a budget allocation rather than for results changes what is meant by performance. Results in the budget based institutions are measured by the budget size. Performance is the ability to maintain or to increase one's budget ... And the budget is not, by definition related so much to contribution as to good intentions ... Not to spend the entire budget will only convince the budget maker that the budget for the next fiscal period can be safely cut.

The argument, therefore, is that performance cannot be expected of public service institutions because they are not paid on that basis but according to how successful they are in the politics of resource acquisition. TQM, as we described earlier in presenting its core concepts, requires the performance of all processes of provision to be revealed by measuring non-conformance and customer approval. TQM would, therefore, positively require a change from budget resourcing to performance resourcing in the public sector; hence, were the public sector to remain as it has been, it would be inimical to TQM.

Why indeed would public sector workers be prepared to make a massive investment in process control enhancement and in the meeting of customer expectations if the results achieved in quality performance did not bring them any benefits in the ways that parallel TQM gains have in the commercial sector? In fact, because rank-and-file workers in the public sector know instinctively that what they do is not resourced on the basis of performance, they are suspicious about any intention to apply TQM. They perceive that unless it is demonstrated to the contrary, that the application of TQM may even be self-destructive; that the sort of savings total quality might make could lead to loss of jobs.

We would see this whole aspect of the basis of resourcing as a substantial inhibitor to the application of TQM in the public sector were it not for the fact that there are now clear moves to make resourcing related to performance. In health and education in the UK or public works in Canada, for example, the rules have been changed to drive financial control of provision down to the local unit level of the individual school, hospital or unit, with funding related to the demonstrated performance of a 'contract' made with a funding or 'purchasing' body. Nevertheless, it is very early days in this regard, so Drucker's crucial analysis has to be faced and overcome. It does seem to us that the force of this 'budget-performance' axiom has even wider implications. To provide a workable context for TQM, not only must budgets follow performance, but a link between the achievement of demonstrated savings and a right to keep them must be established. If, however, the ground rules which apply to the implementation of TQM in public sector institutions do not allow units to receive, by way of increased funding, the savings benefits which have come from enhanced quality performance, the scope for TQM implementation will in our view be limited. Nothing will kill off the promise of TQM more quickly than if public sector workers see the 'savings' they have achieved being swallowed up elsewhere while they go unrewarded, or worse still, the quality enhancements pose threats to levels of professional staffing.

Public sector managers are not rewarded for performance

Another feature of the public sector which can be seen as inhibitive to the reception of TQM is that the pay of its managers has traditionally not been related to performance. Murgatroyd and Earle (1992) summed up the situation as follows:

> ... promotion, rewards and recognition systems adopted by governments are, by and large based on seniority classification systems for positions rather than any pure merit based or team based classification or gain-sharing policy ... Profit sharing, team based reward or pay for learning are not yet the currency of local government.

A ready explanation for this situation has been that in any case there just aren't the performance measures.

Much has also been written in the past about the public service pay ethic to the effect that leaders in public service provisions receive a significant part of their reward *intrinsically*, that is from the satisfaction which flows from having achieved particular service ethic aims. After all, the argument has gone, public service managers have choices for personal satisfaction in their work that are denied to commercial managers who must respond constantly to the external environment for survival; in the public sector, survival is guaranteed, so that action choices can be much more internally or professionally exercised. In any case – so the argument is further extended – even for those public service managers who might have had a leaning towards performance, there has been little development of measures on the part of those who control budgeting that could lead to the improvement of services, or at least costs.

These two linked features have been self-reinforcing, so that energetic and efficient managers have soon learned that achieving better than average performance results does not necessarily bring rewards, because they are not easily demonstrable, because the measures have not received official approval, or because though the basis of the measures may seem all right technically, they are seen to be controversial and there is no consensus about using them. Better in such circumstances, therefore, to depend on politics, bargaining and obtaining the right funding patrons. Public service managers have, then, been traditionally rewarded for their sociopolitical skills in budget acquisition rather than judgements on their measured performance.

This basis of resourcing is, in the early 1990s, starting to be replaced across the public sector, and the advocates of performance measures are becoming more vocal and eloquent. What we see happening at the present time across several countries is that a break with the tradition of no performance measures is first made for the public sector by the external superordinate government funding bureaucracy imposing certain benchmarks, such has been the case in the setting of attainment targets for public sector schools in the UK. In setting some national benchmarks for public sector provisions, government is at the same time tacitly or expressly inviting the 'profession' to go to it and get better measures if they can. What in general terms is the nature of the measures which will, and are, coming about in the public sector?

Van Der Hart (1991) has argued that whereas for industry quality performance is essentially mediated by customers' willingness to pay the appropriate price, so that performance is indexed by the important quantitative measures of turnover and market share, government provisions will have to develop forms of measuring which do not derive from the 'price signal'. He suggests that the types of measures likely to be available will fall within the linked categories of output, reach and results.

Our own experience in a good range of public service contexts is that the politics of resource allocation have ruled in the absence of performance measures, so that managers' pay has not depended on results. A halt has now very definitely been called, and in the face of ever-increasing demands for funds, the traditional public service management mores are now fundamentally challenged. Increasingly in pay bargaining, government is insisting on restructuring the rules so that rewards include performance-related pay. To an extent, therefore, public service managers and workers now have their pay to some extent linked with performance. Moreover, the budget disposers are no longer negotiating for but demanding performance measures and will impose them if the professional constituency resists the whole idea, as has happened with regard to schools in the UK. In the UK, the publishing of school league tables of the raw results of examination performance has been imposed against the fierce opposition of all teaching unions. The plain fact is, then, that both these aspects – performance-related pay and performance measures – are no longer missing elements in public service provisions and are likely to become more widely established.

Public sector managers are not free to enact management in the way that managers in manufacturing or commercial service provisions are

Milakovich (1991), Van Der Hart (1991) and others have drawn attention to certain constraints on managers in the public service sector which do not leave them as free as their commercial sector counterparts to pursue best performance in quality and cost terms. *A priori*, these constraints would be inhibitors to the implementation of TQM in its full expression.

Principally under this heading, these authors draw attention to the nature of political control. Politicians do not necessarily restrict themselves to policy-making; they often wish to involve themselves in the execution of policy, yet the adoption of TQM would seem to assume a clear distinction between making and implementing policy. There is the further constraint which relates to constituency or customer groups. Commercial managers do have to worry a great deal about groups beyond their target customers, e.g. shareholders. But the political controllers of public service provisions must always have a concern (and hence their managers also) not to alienate any group of their constituents. There is not just one target group of clients and shareholders, but the whole community. As a consequence, a focus on the avoidance of alienation may well be stronger than a focus on the satisfying of any one particular group. It could be argued that a TQM approach in the public sector cannot exercise the costly control provision to those services or groups where quality can be guaranteed. It does not have the selectivity associated with the competitive positioning choices available to the commercial sector. Government frequently has to make provision for which there would be little commercial incentive – a healthy environment or safety on the streets, for example. An explicit adoption of TQM would therefore imply a clarification of the 'fudge' between management and politics. This would mean a need to declare what programmes are being acted upon or not, which groups are currently being served or not, rather than a continuance of the traditional rhetoric that everything is being done to the best possible extent for all 'the voters'. In our view, if politicians are to see the adoption of TQM, they will need to live with the consequences of the empowerment necessary for its managers and work teams.

The work cultures of the professionals in the public sector are inimical to TQM

In the previous chapter, we presented a description of the concepts, beliefs and practices of TQM as implying total cultural change in the way an organization works and is managed. For manufacturing in the UK and in other western countries, the degree of adjustment required has been dramatic. When a factory known to one of the authors was taken over in the mid-1980s by a TQM company, the overnight changes were revolutionary. For example, it was announced to all senior managers that reserved parking spaces would be done away with forthwith. 'What if there is not a space available when I arrive' asked one? 'No problem, you must be here first in the morning', was the answer. Along with the reserved parking, three separate canteens were eliminated in the first week, and the whole range of relationships and working practices of TQM quickly established, which all in all meant a total cultural change for this plant. With the advent of TQM, would there be a need for parallel cultural change in the public sector?

Public sector organizations are heavily staffed by professionals and there are some aspects of professional work practices which on first sight appear to be obstacles to TQM. In particular, there are the work practices which have derived from:

- the multiplicity of professional specialisms;
- the primacy accorded the individual professional transaction; and
- the authority (sometimes autocracy) of seniority and status hierarchies.

The multiplicity of professional specialisms

Most public sector provisions are characterized by a range of professional specialisms, each with their own identities. These professional groups can be assertive and protective of their own work areas or 'turf', which they see as territories for their own autonomous action. This posture does not make for the sort of lateral cooperation and cross-functional working arrangements which TQM requires if processes and supplier–customer chains are to be enhanced. TQM is, in its essential nature, subversive of professional exclusivity and requires strong collaborative working. There is no essential reason why the equal and full collaboration of professionals within a TQM-committed organization cannot be achieved, but tradition and history dictate that a full awareness of this aspect is needed together with conscious commitment to undo professional demarcations if needed.

The primacy of the individual professional transaction

This is clearly something which is central to professional provisions such as health, education and social work, even though it may be somewhat more tenuous in an assessment of an individual's housing needs or planning application. The centrepiece of many professionals' work practice is, then, a transaction between expert and client; in health this would be the practitioner prescribing for and treating the individual patient as a unique set of problems to be solved. Professionalism in this sense is primarily individualistic, whereas TQM calls for planning and organization in collectivist expressions. TQM, in fact, seeks to promote the collective and quantitative dimensions of quality so that degrees of quality conformance can be established on a holistic rather than individual or idiosyncratic basis. TQM does not remove the individual professional transaction, but it places that transaction within a wider 'collectivist' construction of practice and standards to be maintained.

Moreover, the practitioner–client encounter is modified under TQM in another way. It also seeks to move from the traditional altruistic relationship between professional and client towards client empowerment and participation as an equal partner in the securing of his or her own health, learning, solution to the social problem or whatever the case may be. In the traditional encounter, the client is expected to be passive and sometimes even deferential regarding the defining of the content and format of the whole transaction, but the assumptions regarding the client's or customer's role in the determination of quality which TQM makes requires modification here.

The TQM challenge to the professional transaction in this regard does lead some to take up the position that TQM can really only be about the administrative or service issues within public sector provision, and is not to be applied to, for example, teaching, clinical care, or any other direct professional transaction itself. There is indisputable evidence, as we show in Part 2 of this book, for the effectiveness of TQM application to the administrative and service aspects of public sector work contexts, but very little empirical evidence so far on which to make a judgement about TQM's usefulness in enhancing core professional processes. In so far as there is evidence, and again we describe this in Part 2, the potential of enhancement to core processes from TQM applications has tended to come from the customer view of the receipt of the experience rather than process control and measurement of the specifically technical or professional aspects of the transactions.

The authority and autocracy of seniority and status hierarchies

Professional provisions within the public sector have traditionally been characterized by the stratification of statuses, with senior role-holders being invested with considerable positional authority and even autocracy. One thinks of the headmaster tradition in British schools, or the distance exercised and deference expected by the medical consultant, for example. In many professional areas of public sector provision, there has traditionally been pedestal power and the autocracy of management decisions which flow from that, however benevolently it was exercised. The rules associated with such status authority dictated that others had no right as part of work practice – rather than gossip – to venture opinion on the work practices of higher status holders. Daily working relations and interactions were held together in a set of superordinate–subordinate rank levels. These may or may not have been officially defined, for even where they were not, the 'rules' were well known by custom and practice. TQM is clearly subversive (i.e. its pyramid of status control) and its adoption would call for radical revision in these regards in its implementation in the public sector. Of course, it is in any case true that the status or rank differentials of yesteryear have been considerably modified, TQM or no TQM, but the point to be made here is that TQM applications would call for modification to be designed-in, so that working relations recognize the needs of supplier–customer chains with full reciprocity of input to the quest for quality improvement.

The discussion of these three aspects might suggest to the reader that the responses to TQM needed by professionals would lead to a diminution of professionalism, an overall deficit. We do not think this is the case, for we see the changes in traditional practices implied by TQM as encouraging an identity of shared reflective practice by professionals rather than promoting an exclusivity to a particular technical expertise. It could well be argued that TQM takes professionalism/professionality more onto a model which demonstrates that the experts are still learning and, moreover, able as well to learn from the client.

In the public sector the customer is a more problematic concept

Many writers have suggested the problematic nature of the concept of the customer in the public sector. Swiss (1992) has put it thus:

> Because government agencies must serve a wide variety of customers who have widely divergent and even contradictory demands, and because the general public remains a 'hidden customer' with yet additional, often incompatible demands, government agencies often have to deliver a service or product that reflects an uneasy compromise. In such cases the [TQM] principle of delighting or even satisfying customers begs too many questions to be a clear or useful goal.

While we take the point being made here, we see it as overdrawn, and for two reasons. First, while government may not be able to satisfy the demands of all external customer groups for the reasons Swiss gives, the principle of identifying customer needs and explicitly meeting some of them cannot be contested. Second, such qualifications as exist regarding 'external' customers in the public sector, do not deflect from the validity of the TQM concept of the 'internal' customer, and the supplier–customer chains which exist within all public or private sector organizations.

There is in any case the more generally and widely acknowledged point that the benevolent paternalism of traditional government bureaucratic provision has not sought the voice of the customer in the past. Given that the public sector provisions were supplying monopoly or near monopoly services, there was in fact no incentive to do so because no challenge of having to retain or attract customers existed. However, in the last decade, government provisions in the UK and North America have seen the effects of two forces. On the one hand, there has been the growth of consumerism, and the fact that people accustomed to the modern 'supermarket' range also want more choice and better service in government provisions, politicians have been swift to respond to this. On the other hand, there has been the re-shaping of government provisions organizationally to give greater financial accountability and measures of performance. In 1994, then, while it may have been once the case that the customer was a problematic concept for the public sector, we see this as being less and less the case.

Public sector provisions are more complicated than manufacturing

In addition to the difference of a multiplicity of professional specialisms characterizing the public sector, the argument frequently advanced regarding public sector complexity compared with manufacturing concerns the relationship between quality and cost. It is asserted that improving service quality without increasing costs is more difficult in the public sector, and hence constitutes an objection to TQM.

This quality and costs 'problem' is allegedly rooted in those very public sector 'obstacles' we discussed earlier. Writers such as Milakovich (1990a, 1990b, 1991) have argued that improving service quality without increasing costs is more difficult in the public sector because: elected officials under political influence must attempt to balance multiple, vague and conflicting goals of diverse interest groups; annual budget battles stress short-term rewards rather than long-term professional values; managers operate in a non-competitive environment with far less control than their private counterparts. The annual budgeting systems place negative incentives on individual departments to improve the process as a whole. There is no incentive to go after cost-effective and process-oriented improvements; departments instead practise resource acquisition and expansion. There has also been little development of measures on the part of those who control budgeting which could lead to the improvement of services, or at least costs. Hence, effective and efficient managers soon learn that these in themselves bring no rewards because they are not easily demonstrable. The consequence has been incremental budgeting, politicking and the building of sectional power bases at the expense of the entire service provision.

All of the above features have been and can still be true of public sector provisions, and they are all inimical to TQM. However, as we have already said, the 'governors' are reinventing the nature of public sector provisions in order to improve quality and seek value for money – something often dictated to the politicians by the level of public demand for money and the limited resources to meet that demand. They are redefining the nature of government regulation and the organizational formats of provision. The political controllers have begun to promote real costing, measures of costs, a modification of monopoly by the development of quasi-market elements, and most radically the complete privatization of what had been entirely public provisions.

Overview: to what extent does TQM 'fit' the public sector

The theme of this chapter so far has been that certain distinguishing features of the public sector, as well as the nature of TQM itself in some regards, makes for a problematic fit of TQM to public sector provisions. Also, that managers wishing to apply TQM in the public sector will need

Table 5 Contrasts between the manufacturing and service sectors

Sector	Prime output	TQM focus	Measures of achievement
Manufacturing	Physical product	Fitness of purpose; customer delight with product	Zero defects; benchmarked standards; market leader; least cost among comparable quality product providers
Services	The service encounter and transaction	Meeting and exceeding customer expectation	Market leader; customer rating; least cost among comparable quality service providers

to appreciate certain apparent 'obstacles' to its application, and achieve answers to the following questions: Are these obstacles in the sense of 'challenges which have to be overcome' by adaptation to the context of the public sector? Or, are they obstacles in the sense that they effectively invalidate the applicability to the public sector of the TQM concepts, beliefs and practices discussed in Chapter 1?

The tenor of our comment has not been the latter, but by way of coming to a balanced conclusion to these questions, let us consider first in broad terms the prime distinctions between manufacturing and the service sector. Table 5 sets out what we see these to be; we recognize, of course, that they are very broad generalizations, but we consider that they do position from the TQM perspective certain core differences between manufacturing and service provision.

What Table 5 brings out is that while there are important distinctions between the commercial manufacturing and service sectors regarding aspects of prime output, the TQM focus and the nature of the measures of achievement, there are equally important common denominator aims. In common between manufacturing and service providers are the ultimate overarching 'drivers' of quality: 'delighting the customer' and becoming the market leader and least-cost provider in their respective markets. In no way do any of the distinctions shown in Table 1 differentiate manufacturing and services in terms of key TQM concepts, beliefs and processes. This is similarly true if we draw parallel contrasts between the private and public service sectors, as in Table 6.

Table 6 distinguishes contrasts in terms of the customer, the nature of the service encounter and achievement measures. In the public sector, the customer is not a direct purchaser of a particular service in the sense that

Table 6   The service sector: commercial and public service contrasts

Sector	Prime output	TQM focus	Measures of achievement
Commercial provider	Purchaser-driven service encounters	Customer acclaim; differentiation of quality service among multiple providers	Market leader – open market
Public sector service provider	Citizen-user service encounters	Professional service standard and client acclaim	Problematic, to be developed – 'internal market' or 'modified monopoly'

money is handed over at the point a particular service is requested on an individual 'shopping' basis, for the customer more usually has the status of 'citizen-user', calling for his or her share or take-up of a provision for which in broad terms he or she has already paid for. The main consequence of this difference for the service encounter, is to potentially weaken the zeal of the public sector provider to please the individual customer and to seek evidence of performance in a context where the public sector customer cannot go to another supplier. However, once again there is in common the all transcending focus of serving the customer and no contrasts are suggested between the commercial and public service sectors in terms of the validity of key TQM concepts, beliefs and processes. In fact, what drawing the contrast from a TQM perspective brings out is the need to align the public sector around the need for agreed measures of achievement.

The contrasts between the manufacturing and service sectors, and between commercial service provisions and public sector service provisions in Tables 5 and 6, are not intended to convey that these are mutually exclusive profiles of types of organizations. More and more organizations do not exhibit the 'ideal' or homogeneous profiles suggested by the labels we have used in Tables 5 and 6. While there are organizations which are essentially manufacturing enterprises, there will still be within them subunits or branches which exhibit all the features of service providers. Similarly, there are companies whose main purpose is to provide a service, but that service may entail in part the manufacture of the components or commodities necessary to the delivery of the overall service. Assuming, then, that most organizations will not be homogeneously manufacturing or homogeneously service, but will exhibit some degree of MANUFACTURING/service or SERVICE/manufacturing mix, it would be invalid to advocate or adopt either a position that TQM is applicable or not applicable, or

Table 7   Applicability of TQM across occupational cultures

Category	Level of applicability
Core concepts, tools and applications	All occupational settings
Adaptive concepts, tools and applications	Most occupational settings
Problematic concepts, tools and applications	Some occupational settings

that there are exclusive models of TQM such as a manufacturing model and a service model. Indeed, we have heard the senior executives of the Ford Motor Company argue that their own manufacturing activities are simply a part of their overall service activity – 'we sell', one said, 'the service of transportation'.

We have just argued against assuming any exclusive distinction between a manufacturing and service organization, and similarly, we take it that there is no longer the exclusive or stark distinction that can be argued to have once existed between commercial and public sector service providers. Many public sector provisions do now also offer services on a market basis, and these may compete with a range of local providers who operate on a wholly commercial basis. For example, to 'citizen-users' in Cardiff where one of the authors lives, the local government authority provides, as anywhere else in the UK, a whole range of services (e.g. street lighting, collection of refuse, etc.) in return for the up-front global payment of local 'rates' or taxes which is made on a regular basis by the citizen-user. However, it also offers, for example, in the open market, drain-cleaning services, which must be ordered and purchased on the same individual encounter basis to that provided by firms wholly in the commercial service sector. There can, therefore, be service components within manufacturing organizations, manufacturing components in service organizations, and open market components of activity within the public sector. There are, therefore, in our view no exclusive models of TQM.

We are therefore suggesting that TQM needs to be seen as a framework which can span all organizational settings, both commercial and public, manufacturing and service, or indeed any particular mix of the foregoing. Our view, exemplified in Table 7, is that there are some TQM concepts, tools and applications which are 'core' because they are essentially concerned with process enhancement whatever the sector, and are thus generic to all occupational settings where TQM is being applied. Alongside the core of TQM, there are other TQM concepts, tools and applications which though they may have originated specifically in manufacturing, in services or even (in the future) in public sector service provision, nevertheless can be *adapted* to most, if not all, occupational settings including the public sector. However, the framework conveyed in Table 7 also recognizes that within the whole range of thinking and practices which TQM has generated to date, there will be problems in 'translating' some TQM concepts and practices to occupational settings wholly different in kind from the environment in which they originated.

It needs to be recognized, therefore, that not all TQM concepts, tools and previous applications can be used in public sector provisions. There are some which are 'problematic', and which might only ever be valid in the occupational setting they originated in. For example, 'zero defects' is the example which comes most quickly to mind in this respect. This particular TQM concept, derived from manufacturing, is the one most guaranteed to incite instant opposition from public sector professionals, and this is quite understandable because it essentially applies to the elimination of defects in a physical product for which precise standards can be set. We would not say that the concept can never be adapted to the public sector, but until such an adaptation is made, its status in terms of the definitions of Table 3 is problematic.

The value of the frameworks proposed in this chapter is that they avoid an evaluation of TQM for the public sector on an 'all or nothing' basis. Such a simplistic dichotomous basis of judging TQM for the public sector would imply that a straight 'yes' or 'no' answer could be given to its validity, and for reasons we have already set out above that is to be rejected because of the mixed realities of organizational activity.

However, there are additional important reasons why our contingency model of TQM best fits the emerging realities. By early 1993, it was already clear that a whole new range of government 'provisions' was emerging. Government had already begun to re-invent itself by initiating new models of public sector provision.

Table 8 gives our view of the four basic provision strategies which had been developed by government by the early 1990s. What had started to happen was a decrease in the supremacy of the Dominant Provider Model. The issues we discussed earlier regarding the fit of TQM to the public sector were essentially about the Dominant Provider Model. The advent of new models of public sector provision, or rather government-inspired but not directly made provisions, increases the scope for TQM, and enhances the validity of the contingency view of TQM concepts, beliefs and applications. The proliferation of provision models does not therefore, in our view, support dichotomous model interpretations of TQM, such as that of Swiss (1992), who has proposed 'Orthodox TQM' and 'Reform TQM' models, and concluded that 'TQM can indeed have a useful role to play in the public sector, but only if it is substantially modified to fit the public sector's unique characteristics'.

We see the reality of the fit of TQM to the public sector as one where within the range of its concepts, beliefs and practices, TQM *has* a core philosophy, some core concepts and some generic tools which can be applied to significant advantage within all public sector provisions. It is intended that the case studies in Part 2 of this book, which describe applications of TQM in the public sector contexts of government, health,

Table 8   Strategic choices open to government regarding the type of provision

HIGH

DOMINANT PROVIDER MODEL	**PATRON–AGENCY MODEL**
Government controls, regulates and makes the provision itself	Government controls and regulates a range of semi- or fully autonomous providers
EXHORTATION MODEL	**MULTIPLE PROVISIONS MODEL**
Minimal control and regulation – minimum or no specification of providers	Low government control of a recognized range of providers

REGULATION

LOW   MARKET COMPLEXITY   HIGH

education and social services, amply illustrate these core and generically applicable aspects of TQM.

It is not uncommon today in the countries of the industrialized world for more than half their gross national product to go on public sector provisions. These provisions, as we described earlier, are characterized by a budget-seeking rather than a performance-demonstrating posture. As Drucker (1988) has noted, there are three common explanations for this: their managers are not business-like; the staff are not as good as they should be; results are intangible and incapable of definition or measurement. Drucker is adamant that all three reasons are invalid and are pure alibi. The real reason he demonstrates is that they have not been managed for performance. Their deadly sins have been: a lack of clear performance targets; trying to do too many things at once; solving problems by throwing money and people at them; a lack of an experimental attitude; a lack of evaluation so that nothing is learned from experience; and reluctance to abandon programmes. These sins or practices can no longer be afforded in the advanced democracies and the modifying of traditional public sector management is becoming more and more a top priority of government. TQM has become the official policy for achieving this across government in some countries such as the USA, and is an officially sponsored policy for particular sectors such as the health service in the UK.

Osborne and Gaebler (1992) have analysed and explained governments' new postures towards strategy and management under the title of 'Reinventing Government'. What they have written argues that public sector provisions and their managements are becoming further characterized by the following twelve features as the 1990s proceed:

- promoting competition between providers;
- empowering citizens by pushing control out into the community;
- measuring performance;
- focusing not on inputs but on processes for their outcomes;
- driven by their goals (vision) – not by their rules and regulations;
- redefining clients as customers;
- offering citizens/customers real choices;
- preventing problems before they occur rather than rectifying them afterwards;
- decentralizing authority and embracing participatory management;
- putting energy into earning money, not simply spending it.

These twelve features reflect both the new strategic choices for government we presented in Table 8, and the beliefs of TQM discussed in Chapter 1.

The application of TQM in the public sector is really just beginning, which makes it important that those who are about to or are already applying it, understand the issues and take a cosmopolitan view of its development. Hence this book on TQM in the public sector and the case histories of early TQM applications in the chapters which follow.

PART
2

Applications of TQM to public sector organizations

Introduction

The first three chapters of this book examined the following questions: What is TQM and what key ideas and constructs inform its practice? Who are the progenitors of TQM and what does each bring to our understanding of the dynamics of TQM? What issues are encountered in the attempt to adapt and apply TQM in the public sector? In developing our response to these questions, we have sought to provide a critical framework and analysis. We have also introduced some new components, most notably the model of strategy introduced in Chapter 3 and the recognition that there are core, adaptive and problematic constructs within TQM which have to be recognized when new applications for TQM are being developed.

We now turn our attention to the specific attempts to apply TQM in the public sector. We need to begin by recognizing that, though what follows is substantive, it is not a complete survey. We have provided detailed statements of the pattern of development of TQM in health, education and social services and have looked at some other developments across remaining government departments. We have not dedicated a chapter to developments in defence and policing, though both are mentioned in the work which follows, nor have we looked at every area of government in turn. This would have been a mammoth undertaking, something that was beyond the scope of this book.

Our aims in the following four chapters are: (1) to provide a description of recent developments in the sectors examined, with case vignettes and critical analysis where possible; (2) to use these specific areas of implementation as a basis for identifying key issues in the practice of TQM which have implication for both the specific service and for everyone concerned with TQM in the public sector; and (3) to highlight possibilities for the further development of TQM in government and allied services. In looking at these territories of work, we have sought to indicate the underlying trends in development in the UK, the USA and Canada in particular.

TQM is a rapid area of growth in government. Between the completion of this text in April 1993 and its appearance in early 1994, many developments will occur. Our concern here was to provide an indication of trends rather than a detailed description of every single instance of TQM being used in government. In looking at new developments and the issues they give rise to, it should be possible to look at the chapters presented here and link these new developments with the key features of current TQM practice.

In preparation for these chapters, many interviews, discussions, telephone conversations, literature reviews and observational visits were made to institutions in the UK, Ireland, Canada and the USA. Our understanding of the developments we report is intended to stimulate debate, understanding and evaluation by others.

CHAPTER

4

TQM and health care

Although we have organized what follows to look at TQM developments in certain occupational areas of the public sector – health, education, social work, and a chapter on developments in government service (the scope of which will be explained in the chapter itself) – we intend that the content of these chapters be studied with benefit by all readers. In shaping the material we present in these chapters, we have assumed that the reader is likely to have a detailed knowledge of one of the occupational areas covered, but will want to know two things. First, about the range of issues and problems which can be faced in implementing TQM in the public sector whatever the particular occupational context. Second, about public sector TQM case histories, even though they may not be in the reader's own particular occupational area. Cases from other contexts are often helpful in suggesting approaches and ideas which can be transferred to one's own situation.

Our overview of TQM developments in the public sector by the early 1990s shows that TQM was being initiated on the basis of one or other of the four 'implementation/dispersion' models set out in Table 9. Each of these models is shaped by a differing value position and commitment posture to TQM and its implementation. We would not want to exaggerate these models, but from our observations it would appear helpful for managers to clarify exactly which model they wish to enact. Sometimes we have gained the impression that the approach is an unclarified mixture of several of the models, or one where commitment seems to move from one to another.

Table 9 Models of TQM implementation

Model	Value Stance	Implementation approach
1. System-wide commitment	'TQM will bring benefits'	Experimentation across the board
2. Exhortation/demonstration – 'Parable of the Sower'	'TQM should help'	Selective – strong focus on customer audit
3. 'Lone-ranger' innovator	'I am a believer'	Across-the-board commitment with some process focus
4. Token attempt	'Been here before, – 'it will go the way of all gimmicks'	Enclave approach – 'relegate it to a ghetto'

The health sector has seen its share of 'lone-ranger' innovators, but by the early 1990s in the countries covered by this study, health was also characterized by both 'system-wide' and 'exhortation' models of TQM implementation.

The crisis of health care in the 1990s

In 1993, all the advanced democracies are in both financial and value trouble over health care and almost everywhere policy-makers and managers are searching for new ways to achieve better productivity and efficiency for the expenditure. In the UK, where only a minority of people have private health care arrangements, the publicly provided National Health Service (NHS), long held to be one of the country's proudest national assets – and certainly in 1993 still one of Europe's largest employers – does not have the money to meet the demand of a growing population of senior citizens and rising expectations. Many more stories such as the following are appearing in British newspapers:

> In most businesses attracting new customers would count as a success. But for Britain's largest cancer hospital it is a trial not a triumph. Over the past two years the Christie Hospital National Health Service Trust in Manchester has treated 16 per cent more patients, but the health authorities which buy care on behalf of their patients cannot afford to pay for the extra workload. As a result of this, and rising drug costs, the hospital is currently £500,000 overspent. [The Chief Executive] has been told by the Department of Health he is 'overtrading': the doctors are seeing too many patients.
>
> (Ormell 1993)

In Canada, the health care sector is also in serious trouble because of rapidly rising costs as well as problems of focus. In the early 1990s, some provinces are spending over a third of their budgets on health care, and cannot afford to spend any more. Ontario, the centre of some of Canada's key business and industries, has been spending one-third of its total provincial budget on health care annually, yet as an observer of the scene has commented, 'the demand for the services of doctors, hospitals and extended care facilities will continue to grow, as Canada's population ages' (Warner 1991).

At the same time, the USA is faced by similar policy dilemmas regarding health care. Although widely believed in Europe to be virtually a private provision, America has in fact a 'mixed' system of health care resourced from public and private resources. In 1993, the US government subsidized care for nearly one-half of the general population: the elderly, the poor, the disabled and those whose incomes fell below the poverty line, though this is far from being a national health service.

Industry has also borne much of the direct cost of providing health care for its workers. W. Edwards Deming, one of TQM's gurus, has likened American health care costs to a deadly disease sapping the productivity and international viability of business. The Chrysler Motor Corporation, for example, has estimated that health care adds more than $600 to the cost of every car made in the USA (Warner 1991). In 1990, US health expenditure totalled $600 billion, or 11 per cent of gross national product. By the early 1990s, 80 per cent of health care costs in the USA were in fact driven by less than 3 per cent of the population. In 1993, President Clinton, who had pledged to provide universal health care, recognized the dilemma of costs and growing public demand when he said that 'curbing health care costs and providing universal access was the single most pressing problem of his presidency' (Nicholls 1993).

This picture of crisis facing health care is also true to some degree in the other advanced democracies in Europe and Scandinavia. Government-funded health care in the 1990s therefore faces a management problem: how to deliver more at a cost the taxpayer is willing to pay while demand continues to rise.

Some observers are of the belief that within health care there is a chronic waste of resources, a confusion on the part of the delivering organizations – principally the hospitals – regarding the fundamental nature of their roles, and a lack of incentives on the part of professionals to deliver high-quality customer care on a cost-conscious basis. Hospital, medical and health care services have traditionally emphasized quality assurance and externally imposed regulatory standards from a strict clinical–medical standpoint. It has generally been assumed that the monies will become available to meet these requirements on a demand-led basis.

Others have suggested that hospitals (more particularly the small 25–30 bed community hospitals in North America) have presented confused missions and objectives, with a resulting impairment of effectiveness and performance. Should hospitals focus on the major health needs of a community or try to do everything and be abreast of every medical advance, no matter how costly and how rarely used the facility might be? It has been suggested that what many hospitals do, is to pretend that there are no basic questions of strategy to be answered.

For all of these reasons, quality and TQM have taken a prominent place in the health discussion agendas of the UK, the USA and Canada. In fact, it is our view that of all the public sector contexts discussed in this book, it is the health sector which to date has seen the greatest range of thinking and activities in connection with quality and TQM. In any case, as several writers have been at pains to point out, quality is not a new idea in health. It is the nature of health care that all the professionals working in it have a commitment to 'quality care' for the patient. What the discussion of quality here does not intend to suggest is that quality is a recent and new idea for health professionals. The distinction needs to be drawn between concern for quality, and the systematic management of quality (Morgan and Everett 1990). This book does not suggest that there has been in any of the public sectors a lack of commitment to quality in the general professional sense, rather that the systematic management of quality needs an intentional framework. Our essential approach is therefore to evaluate the extent to which the concepts, tools and applications TQM are currently influencing health care.

Policy and management responses to the health care crisis

By early 1993, the most dramatic responses to a perceived developing crisis in health provision on a nationwide strategic basis have taken place in the UK. The responses have taken several forms: a major restructuring of the organization of the NHS from the usual layered bureaucratic pattern to create 'purchaser' and 'provider' units; the establishment of contracting between purchasers and providers; and the encouragement of provider units – whether hospitals or general practitioners – to act as their own cost centres and operate as wholly self-managing trusts instead of being managed by a superordinate health authority structure. Perhaps the central feature is that in the future, a purchaser will have to place a contract with a provider for a service to be made available to a district's residents, thus creating a quasi- or internal market (the term usually deployed) in which a degree of competition can drive quality.

The 'provider' units will be expected to pursue an active and expanding programme of market testing, and purchasing authorities will be encouraged to place contracts with providers who can demonstrate clearly and publicly that through market testing they have taken action to drive costs down while improving the quality of service delivery (Welsh Office 1991; Ferlie *et al.* 1992).

The creation of purchasers is both new and different for the NHS in the

UK. The intention is that these purchasers will be psychologically separate from the provision of service, and thus insist on better value for money and higher quality of service. The new policy intends that purchasers should also take into account the preferences of consumers. In addition, purchasers will have to find new ways of assessing the health care needs of the population and to reflect this in the contracting process. The new purchasing authorities will therefore in effect be managing through contract rather than through hierarchy or classical bureaucracy.

It is early days in the context of developing the internal market for health care in Britain, and as yet there is only one significant purchaser in the market, the district health authority. However, if the number of general practitioner fund-holders grows substantially in the 1990s, as the government intends, there will be a large number of other purchasers. One scenario would be that these purchasers would have little contact with each other, and that this would better approximate to a classical market as long as there continues to be a large number of alternative providers offering the same services (Ferlie *et al.* 1992).

The government-planned emergence of a quasi- or internal market is the first of the major responses in Britain to the health care crisis. We have indicated its features here (the creation of self-managing cost centres, the bringing in of market forces, and financing according to results) because of its generic validity in terms of direction of change for other public sector contexts.

There have been two other significant features of change to British health care provision, a formal policy of 'quality' and specific advocacy of TQM. The first of these has been the formal declaration of a 'quality' policy for the NHS. In 1991, the government's 'Citizen's Charter' on health stated:

The Government is committed to:

- improving the Quality of NHS provision at all levels;
- increasing the Choice available to everyone within the NHS;
- raising the Standards within the NHS, describing clearly what those standards are and what can be done if they are not achieved;
- ensuring as taxpayers we receive the best possible Value For Money.

The second main feature of government's reformulation and restructuring of health policy in Britain has been the setting of choice, quality, specified standards and 'value for money', as the expectations of consumers. Astute readers will already have noted that the two main features of health reform in Britain reflect many of the key elements of the twelve hallmarks of 'Re-inventing Government' which we set out in Chapter 3.

The third feature alongside the strong explicit 'quality' policy and the introduction of structures for market forces and the contracting provision in response to the crisis facing public sector health provision in Britain, has been an explicit recognition of TQM as the desirable way forward for managing efficiently to provide consumer choice at best standards and least cost. In England, this has meant the establishment of a whole range of TQM demonstration projects. At the time of writing, these are being systematically evaluated, but some independent researchers have described some clear gains and some implementation issues, examples of which we discuss later. In Wales, the government health service directorate has already indicated TQM as the management policy which should be enacted throughout the principality: 'the recommended approach to this challenge is Total Quality Management. Total Quality Management is now regarded worldwide as an operational philosophy vital to the successful development of most large organisations... "customer centred"... "measurable standards of performance for all aspects"... "reinforced by robust and reliable processes",' etc.; etc. The policy document also gives a clear view of 'quality':

> In looking at the way in which needs and expectations are fulfilled, three components can be considered:
>
> - the quality of technical care, which links directly to its effectiveness or ability to achieve improvements in health (health gain);
> - the quality of inter-personal relationships with all 'customers' needing to be treated with sensitivity;
> - the quality of amenities, that is convenience, creature comforts, and the quality of the environment in which the care is given.
>
> (Welsh Office 1990)

Although the commendation and development of the application of TQM to health on a system-wide basis could only perhaps have been expected in Britain because of its nationally funded system of health care requiring national strategies, TQM has also been developing fast in health care (if only, on a dispersed basis) in Canada and the USA. The successful implementation of TQM has been reported at the Massachusetts General Hospital, Butterworth Hospital and the University of Michigan, with West Pace's Ferry Hospital in Atlanta seen as a leading example of successful TQM implementation (Masters and Schmele 1991). In New England in 1990, a national demonstration project implementing TQM in hospitals was set up, linking twenty hospitals with twenty industrial quality management experts. This followed on from a pioneering of TQM in the Harvard Community Health Plan by Burwick (1989). In Canadian health provision, TQM has become prominent at the University of Alberta Hospital, the Sick Children's Hospital in Toronto, and in many smaller initiatives in the hospital system in British Columbia.

There is a growing body of research and publications on the topic, and specialized journals concerned with quality in health care have become established, carrying papers that discuss the nature of TQM and health, and report applications of TQM in health care settings. By 1993, then, TQM has very much come onto the health care agenda in the advanced democracies, but what issues for health professionals did this raise?

TQM and health care culture and conditions

We indicated earlier that by the early 1990s, it looked as though health, of all the public sectors, had seen the greatest discussion and application of TQM, both in Britain and North America. This is not to say that we see TQM as ubiquitous in health care, far from it. What we do suggest is that TQM has in some places become the officially sanctioned policy for the whole system; in many countries and places it has very clearly become established on the agenda of management thinking and action in health care; and that across several countries there is a significant scatter of health care sites where TQM is being applied seriously though with different emphases. Altogether, then, TQM has clearly arrived in health care and the extent and eventual forms of its viability will be demonstrated by experience and replicability as the years unfold.

Given the nature of health care work traditions and activities, what does TQM have to contend with or overcome in order to achieve the sort of start-up and developments which became evident by the early 1990s? We have found from our own direct experience in recent times, as well as from the observations of practitioners and consultants in the health care field, that the difficulties are very likely to be: early cynicism, issues of cultural fit to the complex nature of the health sector itself, and resistance from the traditional professional identities of key role-holders in the health workplace. In this latter respect, the health care experience of importing and applying TQM to its own management and professional needs, can be seen as something of a trail-blazer and mentor to all other public sector work contexts which are characterized by substantial professional inter-action on a one-to-one personal basis, and a multiplicity of professional identities.

First, and perhaps foremost, we have noted that an announcement to start up TQM in the health care setting is likely to evoke cynicism about quality initiatives among middle managers and rank-and-file workers. This is not because those concerned have no interest in improving service quality – they very definitely do – but because first reactions are to believe that TQM policy is in reality a management ploy to reduce costs and cut standards. Because of their commitment to care, health workers react from the assumption that their health authority or organization should be investing more in order to reduce or eliminate the chances of a defect occurring. Such a reaction is often based on a 'history of the situation', where management has been seen to cut expenditure or staffing levels, with the perceived result of having cut the quality of care. There is no realization that what is being proposed in TQM is wholly different in kind from what has gone before.

At best, even, the announcement of a TQM initiative invites a cynical response to yet another 'innovation' on the part of management. We saw a good example of this phenomenon when we took part in a TQM in-troductory workshop for some 60 middle managers in a district health authority in England. As the chief executive proclaimed the virtues of TQM against a background of where the health authority would have to achieve a certain level of savings over the coming years, hardly anyone in the audience was in eye contact with him, bodies were turned forty-five degrees away, eyes were everywhere but at the lectern, faces were grim, and the cynicism was palpable. To the observer of these deeply committed caring people, the announcement of TQM seemed for them to mean 'more pain'. The message to ourselves – we were to follow-on after the chief executive – was clear. There is a need to ensure that in initiating TQM in such highly professionalized and committed contexts, both its fundamental difference to previous management practice and its people empowerment focus must be stressed and emphasized. Any early reactions that TQM is just another technique to 'dig management out of a hole' must be replaced by a vision of the potential benefits for the patients and themselves.

Traditional autonomy of the professionals

Health care establishments have in the past had a stratification culture in which the senior professionals had considerable autonomy and held considerable distance from other groups or from the notion of management responsibility in any financial sense at least. The hospital was therefore organized around hierarchical lines with self-contained medical disciplines and pockets of management. Departments or separate disciplines lacked regular opportunities to communicate and meet each other.

TQM is certainly subversive of traditional hierarchical health culture. As Merry (1990) put it:

> It should be understood that both the [TQM] process and the implicit higher level of institutional accountability bring a true culture shock to physicians. As members of an ancient and respected profession, they have come to expect autonomy and accountability only to themselves as the norm. Heretofore the complexity of medical care and practice of focusing on individual cases to define quality kept physicians essentially immune from outside challenge. Further, the essential concept of professionalism as a special status granted by society, earned through a long period of dedicated study and service has traditionally guaranteed relative autonomy to those who have been able to gain professional status. The TQM generation of physicians, however, is the first to be exposed to the 'microscopic power' of modern quality process tools and techniques. It should not be surprising that their reaction to such perceived intrusion and exposure would be initially less than enthusiastic.

Our own observations certainly confirm the above view. Where TQM is being introduced, there is a view among doctors and consultants that 'this TQM thing is really just another management ploy to erode our professional independence'. The consequence of this response is to restrict the initial scope of TQM innovation so that 'it doesn't affect their world too much', as a hospital TQM facilitator in England told us. However, 'when we have shown them the benefits of our customer audits and so forth, they are usually amazed that their patients can have a different view of things from themselves, and then start taking an interest in TQM'.

However, even prior to the introduction of TQM the stratification culture in some health provisions had already begun to erode due to mechanisms such as clinical audit. This means, as one senior government health administrator told us in Wales: 'no longer can, for example, a consultant say "I am just concerned with the medicine", they must now learn to contribute to the decisions about the money as well!' In related fashion, a senior nurse in England observed to us: 'a lot of stratification has gone in the health services, there is now no longer the amount of deference there was. However, there is still scope for empowerment even though there is a lot more interchange now, as the hospital environment is more subtly controlling. All this challenges one-way control.'

Language and cultural symbols

Allied with traditional culture in relation to stratification and professional identities, are traditional views concerning the patient. Generally speaking, the patient was essentially a passive receiver of the treatment determined by professionals. Though the professionals were certainly committed to the patient's quality care, he or she was not seen as a customer. In initiating TQM in Britain or North America, both the language and the concept of the patient as a customer can be a difficult one for professionals to accept. TQM facilitators in health care have told us that the idea of 'the patient as customer' is quite new, and that the very idea of asking customers what they value is seen by some to be revolutionary. For the public sector there is therefore a challenge in managing the introduction of TQM in terms of cultural and language traditions. On this point, evaluators of the TQM demonstration projects in England have observed:

> Problems and difficulties with the concepts of TQM and with specific implementation processes were also reported. These covered many areas including some lack of progress in breaking down barriers between different disciplines, particularly between medical and non-medical staff . . . Specific criticism . . . revolved around inappropriate jargon and training materials, overemphasis on mechanistic implementation, and quantitative indicators of quality and the costs of consultancy.
>
> (Kogan *et al.* 1991: 4)

TQM invokes empowerment and inverts the management pyramid (as we made clear in Chapter 1), for if it is to achieve results it must work horizontally across the organization, across disciplines and departments.

The existing culture and structure in the public sector can therefore potentially be a substantial block to TQM, so this must be recognized and managed, sometimes even confronted. Although the point being made here arises within the health care context, the issue is a generic one, and something that needs to be taken into account within the different occupational areas of the public sector.

The challenge of fragmentation and complexity of work flows in health care

The initiation and implementation of TQM in health care can face a particular problem of fragmentation. We are here defining 'a problem of fragmentation' as (1) a lack of awareness of how the system as a whole works, (2) the challenge of effective linkage at the interfaces and (3) the negative effect of narrow or restricted, rather than extended, professionalism.

It is generally acknowledged that in the typical hospital, the workforce is fragmented. There are many departments – disparate groups of people doing different tasks from one another. The range of work carried out can be quite astonishing. There are, for example, doctors, chaplains, dieticians, haematologists, numerically controlled machine operators, radiology technicians, clinical physicists, pathologists, pharmacists, psychologists, nurses, radiation oncologists, microbiologists, photographers, systems analysts, librarians and many others with a different occupational identity. The implications of this degree of professional differentiation and fragmentation from the TQM perspective are that there are many interfaces relying on the interaction of many workers. There are likely to be many, and possibly complex, customer–supplier chains.

Related to this will be the fact that work-flows are patient-driven, they cut across departments in different ways, and will often depend on the needs of the particular patient. To take a quite ordinary example of this, patients in hospital beds need medication. Involved in the process of determining the medication and its ultimate delivery to the patient will be at least a doctor, a nurse, a ward clerk, a porter and a pharmacist. The handling of drugs and other medicines is just one of the many tasks these different people accomplish in a given time period. The people who work in hospitals take all this for granted, of course; it perhaps only looks complicated to those on the outside. However, it is accepted that this process of delivering drugs to patients on wards can lead to medication errors. On an acute ward of a general hospital, it is said that this may be in excess of 1 per cent (Warner 1991). In terms of the potential for error, supplying patients with medications is therefore a complicated process which involves a complex customer–supplier chain. This is therefore a good example of the many processes in health care for which quality can be enhanced by reducing errors. On page 91, we give an example of how the efficiency of hospital pharmacy delivery was enhanced by the application of TQM process mapping and statistical control methods.

Core health professional work and the applicability of TQM

A particular challenge in such highly technical and specialized work environments as health care is the issue of whether the core professional work – the doctor-patient interface, for example – is susceptible to TQM. Whereas it can more readily be accepted that the customer–supplier processes connected with the managerial or organizational context lend themselves to TQM approaches – in health or any other type of organization – there is often considerable resistance to the very idea that TQM can apply to the 'core' or centrepiece of health care, namely those highly individual personal interactions between physician and patient or nurse and patient. It is argued that the salient difference between a physical product of TQM manufacturing such as a motor car and the human body is that patients, while very much more complex in terms of number of parts than motor cars, also vary a great deal between themselves, with the consequence that one cannot define an unambiguous process. The objection, then, is that 'quality' in the core work of health care is problematic, because what must be done for the individual patient becomes a matter of judgement on the part of highly trained professional staff.

Put in this form, the 'objection' is a valid statement of the reality. However, it does not take account of the translation of TQM thinking into the service context. While the processes of interaction cannot be standard because of human variance, they can be designed to meet explicit service standards even though they are customized to the individual. On page 88, we supply a template for doctor–nurse relationships when delivering health care.

In any event, there are now sufficient examples of health professionals who, as TQM pioneer innovators, have assessed the validity of TQM to the central professional processes of health care and found that they are not 'no-go' areas for TQM. Arikan (1991), for example, has proposed a paradigm for TQM in nursing, and believes that 'by adapting and putting into practice the basic principles of TQM, nurses can set examples for other members of the health care team'. Gillem (1988) has translated Deming's 14 points into a broad health care organizational approach. Schmele and Foss (1989) have discussed the nursing application of Crosby's TQM approach, and many other writers on TQM and health care have made it clear that core professional work is viewed as being part of the scope of TQM. For example:

> Quality Process [in health care] encompasses major departures from traditional practices. In place of retrospective review of individual patient charts, analysis of statistical data is now the primary focus

of reviews. Case review is not unimportant, but the focus is now epidemiologic. In other words the question now is less 'What went wrong with this individual case?' and more 'What might be the common denominator of this high infection rate' or location, organism, anatomical site of infection, physician etc. etc.

(Merry 1990)

Merry also adds that the very act of looking at core professional processes from the TQM diagnostic viewpoint together with the implicit higher level of institutional accountability associated with doing this, can 'bring a true culture shock to physicians'.

Using analysis and case experience, therefore, the instinctive reactions of some professionals that TQM cannot touch core professional work cannot be sustained.

Appropriate focuses to TQM in health

If, as we have stressed already, there has always been a commitment to quality in health care, what is the new quality dimension all about? What extra does TQM intend bringing to health care. Bull (1992), a British health service professional, has defined quality in health care, and his five points certainly would make all core medical activities, as well as organizational, managerial and administrative matters, part of the scope of TQM enhanced quality:

1. Guarantees of adherence to legal requirements, national codes of practice and standards.
2. The provision of systems to ensure quality, such as medical audit, nursing and other audit surveys of patient opinion.
3. The setting of specific standards as key indicators of performance on matters of general or specific concern.
4. The setting of specific clinical outcome requirements, both generally and those related to specific clinical conditions.
5. Consumer law, a general assumption of standards which could reasonably be expected from a hospital operating in a modern medical environment.

Overall, regarding the fit of TQM to the health care context, what we have found is that, despite initial cynicism, the cultural traditions and the range of initial objections to the substance and scope of TQM in health, when TQM initiators are sensitive to these issues and translate them with patience into the culture and working environment, TQM can be easily accepted. As was noted by a health care worker in a hospital where TQM had taken root:

Staff come to find that the underlying concepts are really quite simple and in line with their own philosophy of working, also they are intrigued to discover gaps between what they believe is the quality of professional care they provide and the perception of that care articulated by their customers!

Some TQM applications in health care settings

In surveying the applications of TQM which have so far been made in health care in Britain and North America, the focus seems very clear. Customer audit – understanding the customers – has become the pre-eminent focus with the development of clear service standards in close linkage. The process focus has been subordinate to these, as is perhaps to be expected in a highly professionalized public sector occupation where the processes are complex. Nevertheless, there are interesting examples of process refinement and measurement and of the application of classic TQM tools.

Customer audit in health care

Traditionally, the client has been viewed as a patient but not as a customer. It is the *customer perspective* of understanding which first needs the focus of TQM in health and the need for a customer focus requires careful explanation and argumentation. Client satisfaction is of fundamental importance as a measure of the quality of care, because it provides information on health care providers' success at meeting those client values and expectations which are matters on which the client is the ultimate authority. The measurement of satisfaction is therefore an important tool for surveying and planning improved provision.

It may be objected that patients generally are not in a position to understand the technical and medical aspects of care, so that their judgements are not to be relied upon. Also, of course, clients can sometimes expect and demand things that it would be wrong for the health professional to provide, either because they are socially forbidden or because medically they are not in the client's best interest. However, even these arguments do not take away the validity of patient satisfaction as a measure of quality. For example, if a patient is dissatisfied because his or her unreasonably high expectations of particular medical care have not been met, the 'total quality' perspective would argue that the professional practitioner had failed to inform and educate the 'customer' patient.

We see customer audit as the logical starting point for TQM in a professional public sector setting such as health. Although we may have in mind here the external customer (i.e. the patient), this applies equally to any internal customers in the health care setting. What customers (both external and internal) reveal are the key indicators of quality within the total detail of processes which go to make up health care. Having obtained the indicators of quality from the customer, these can be measured and the data used as part of the totality of factors used in discussion by professionals to produce a service standard. An example of an indicator of quality dear to the heart of one of the present authors when visiting his general practitioner is 'average waiting time'. This local general medical practice has a very explicit appointment system and excellent doctors who take time to discuss thoroughly the patient's problems. Unfortunately, the practice is hopeless at sticking to appointments; it is rare for a patient to be seen within twenty minutes of his or her specified time. It is doubtful whether the doctors themselves actually know how long people are kept waiting or whether this matters to patients, which it clearly does. Customer survey and data collection could easily resolve this problem to produce a better service standard in terms of waiting time. This would turn a good service at the present time into an excellent one in the eyes of many customers, and cumulatively save hours of peoples' wasted time.

Service standards

The second major emphasis of TQM development in health care has been the defining of 'service standards'. We would define a service standard as 'a customer-driven agreed level of performance appropriate to the population addressed, which is observable, achievable, measurable and desirable'. The service standard has two main purposes: first, as a yard-stick against which current performance can be compared; and, second, as a prompt to the methodical planning of services to ensure the standard is achieved. The type of questions which need to be answered in developing service standards are: For what particular aspects of care do we wish to produce standards? (focus). What organization and resources do we need to achieve the standard? (structure). What do we need to do to achieve the standard? (process). And, what result will we see from its achievement? (outcome).

Morgan and Everett (1990) have made a useful distinction between a service standard and a service convenience. A statement of service standards includes a specification of the values to be associated with that feature; anything specified must be capable of observation and measurement. For example, with regard to the availability of a general medical practitioner locally, the standard of availability would include such elements as the times when the surgery was open in the week, the appointment system adopted, and a commitment to be seen within a specified time. The service convenience aspects would cover elements which are more subjective and which can be perceived differently by different people. For example, with regard to the local surgery waiting room, the physical arrangements of the facilities and the buildings.

The core of the service standard definition is – as we set out above – 'customer-driven levels of performance', and these can be derived in two ways. First, there is the lesser and easier way of accepting standards laid down by national professional bodies. Of course, these will tend to be more generic and less tuned to the local situation or professional sub-specialism. The second is for the practitioners themselves to determine their own local standards, taking into account national standards where these are available (Williamson 1991). It is this latter approach which is called for by TQM.

Some of the TQM demonstration sites within the UK National Health Service referred to earlier have been initiating and implementing TQM with a strong 'customer audit' and 'service standard' approach as we now illustrate with the case of Trafford General Hospital, Manchester.

TQM case study: Trafford General Hospital

Trafford General Hospital operates in an area where there is distinct competition between providers. The hospital is close to an area which is a leading innovator in everything in health care, and only a couple of miles down the road is a teaching hospital with the advantage of superior facilities and resources. Trafford's own catchment area is a mix of urban and rural, with a poor northern part and some well-off middle-class areas. A TQM policy was chosen by the district general manager for commercial reasons – in order to compete. To initiate TQM, outside consultants were brought in from the commercial and business worlds to advise and help with setting-up. A gradual approach was used to spread the idea, and it was decided that the initial 'quality attack' would be on clinical care at the hospital ward level. After the initial set-up with the consultants, implementation of TQM was led by a quality manager, TQM facilitators and forty trained auditors who are all senior nurses.

The approach to TQM adopted at Trafford General Hospital was to eschew the more industrial-oriented 'right first time' philosophy, mention of which we ourselves have found to lead immediately to cynicism on the part of public sector audiences. This response is based on the view that 'because there can be no such thing as "right first time in our kind of work", the whole idea of TQM is obviously daft'. Trafford General Hospital, therefore, adopted a strong 'customer focus' approach by applying the audit mechanism, and every ward has been audited. The central strategy in Trafford's audit approach is for the peer group to set the 'service standard' from what they make of the audit feedback, 'instead of having to meet some arbitrary standard set from the top by management'. A range of audit tools has been the strategy for introducing total quality at Trafford: formal audit instruments, observation, listening, viewing patients' ward records, etc. The rhetoric here is of TQ (total quality) not TQM, thereby not stressing 'management', a word which can have very negative connotations in Britain.

The whole approach adopted at Trafford General Hospital has therefore been one of customer audit and service standard setting. As described to us by one of the facilitators, the approach has been to 'get the data to see what is happening, to see what problems we have if any'. In some cases, the findings revealed a state of affairs which was unknown and which created astonishment. For example, an audit was undertaken of waiting times in the out-patient department, something which senior managers concerned with purchasing had set down certain theoretical standards for.

'Purchasing' had set a standard that a patient would be seen every twenty minutes; in reality, it was not known how many were being seen. The front-line staff who worked in the out-patient department undertook the data collection. Their findings showed that what was happening with regard to waiting times was not at all close to the service standards which had been arbitrarily set. The data disclosed that 27 per cent of patients did not turn up for their appointment and a significant percentage turned up late. The consultants in the department were amazed to discover this.

An important general point regarding the implementation of customer audit was confirmed at Trafford, namely that the audit instruments and methods need to be tailored to the work contexts of the different disciplines. What will work with one group will not necessarily work with another, as the philosophy of care can vary according to the professional group in question. The whole process must also involve 'credible peers' in its implementation. The type of formal audit instrument used, though customized to the particular department, covered the following template of items: a 'profile of activity' (the environmental features in which the care is delivered); the physical and human resources available; care processes; and measures of patient satisfaction. At Trafford General Hospital, the benefits were very much seen to be as follows: 'people at ground level become aware of the total situation and you obtain data which were previously concealed, data which are vital to the setting of service standards'.

The quality managers and facilitators at Trafford became aware of certain distinct public sector features or issues which needed to be taken into account and managed when implementing TQM in a health setting. These were: visibility of quality shortfalls, empowerment differences, 'defining what is best' and 'fit to the ethos'.

Visibility of quality shortfalls

The quality practitioners at Trafford felt that the quality problems that exist in health settings are not as visible as they are in manufacturing. They judged, as we ourselves do, that 'quality problems' in industry are explicit and more obvious, whereas in the public sector they are generally 'hidden' by the complexity of the professional processes. As a consequence, they saw the introduction of TQM in health as requiring much more initial mapping, auditing and surveying of customer needs in order to reveal or demarcate the 'quality issues'. Hence, in a systematic total quality approach, they began with customer-focused activities rather than, for example, customer chain analysis or process measurements. In short, the Trafford experience demonstrated that the standards to be met were not self-evident, they were to be discovered!

Empowerment differences

The Trafford experience underlines the fact that, in the public sector, as distinct from industrial settings, traditionally front-line workers are not mere operatives but professionals; they have always had to use interactive skills. In health and the other public sectors, the front-line workers have never been disempowered automatons in the way that so many industrial workers have been. The TQM concept of empowerment must therefore have a different emphasis in public sector contexts such as health; it is not so much concerned with empowering the individual 'as of right' *per se*, but with the maximization of reciprocal relationships in the cross-functional sense, and the guarantee of more support from management. Apart from this, there is also the sense of a 'local' emphasis to empowerment – as it applies to the nature of the particular ward, department, professional group, etc. This is particularly important when defining service standards. The same service standards do not necessarily apply across all of the groups, so the empowerment concept enacted must allow scope for a TQM facilitator and peer group to set the service standards for the specific professional areas within nursing care.

Defining what is the best

The health practitioners of TQM at Trafford and elsewhere, feel that defining the 'best' is different in a public sector context than in an industrial context, where there are more external objective benchmarks. What exactly is the best? Or, to put it another way, that which constitutes quality in health, or in any of the other public sector provisions, has a problematic status and there are several parties to its resolution. People like Steffen (1988) have defined it thus: 'For the physician and the patient, quality medical care can be defined as that care that has the capacity to achieve the goals of both the physician and the patient.' However, this statement does not include other key stakeholders in health care – the taxpayers if it is a public provision or the shareholders if a private one. We take the discussion of this matter further towards the end of this chapter.

TQM fit to public sector ethos

TQM ideas must be made to mesh with the ethos and real world of the particular professional service being delivered; there are things that are distinctive to the ethos of mental health care compared with general nursing, for example.

The whole approach to the implementation of TQM at Trafford has been to sell the product of customer audit not the theory of TQM to the rank-and-file professionals. The importance of customer audit is therefore something which must be stressed, and a topic which we analyse further below. At Trafford, as a consequence of customer audit, the hospital had by mid-1992 created seventy-six service standards, in addition to determining some generic standards which affect the work of all groups. In fact, the approach to implementation at Trafford has been to use the 'rank-and-file' to produce evidence to later involve senior management and physicians, and in this respect the evaluation of TQM health projects in Britain points up the importance of the sequence of implementation in terms of role-holder groups:

> In TQM, therefore, the sequence of introduction and implementation becomes a prime concern. 'Top-led and Bottom-fed' attempts imply an iterative process, perhaps a helical one, in which the 'top' moves into quality only after it has created a joint agenda with those working at the base. It does not begin to move towards the more formal description of requirements, standards and conformance until it has recruited the support of the operational levels. Once that is done, the 'top' is able to move more firmly along the lines of total quality management implementation in which all of its components, organisational and setting of standards, can be included.
>
> (Kogan *et al.* 1991: 13)

The importance of customer audit

Aside from the exhortations of government, and the diligent applications at ground level such as by the people at Trafford, customer audit has received some interesting theoretical treatment in Britain from health care professionals writing about quality. They stress its centrality for achieving quality in health care and have conceptualized why it is very important. The perspective set out by John Morgan and his colleagues (1992) is, we think, very helpful, for it recognizes that the professional service encounter or transaction in a public sector provision such as health care is inter-actionist, and as a consequence the experience just cannot be the same for both parties. They encapsulate very well in our view the customer–patient situation:

> Professionals can misinterpret what users say about the service simply because their experience and perception of the service are different. Because they are familiar with the service, it is easy for them to assume that users perceive it in the same way, and speak the same language. Daily they make clinical and other judgements based on the information users give them, at the same time bringing professional knowledge and judgement to bear on the situation. It can therefore require a conscious effort to stand back and ask 'what are users really saying?', 'what does this mean to them?'.
>
> (Morgan *et al.* 1992)

Morgan *et al.* have provided a useful table which contrasts the features of the provider's and customer's experience (Table 10). We think this formulation (with necessary adaptations) would describe most professional

Table 10 Features of the provider and customer service experience

Provider's experience	User's experience
Their job	Distraction from normal life
Familiar:	Strange:
– setting	– setting
– language	– language
– people	– people
– behaviour	– behaviour
– conventions	– conventions
Feel confident	Feel anxious
Not in pain	In pain
Knowledgeable	Limited lay knowledge
In control of events	Limited or no control

service encounters in the public sector and hence has a great deal of generic validity.

The contrasts displayed in Table 10 convey very well why it is important to understand the world of the customer, and to bring about a situation where this is done on a systematic basis using reliable instruments; hence the development in health care in North America and Britain of a range of audit instruments. It again seems to us to be the case that health care is significantly ahead of the other public sectors in this regard. The following are some of the instruments that are available for auditing nursing:

- PHANEUF: a fifty-item scale from the USA 'designed to measure retrospectively the quality of care received by a patient during a particular cycle of care'.
- MONITOR: an index of the quality of nursing care for acute medical and surgical wards. This is a British index which consists of four separate patient-based questionnaires, each of which relates to a different category of patient dependency, and a further ward-based questionnaire.
- NATN: an instrument developed in the UK in the mid-1980s by the National Association of Theatre Nurses. It has five main areas: preoperative patient care; preparation of personnel; operating room care; postoperative patient care; departmental organization.
- PA Quality Scale: the aim of this scale is to assess the overall quality of nursing care received by clients in a variety of specialized medical care conditions.

We include reference to these instruments because we think the systematic management of quality in health, though still in its early stages, is ahead of education, social work and other occupational areas in the public sector in this regard, and managers in other occupational sectors may wish to look at these as exemplars of customer audit which could be useful to them in designing their own instruments.

Although we have emphasized that customer audit and standard setting characterized the work of the early TQM pioneers in health care, in Britain at least, there have been a whole range of other TQM applications. In the remainder of this chapter, we give case examples of some of them in order to show the extent to which TQM exponents in health care are adapting and applying principles and techniques that were once exclusive to industry.

Cross-functional team and empowerment: Lakeland Hospital case study

The following account of Lakeland Hospital is taken from Berry and Parasuraman (1991), which provides a whole range of useful insights into service quality for managers in the public sector. Lakeland provides a good vignette of the application of the principles of empowerment and of the cross-functional team which we described in Chapter 1.

> Lakeland Regional Medical Center, an 897 bed hospital in Lakeland, Florida, is one of an increasing number of service organisations that are creatively applying the team concept and are reaping handsome returns as a result. Each Lakeland patient in a 40-bed pilot unit is assigned a 'care pair' – usually a registered nurse and a helper – that caters to all the patient's needs from check-in to discharge. The care-pair teams are cross-trained in functions ranging from EKG monitoring to housekeeping chores to reading patients' costs. Moreover Lakeland has equipped patient rooms with computer terminals and mini-pharmacies so that the care pair has ready access to most necessities for providing quick, dependable service. Per-bed operating costs at the pilot unit are more than 9 percent lower than at conventionally organised units. Apart from this productivity boost, Lakeland's pilot unit is also enjoying higher patient satisfaction levels. As this book goes to press, Lakeland Regional is expanding its successful pilot program to other units.
>
> (Berry and Parasuraman 1991: 29–30)

The use of TQM tools and modelling in health

In searching the international literature for reports of TQM applications in health care, we found examples of the use of all the main TQM tools. 'Fishbone diagrams' have been used, for example, to analyse the causes and effects of the problem of wrong hospital meals, and 'scatter diagrams' have seen a range of applications. For example, Merry (1990) cites the use of a scattergram to determine a possible relationship between two variables: the percentage of mortality coronary artery bypass graft operations and the number of operations per year. The use of the scatter diagram showed a correlation between the mortality rate for this surgical procedure and the number of times the procedure is performed over a twelve-month period. This data invited the professionals concerned to improve quality by actions which would reduce the mortality rate.

Similarly, 'Pareto' analysis is in significant usage. Morris (1989) has applied Pareto analysis to all of the complaints logged by a district health authority in the UK over a given period. Pareto analysis consists of listing all the types of complaint, and then determining the volume of each type. These are expressed as percentages of the total number of complaints, and then ranked in decreasing order. These percentages are then plotted against the types of complaint expressed as percentages of the total number of types. Pareto analysis is named after an Italian economist who first illustrated that about 80 per cent of cases of a given class of phenomenon (in this example, complaints about the health service), are attributable to about 20 per cent of the range of possible causes (i.e. in this example, types of complaint). In everyday organizational life, the causes of problems are often attributed on the basis of anecdote, 'what everybody knows', or generalizing from an insufficiency of cases, etc. The stance of TQM in the public sector, or in any type of occupational sphere, is that the systematic management of quality must proceed on the basis that decision-making for quality is based on sound data and not best guesses or impression. Pareto analysis is therefore an ideal tool for directing attention to those causes on which the improvement of quality can be concentrated.

Morris's study did indeed confirm the 80:20 relationship of Pareto analysis – 76.43 per cent of all complaints received by the health authority derived from 21.28 per cent of causes. In fact, 60 per cent of all the complaints derived from just six complaints categories: inadequate treatment; unsatisfactory staff attitude; unsatisfactory care; poor or inadequate communication; errors in procedure – discharge; errors in procedure – communications.

Customer focus and flow modelling for quality re-design

Another TQM application for enhancing the quality of the customer's experience which fits the public sector professional transaction is flow modelling. Ovreteveit (1990) advocates the application of flow modelling in health care and the general principle behind it is to view the particular health service or transaction as a process with a series of stages which the customer passes through over time. Taking a hospital out-patient service as an example, a flow diagram would be made of a typical patient from entry to the service through each stage to departure. The model would show how the service was selected, the decisions to be made at each stage of entry and delivery, the information and services required from other departments and the opportunities for error at different points. Using the flow model as a guide, investigations would then be made of what actually happens to the patient/customer – the 'patient's journey' – in order to find out where the most frequent and costly errors occur. By matching what actually happens in the service with what is intended could then be used to re-design the process and procedures to avoid errors and wastage, and to reduce waiting times.

The concept of modelling the ideal flow of a service or analogously the ideal structure of a process has received interesting treatment in health care. For example, Musfeldt and Collier (1991) have modelled the processes/issues related to quality for: patient pathways, pharmacies, operating rooms, ancillary services, emergency rooms, laboratory services, radiology services, critical care units, out-patient services, obstetrical services, doctor–nurse relationships, children's hospitals/pediatrics, medical technology, post-hospitalization home care, and post-hospitalization complications resulting in re-admission. For each of these, the authors advocate that 'quality improvement outlines' be developed. Table 11 shows the quality outlines Musfeldt *et al.* have produced for physician–nurse relationships.

We think the approach of modelling, of creating quality outlines, as shown in Table 11, has good generic potential in the public sector. The elements of this approach could be used as a template for work outside health.

What is quality to mean in health care?

Having considered some of the key applications of TQM to health at the present time and given examples of some of the TQM techniques in use, it is relevant to consider the whole question of what constitutes a comprehensive definition of quality in health care. However, before doing so, we should remind ourselves that the word 'quality' needs to be pinned down with some conceptual clarity, as otherwise it may take on different meanings for different users.

So far in this chapter we have emphasized the customer perspective as a critical constituent of quality, because in TQM thinking the customer has a central role. The taking into account of the customer's perspective provides an important redress to the traditions which have existed in health and the other occupational areas of the public sector. Traditionally, quality has been defined on the basis of the views of the professionals alone. It is only in the last decade or so that Avedis Donabedian and others have brought the patient/client centre-stage:

> Client satisfaction is of fundamental importance as a measure of the quality of care because it gives information on the provider's success at meeting those client values and expectations which are matters on which the client is the ultimate authority. The measurement of

Table 11   Quality outline for physician–nursing relationships

---

Importance
The physican–nursing relationship will be reflected in the quality of care, philosophy of care and job satisfaction of the nurses and physicians. Effective communication between physicians and nurses will increase the speed and accuracy with which care is given.

Problems
• Delays/errors in care due to physician–nurse miscommunication
• Delays/errors in care due to physician–nurse hostilities

Potential causes
• Understaffing of nurses
• Perceived attitude of nurses
• Perceived attitude of physicians
• High turnover
• Nurses and physicians leaving the profession
• Agency staffing
• Compensation issues
• Role identification

Quality improvement opportunities
• Nurses can identify physician prescribing errors in orders and correct in advance
• Physicians can anticipate nurses' questions or confusion in dispensing medicines or treatment and correct in advance
• Nurses can notify physicians sooner of changes in patients' condition, lab results, radiology results, other physicians' orders or consulting opinions as well as family issues

Potential methodologies and solutions
• Physician–nurse conferences
• Co-ordination arrangements of information transmission between nurses on the hospital floor, card clerks, physician's office staff and physician
• Establishment of physician–nursing relationship committee for the hospital
• Remove all obstacles to physician–nurse communication
• Greater recognition of nurses' clinical skills and achievements
• Greater nursing role in physician–patient rounds
• Specify clinical roles for registered nurses, clinical psychologists, nursing aides, technicians and students

Impact of resource centre
• Seminars on communication for physicians and nurses
• Computer programs linking physician offices and hospital floors

Patient surveys
Applying tools to identify the causes of quality problems

---

satisfaction is therefore an important tool for research, administration, and planning.

(Donabedian 1980: 25)

With serious consideration now being given to the customer perspective, the definition of quality can therefore be taken a stage further: quality medical care can be defined as that care that has the capacity to achieve the goals of both the physician and the patient. This is to give quality in health a 'dualist' or interactionist basis. Others have defined this dual perspective definition in more detail and a North American view has suggested that quality medical care: produces optimal improvements in the patient's health; emphasizes the promotion of health and the prevention of disease; is provided in a timely manner; seeks to achieve the patient's informed cooperation and participation in the care process and decisions concerning it; is based on accepted principles of medical science; should provide sensitivity and concern for the patient's welfare; makes efficient use of technology; is sufficiently documented to allow continuity of care and peer evaluation; and gives an important place to the assessment of patient goals and values.

The only item in the above list that we would seriously question is 'based on accepted principles of medical science', for that in itself raises the question of who is defining the 'accepted principles'? This element of the quality definition could be a support for orthodoxy ('political correctness') and be used to reject a treatment which, in the view of the patient and doctor, has been beneficial even though it is new to the accepted principles of medical science.

The 'dualist', professional–patient/customer definition of quality which we have now arrived at, is essentially about benefits as perceived by the two parties. What though about costs? Even in the early thinking about quality, Donabedian saw it as involving a balance of benefits over harms, efficiency and cost:

> I believe that in real life we do not have the option of excluding monetary costs from the individualised definition of quality . . . Given a specified quantity of resources devoted to medical care (e.g. by the state), the highest quality of care would be that which yields the highest net utility for the entire population.
>
> (Donabedian 1980)

We need, therefore, to bring costs into the equation, and Ovreteveit (1990: 34) has put the issue succinctly, by stating that a service must meet a customer's needs as perceived by that customer and the professionals, but not be wasteful of resources, resources which could be used to treat other customers. In our view, Ovreteveit has produced a definition of quality in health care which balances the stakeholder's interests with management realities.

We recognize at the present time, though, that many quality practitioners in health care – in the UK at least – are wary of the resources/cost dimension associated with process quality. There is every good reason for the British health care professional to be wary in our view because the full requirements of an 'internal market' have not yet been put properly in place by government, and there appears to be no guarantee that the quality savings produced by TQM would accrue to the provider, even in part. Some observers have even suggested that the government-inspired market is in fact a guise for an administrative form of work control (Riggs 1992).

The implication of the purchaser/provider model in the UK National Health Service is that those who demonstrate better productivity and efficiency will be rewarded in resource terms, in parallel fashion to the way they would if they were in a commercial venture in a true marketplace. This is not happening. To return to the Manchester cancer hospital example cited at the beginning of this chapter, here is an establishment which since it became a trust in 1991, has started two income-generating projects, has increased its income from private patients to more than £1 million, and opened a drug manufacturing plant on site in collaboration with a drug company to manufacture some of the hospital's cancer drugs. Yet as Mike Fry, its chief executive observed: 'we have an increasing number of patients/customers but we are not rewarded for them. If anything it is an inverse market because as demand increases there just aren't the resources' (Ormell 1993).

This raises a wider point about process quality cost savings and the public sector in general. We fail to see what would be the incentives for any health care organization or department in the public sector to implement process quality studies with a view to cost savings, unless the health service professionals in the organization as a whole, or in the department, are allowed to keep and use for their own plans, a significant slice of the cost benefits of quality. In other words, unless government treats health (or any other public sector provision) as a real internal market and rewards productivity, health service professionals will remain shy of the process quality dimension and be suspicious of TQM in general.

In summary, regarding quality in health care, we see the Ovreteveit's (1990) definition as comprehensively informing the development of TQM:

> ...we can define quality in health services as meeting customer requirements at the lowest cost, and as involving three elements: first customer quality, which is whether the service gives customers what they want as measured by customer satisfaction and complaints; second professional quality, which is whether the service meets customers' needs as defined by professionals, and whether the professional standards which are believed to produce the required outcomes are observed; and, third 'process quality', which is the design and operation of the service process to use resources in the most efficient way to meet customer requirements.

In the discussion above, we have emphasized the customer focus aspect of quality because for us it most characterizes the implementation of Total Quality Management in health to date. We do not, however, wish to give the impression that what Ovreteveit termed above 'process quality' and the cost dimension has been ignored by practitioners, because this is not the case. The evaluation studies of the ten TQM projects in England provide evidence of process improvements and cost savings:

> Many examples of process improvement and resource savings were noted during fieldwork ... There were examples of savings on one ward for the elderly of 30% in the pharmacy bill in the last two years; a major saving in resources on an ophthalmology ward by instituting a pre-admissions clinic to screen out unfit patients; large savings by a physiotherapy quality circle as a result of better control over crutches and other aids, and a cost of non-conformance study showing the potential for 18% saving in the running costs for a Medicine for the Elderly Ward. These initiatives were based on, and resulted in, improvements in quality of service, not just in reduction of costs. There were also examples of empowering patients and relatives including a programme to give patients more control over their own pain relief, and a thematic study to improve contributions made to the handling of relatives and friends of the dying and deceased. These exemplified the TQM principles of customer focus, systematic analysis, and multidisciplinary cooperation.
>
> (Kogan *et al.* 1991: 4)

Kogan *et al.* also reported on TQM applications in health which applied some of the more demanding concepts of 'process quality', such as non-conformance for example (see p. 22):

> One authority did carry out an exercise to tackle the complex issue of non-conformance. A team was set up which involved staff from the ward as well as a business manager and a clinical nurse manager. Twelve areas of potential non-conformance were identified and following further discussions with ward staff a further three areas were added. Detailed data collection was carried out and non-conformance was costed on the basis of lost bed days per year. On the basis of seven areas alone, costs of non-conformance were calculated to be some £116K per year or 18% of the £681K costs of beds and staff time. This is within the range claimed by Crosby and others for non-conformance in service organisations.
>
> (Kogan *et al.* 1991: 72)

Process quality improvements in health care have also been reported from North America. For example, Kleefield *et al.* (1991: 409) have documented a case from the Brigham and Women's Hospital affiliated to the Harvard Medical School in Boston, which distributes from its in-patient pharmacy 4.3 million doses of medications per year to service the

700 plus beds of its four satellites. In 1988, nurses began complaining to their supervisors about delays in medication delivery – that they were sometimes taking many hours, or that delivery was unpredictable.

In response to the complaints, teams were set up to resolve the situation. They began by surveying systematically the nature and extent of the problem. The survey revealed that only 39 per cent of nursing staff knew when pharmacy personnel made their rounds; 28 per cent thought rounds were made randomly anyway; 74 per cent perceived that medication delivery time averaged two to three hours; and 36 per cent were dissatisfied with the medication delivery service. A team was specifically charged with reducing the variation in delivery of medications to the nursing units, ensuring delivery within one hour of the order. The results of process improvements included: significant reductions in the variation in times at which medications were ordered and delivered; specification of routes so that floor nurses could predict arrival times, and these now consistently arrive within seven minutes of the due time, whereas this could have been as much as twenty minutes in the past; a new process for preparing frozen antibiotics can be completed in 1.3 hours, whereas the old process took four hours; relocating certain processes has enabled much greater automation and computerization and medication errors have reduced from 'an average of six to ten per day to nearly zero'. The steering committee of this quality project computed the quality costs using conservative estimates. They determined that the changes were saving 17 000 dollars a year from the elimination of errors, and a saving of 38 000 dollars a year in personnel costs because of the new working processes.

What Kleefield and his colleagues concluded about this and other TQM applications was that 'health care organisations can apply certain technical elements of TQM and that doing so can lead to process improvements comparable in magnitude to those achieved in other industries'. After two years of TQM application at the Atlantic City Medical Center, for example, 'specific improvements such as increased teamwork, improved physician relations, increased patient satisfaction, and a substantial increase in profit margins have resulted' (Kleefield *et al.* 1991).

In early 1993, the evolving picture regarding TQM and health care in the advanced democracies seems to be clear. Where TQM is being adopted, customer audit and service standards are the focus, with 'process quality' applications yet to be fully explored. The demographic and life-span trends are increasing pressures for quality in the utility or cost savings sense, so that process quality is likely to come to the fore. What is already clear for health care in the public sector is that TQM has already shown that it can produce more satisfied clients and better provided for clients with resource savings.

However, it is still early days for TQM in health care. Kogan and co-workers' (1991, 1992a, 1992b) evaluations of the UK demonstration TQM projects, for example, have shown that while there has been significant successes in the implementation of changes in some areas at some hospitals, on most sites it is still patchy and there are many quality improvements unconnected with TQM.

Overall, though, taking Britain and North America together, it would be fair to conclude that by the early 1990s, the potential – if not yet the system-wide *achievements* – of total quality approaches to health care has been established. We anticipate an explosion of TQM applications in the health care sector as the 1990s proceed.

CHAPTER

5

TQM and education

TQM and education: the general context

As with the policy crisis in health provision in the advanced democracies, there is also widely perceived to be a parallel but differently based crisis for government-provided education. In Britain, Canada and the USA, and many other OECD countries, significant changes are emerging in the way government makes educational provision. Though these changes are not similar in nature in each country – indeed, as we indicate below, they can often be in opposite directions – they are nevertheless a response to a very similar set of concerns.

These concerns are financial, educational and economic: to do with controlling government expenditure on education; to do with enhancing students' levels of educational achievement in all age groups; and to do with ensuring that the student experience encompasses competencies and skills necessary to the world of work.

In each of the three countries which provide case examples for this chapter, there has been the important realization in recent years that the level of government expenditure as a proportion of gross national product cannot be allowed to continue at its increasing pace if these countries are not to bankrupt themselves, hence educational policy-makers have become preoccupied with the return on educational investment. Moreover, there are the additional special context features regarding educational provision of certain social and demographic trends affecting schooling. There is an ageing population with fewer people in work being asked to support those in school or retirement. There are also many households who have no stake in schooling. In the UK in 1992, 60 per cent of all households were either single-person households or consisted of a couple without children. In several countries, the willingness by the 'Dinkies' (the double-income, no-kids households) and the 'Woofies' (well-off older folks) to pay more taxes for education has evaporated.

The advent of the global economy and the ubiquity of information technology have caused the OECD countries to question educational curricula and standards in the face of the economic success of the Pacific Rim. There has been a concern to improve or reconceptualize what should be the vocational or work-related constituent of schooling, and there is an overriding anxiety about the overall levels of educational performance in comparison with others. For example, the sort of data provided by the World of Differences Study (see Table 12) have concentrated the minds of those who advise government ministers, with regard to how schools are best controlled and managed, to enhance the performance levels of students in a world of competitive economy (Porter 1990).

The response in England and Wales has been one of far-reaching gov-ernment-driven changes in the control system and in the specification of the curriculum which must be taught. Some of the systemic features of a quasi-market have been developed. The controlling powers of local educa-tion authorities (the analogue of school boards in North America) have largely been taken away by the devolution of management powers and financial control to the individual school and its own board of governors. Parental choice and open enrolment to schools have been legislated for, and a policy on performance measures through the publication of the examination results of individual schools has been enacted. Regarding the curriculum, whereas this was previously largely left to the individual schools in England and Wales, a centralized national core curriculum has been instituted, with a prescribed content and attainment targets across a large number of subjects and national testing and assessment of results at the end of key stages such as seven, eleven, fourteen and sixteen years.

In the British responses to the 'crisis' of educational provision, there had until very recently been little mention of the word 'quality', whereas this had been a feature of the response to health care concerns. Neither had there been any indication by government of TQM as a management strategy desirable in the new circumstances.

During this same period in the USA, there have also been expressions of a crisis in the public education system. In April 1991, the White House set out 'Education 2000', a statement of six national education goals to be achieved by the year 2000, and which generally called for 'better and more accountable schools', 'schools that will reach the national educational goals'. It is widely believed that this policy initiative of President Bush fell by the wayside because of the Gulf War. However, what has been influential in response to the perceived education crisis in America, has been the growing

Table 12 'World of differences': average mathematics and science proficiency, age 13[a]

Mathematics	Science
Korea, 567.8	British Columbia, 551.3 Korea, 549.9
Quebec (Fr), 543.0 British Columbia, 539.8 Quebec (Eng), 535.8 New Brunswick (Eng), 529.0	UK, 519.5 Quebec (Eng), 513.7 Ontario (Eng), 514.7 Quebec (Fr), 513.4 New Brunswick (Eng), 510.5 Spain (503.9)
New Brunswick (Fr), 516.2 Spain, 511.7 UK 509.9 Ireland, 504.3	USA, (478.5) Ireland, (469.3) Ontario (Fr), 468.3 New Brunswick (Fr), 461.1
Ontario (Fr), 481.5 USA, 473.9	

[a] Differences in performance between the groups in both columns are statistically significant.

Source: Compiled from data in Lapointe, A.E., Mead, N.A. and Phillips, W.G. (1989) *A World of Differences: An International Assessment of Mathematics and Science.* Princeton, NJ: Educational Testing Service.

exhortation and statementing of policy with regard to the teaching of workplace skills. The 'SCANS' Report (1991) noted that education must teach the skills needed in a world economy increasingly driven by TQM:

> This report identifies five competencies which, in conjunction with a three-part foundation of skills and personal qualities, lie at the heart of job performance today. These eight areas represent essential preparation for all students, both those going directly to work and those planning further education. All eight must be an integral part of every young person's school life.
>
> (SCANS 1991: vi)

Table 13 sets out the skills identified in the SCANS Report, and we have displayed them here because they reflect many of the precepts of TQM and because of their general applicability to training for TQM implementation in the public sector.

What is interesting about the American response when compared with the British, is that while it also aimed to change the status quo significantly, it did so in the opposite direction – away from a mandated curriculum in the subject sense to a situation of freeing-up schools regarding the way

Table 13 Competencies and skills identified by SCANS

Competencies needed by effective workers:
- *Resources*: allocating time, money, materials, space and staff
- *Interpersonal skills*: working on teams, teaching others, serving customers, leading, negotiating, and working well with people from culturally diverse backgrounds
- *Information*: acquiring and evaluating data, organizing and maintaining files, interpreting and communicating and using computers to process information
- *Systems*: understanding social, organizational and technological systems, monitoring and correcting performance, and designing or improving systems
- *Technology*: selecting equipment and tools, applying technology to specific tasks and maintaining trouble-shooting technologies

Foundation of skills and personal qualities
- *Basic skills*: reading, writing, arithmetic and mathematics, speaking and listening
- *Thinking skills*: thinking creatively, making decisions, solving problems, seeing things in the mind's eye, knowing how to learn, and reasoning
- *Personal qualities*: individual responsibility, self-esteem, sociability, self-management and integrity

---

they manage the subject curriculum when compared to the past. The American response to education crisis has been to emphasize cross-curricular competencies and the role of empowerment of participants. The vision statement of President Clinton for education emphasizes:

> the leadership responsibilities of *all* actors in the learning process . . . [and] . . . seeks broad political empowerment to change the direction of our schools at the expense of bureaucratic maintenance and intellectual conformity . . . Therefore the essential next step for education reform is to empower school boards, superintendents, principals, teachers, and community members with the tools they need to create a new climate.
>
> (Clinton 15 January 1993)

At the beginning of his tenure, President Clinton saw education then as in need of radical change, and the whole vocabulary of his position echoed the canons and concepts of TQM, as well it might, for the State of which he had been governor, Arkansas, was in 1993 the leader in applying TQM to state government.

Education in Canada was equally in crisis. In Edmonton, Alberta, the School Board announced in April 1993 that it would reduce its budget by some 10 million dollars, mainly by laying off about 175 teachers and thirty other staff. Alongside budget issues, there was concern about performance. In its annual review of the education system, the Albertan government had given the province a 'B−' for its overall performance. School systems across Canada were similarly facing budget reductions, major changes to services, and new demands for improved performance. The concerns were not confined to elementary and secondary schools. At the post-secondary level, governments across Canada were reducing expenditure, encouraging innovation so as to do more with less, and requiring some staff to accept voluntary pay freezes.

Taking these western democracies as a whole, then, government provision has everywhere been seen to be in crisis, and in need of a dramatic response. The difference compared with similar levels of crisis perceptions in health, has been a less explicit designating of 'management' as the direction of the needed response, and an absence of the recommending of TQM as something to be considered or recommended as a management strategy. The need for enhanced performance, though, has increasingly been emphasized in education in each of these countries in recent years, but this has been more implicit in a range of context changes, rather than explicit as management strategy, as has been the case in health care in each of these countries. Although by 1993 there has been no direct government sponsorship of TQM, whether central (federal) or local (state/provincial), as there has been in health, some leading academic writers have advocated the application of TQM to education (Murgatroyd 1989, 1991; Hill and Taylor 1991; Taylor and Hill 1992; Murgatroyd and Morgan 1993).

Challenges to the adoption and implementation of TQM in schools and colleges

Many writers, including ourselves, have set out the particular challenges which the world of education needs to overcome in adopting and implementing TQM. These are essentially challenges for cultural change, for the revising of the existing cultural mores of the school or college organization, and of the sub-cultures of professional identities within them, so as to create an environment in which TQM can become rooted and flourish.

We see six categories of 'cultural' challenge to the adoption of TQM in education, and we consider that each of these categories has its analogue in the other occupational provisions of the public sector, hence the foregoing discussion will have some generic validity for the reader from any 'government' background.

The rejection of industrial models and vocabulary: an anti-management tendency

In all three case-study countries, there has in the past been an anti-industry, anti-management, anti-measurement and anti-'pursuit of effectiveness' posture to the occupational culture of schooling. This has stemmed, we believe, in part from accurate perceptions of the dehumanizing aspects of earlier mass production industrialization and a failure to recognize the liberal and humane benefits which derive from very good systematic management techniques.

An anti-management posture, and with it a rejection of the vocabulary, has also derived from the sentimental philosophy in which most teachers were trained and acculturated into the profession. The initiating philosophy has been very much one of:

> we are very caring people, altruistically concerned with the individual child and the whole person, and are not to be driven by the impersonal demands of economy. Also, given the fact that the dice is loaded against some children because of their social backgrounds etc., only we, the teachers, can compensate for that by showing we value them, and by giving them certain values and experiences and these may well have nothing to do with success in specific skills or crude performance as understood in the outside world.

To some extent, therefore, a false and dichotomous view of caring and learning, or learning and effectiveness, has in our view arisen in the occupational culture.

Hence, certain vocabularies thought by many elsewhere to be part of generic management thinking, can receive cultural rejection: 'performance', 'product', 'customer', 'measurement', for example. These are seen as industrial or commercial terms irrelevant to the educational world and the learning process. Such a value posture to the culture of schooling potentially sees TQM as alien because of its industrial origins and connections. It is not immediately understood that TQM is a whole new paradigm in the way that we discussed in Chapter 1. What needs to be set forth is the whole idea that TQM is as far removed from 'industrial revolution management culture' as is the personal computer from the work context of the early Ford production line.

A main consequence of the anti-industry, anti-management cultural posture has been the position held by many that what is to count as 'quality' in schools is to be defined by the professionals and not by the consumers. More frequently, though, teachers are becoming conscious that the expectations for schools have changed. The community at large and its stakeholders are no longer prepared in most advanced countries to let the schools get on with it, to trust the professionals to deliver the goods. The expectation now is for schools to demonstrate their performance or 'value added' and to make explicit their satisfaction of customer expectations, as government in many countries is specifying. The TQM perspective focuses on the customers in all their 'internal' and 'external' manifestations and calls for the abandonment of crude anti-management tendencies.

A tradition of individualist rather than collectivist responsibility for quality

The core of professionalism in teaching (as in health and certain other government provisions) has always been connected with the autonomy of professionals in their own arenas, such as the teacher in *his or her own*

classroom. 'Quality' was therefore individualistically defined by the professional in his or her altruistic dealings with students as a unique encounter
and relationship. In contrast to this, TQM seeks to promote collective or
organization-wide dimensions of quality, and where possible wishes to
quantify 'quality' so that degrees of non-conformance can be established.
For example, in a school where TQM has started to be applied, the head
has noted how individualistic procedures defeat consistency of procedures
and a coherent view of quality. He cites the case of the criteria being
applied for sixth-form students being allowed admission to A level courses
(equivalent to grades 11 and 12). 'One [teacher interviewer] allowed entry
to A level courses with a GCSE entry grade of "D" (or even in one
instance an "E"); another insisted on the minimum of a "C" etc.' (Samuels
1991).

The organizational context of the school but not the classroom can be a focus for TQM

Traditionally, classrooms have been viewed as islands of professional
autonomy with the processes of teaching and learning too esoteric and complex to be the subject of management scrutiny or technical analysis to any
extent. As a consequence, there is a disposition for the professionals in
schools to concede the possibility of improving administration and other
organizational processes, such as canteen arrangements or rules of behaviour
and discipline for example, but to exempt the activities within the classroom. When such views of professional autonomy and 'sanctity' of the
classroom are allied with a traditional management perspective, then the
school is viewed as a collection of separate, highly specialized individual
performers and units, though linked administratively within a functional
hierarchy by lateral connections being made by the mediating roles of
senior managers and heads of department.

In contrast, the TQM perspective, with its focus on the customer and on
process improvement, insists on applying these equally to the classroom as
well as the context, and from this foundation revises the whole concept of
management in the school. Tribus has defined quality in education as that
which makes learning a joy and a pleasure to the students. However, he
adds:

> . . . joy is ever changing. What is thrilling at one age is infantile at
> another. Teachers must [therefore] be ever alert to engage the stu-
> dents in the discussion of what constitutes a quality experience. The
> negotiations and discussions are never done.
>
> (Tribus 1992: 7)

The students learn within the systems and processes of the classroom and
can give their views of these. Teachers can study the systems and processes
they use for consistency of performance and effectiveness, with the prime
aim of improving the quality of learning. With such customer and process

perspectives as these, the job of the teacher refocuses onto the learning systems in order continuously to improve them with the students' help. Similarly, the job of the principal and senior managers changes from the traditional bias of the enactment of established rules and procedures where staff are the customers of the 'book', that is essentially defined by the positional hierarchy, and become instead leaders and facilitators who work on the school systems and processes within which the teachers work, so as to improve them with their help.

Traditional belief that performance achievement is the product of inputs

Another feature of 'held belief' in much traditional school culture is that learning performance achievements are the products of certain key input factors such as the pupils' intrinsic competences, or certain levels of resourcing such as class size, the amount of money available for books, etc. A range of significant and authoritative researches into school effectiveness in recent years have shown that there is no simple, straightforward relationship with input factors (Rutter *et al.* 1979; Reynolds *et al.* 1980; Smith and Tomlinson 1989). These researchers have demonstrated beyond dispute that there are 'school effects' which are unrelated to input factors. They have shown that when input factors are controlled out of the comparisons, some schools achieve more for all of their children, *whatever* the basic abilities of the children.

While the causes of such enhanced achievement have not been pinpointed exactly, the researches indicate that 'ethos' and 'managerial process' factors are likely to be responsible. The position of TQM, and the evidence of its track record, is that to concentrate on process enhancement will achieve important output gains.

We are doing very well as we are under the present circumstances

Many educational establishments (or any other type of public sector provision for that matter) can demonstrate that in terms of the measures conventionally used, they are doing very well as they are. They point to their position in examination league tables, in school attendance leagues, or in respect of how many parents turn up to parents' evenings, etc. There are no apparent grounds for dissatisfaction by their stakeholders.

These situations just described can be presented as firm objections to TQM, reflecting the stance that 'if we do what we always do we will get what we always get and that has been quite satisfactory for us!'. Apart from saying something about risk avoidance, this stance of course does not recognize that even greater achievements may be possible. The TQM perspective calls for improvements beyond comfort levels of achievement, and argues that the continuing search for quality challenges the setting of goals in education or elsewhere which are outrageous in comparison with previous standards. The absence of dissatisfaction is not necessarily proof of positive customer satisfaction; it says nothing about the levels of quality and customer satisfaction which might be achieved.

A tradition of management by centralized decision-making: the 'headmaster' or 'superintendent' tradition

In Britain, it is recognized that there has been a 'headmaster tradition' in the running of schools. This label refers to what was once a management style of benevolent autocracy on the part of the school principal (possessing many of the attributes of a nineteenth-century employer according to Baron 1975), but which in recent decades has become very much consultative. Even in North America, a wholly collegial approach has hardly been a notable feature of managing schools.

By and large, school principals in each of these countries have stood between their staffs and the education office, whether of the local education authority or of the school board, mediating the policy and rules of the system. The principal's job has been to plan for subordinates and to appraise their work to ensure plans are followed, for in any particular phase or age level of education, schools were expected to perform to certain given system-wide norms, they were not seen to be much in competition with each other, or to be run on lines which might differentiate them greatly from each other in terms of what they offered. In all of the advanced democracies, this traditional context is being changed by government-driven system changes intended to secure better performance and enhanced quality in the eyes of the stakeholders. The context is now one of a quasi-market which requires very different management strategy and practices.

This new context calls for the abandonment of 'decision centralization' in the hands of senior management and a TQM culture with empowerment of staff and students – a culture that encourages individual initiative, risk-taking, tolerance of conflict and high levels of horizontal communication. Instead of a leadership which commands, it calls for a leadership which facilitates and mentors. As we described in Chapter 1, there needs to be an inversion of the triangle of management. By and large, then, there is the challenge of changing school management from a top-down consultative model to a wholly empowered and democratized one. Schools' senior managements, therefore, have the challenge of breaking the management tradition and consciously eschewing decisions solely justified by the positional power of senior management role-holders. The embedding of TQM requires a leadership which creates a system or environment that makes every person a process manager, presiding over the transformation of inputs to outputs of greater achievement and value to the customer.

Teachers' attachment and 'corporate' endeavour

Another challenge for TQM in the cultural context of education is the tradition of teachers' strong attachment to their own subject or to their own pupils, while sometimes being uncommitted to other customers (both internal or external) or to the corporate strategy of the school or college – assuming they know about it. This traditional or 'restricted' perspective has gone hand in hand with the first challenge we dealt with above, namely that of an individualist rather than a collectivist or corporate concept of quality. The same point can be made about school administrators, not just teachers. A school's senior managers may be so committed to the particular rules and procedures they are responsible for implementing, that they may lose sight of commitment to overall 'corporate' objectives. The challenge for TQM implementation, in this or any other public sector, is to recognize the potential block of traditional culture and manage the change. In this example, it would mean creating an alignment of individual approaches to quality with the school's overall strategy for its 'marketplace'.

Challenges to TQM in education: managing the culture, a summary

We have found from our own work in schools, colleges and universities that the challenges which the existing cultural mores of the educational world present to TQM can find expression in:

- a disposition to keep the definition of quality abstract, and to avoid the conceptualization of quality as customers' perceptions;
- a tardiness to accept fully the notion of internal customer–supplier chains, and to explore the perceived quality of these;
- an absence of systematic evaluation in general, and in particular of internal 'products', either by the immediate customer or preferably by the preceding supplier. There is generally a bias to depend on impression and reluctance to collect hard data;
- an absence of a defined strategy for its local 'marketplace'.

These and the points we raised earlier, lead to the need for managing the culture to receive TQM, and this is a generic point irrespective of the particular public sector. TQM represents a paradigm shift from traditional management to a whole new way of managing organizations (see Chapter 1). Consequently, all public sector occupational contexts will have the challenge of overcoming certain cultural mores which are inimical to TQM. In this respect, the framework for understanding organizational culture developed by Hofstede *et al.* is insightful and extremely useful.

Hofstede and co-workers (1990) have demonstrated that organizational culture manifests itself in four ways, and we illustrate these below in terms of the school, but they are equally valid constructs for all public sectors and other organizations. The four manifestations of culture are:

- *Symbols*: these can be words, gestures, pictures or objects that carry particular meanings of what is valued, e.g. the school motto.
- *Heroes*: individuals who possess characteristics highly valued in the school

and who therefore serve as role models for desired behaviour or performance. In this category, we traditionally tend in the school situation to think of students being held up as heroes for their academic or sporting success, but more recently of course also for their social care concerns.

- *Values*: these can be specific, but are often non-specific feelings of good and evil, normal and abnormal, rational and irrational. They are rarely discussed explicitly but are to be seen as the core of a culture. Values are very strongly attached to the key concepts and beliefs of TQM, which we discussed in Chapter 1. For example, take empowerment. Attached to this is the value of the equal validity of anyone's technical view or experimentation and the right to demonstrate quality enhancement whatever their position in the organization. Indeed, empowerment seeks to celebrate the importance of the 'front-line' worker. Also in TQM, the whole concept of the primacy of the customer is equally bound up with a range of values. TQM defines the customer's view of his or her transaction with a teacher or physician as of equal importance to that of the professional, a radical revision of the traditionally held view of the student or patient.
- *Rituals*: these are collective activities which are technically superfluous but which are seen to be socially essential. The school assembly is the most obvious expression of this aspect of the culture. The rituals are events where symbols, heroes and values are paraded and rehearsed in some ceremonial and integrated form.

We have sought to show in this section that there are traditional mores to the culture of education in the public sector which present themselves as challenges to be overcome in the adoption of TQM. Also, we have demonstrated that the management of occupational cultural challenges can be assisted by an awareness of symbols, rituals, heroes and values. Indeed, the adoption of TQM is likely to require new symbols, heroes, values and rituals.

Applications of TQM in education

The picture which emerges from surveying the application of TQM in education in Britain and North America in 1993, is not all that different from the one which we characterized for health care provision. The focus of TQM activity is very definitely on the customer rather than the process perspective. Most TQM applications in educational settings have been concerned with empowering the customer and creating an awareness of customer–supplier responsibilities, by way of the application of customer surveys. Alongside this customer focus, the setting of service standards has also begun in those schools taking a systematic approach to the management of quality. All this is not to suggest that there are many school and college sites in Britain and North America that are applying TQM. Though there are no data available which indicate exactly how many schools and colleges have officially adopted a quality policy with a total management approach, our estimate is that it has not reached 1:1000 educational establishments, though there is a growing interest to find out more about TQM. What is clear is that the tertiary level educational institutions in North America and Britain are ahead of the primary and secondary schools in the adoption of TQM.

In contrast to the customer focus of these early TQM applications, the whole area of process conformance studies is virtually undeveloped, although there are occasional cases of process mapping and measurement, which have essentially concerned themselves with organizational, management and ancillary professional issues rather than with classroom processes. A number of government bodies, though, have signalled to the educational world the need for some process studies. We have not yet found one case of the application of TQM to classroom processes *per se*, but there has been some very interesting research on 'customer–supplier' chains, and we discuss this below.

We see the customer focus of TQM in education as providing data to disclose exactly what the quality issues are, as well as to answer such questions as:

• To what extent are teachers able to accept some of the central concepts of TQM?
• Do teachers recognize they have customers in the TQM sense?
• Is the whole idea of 'customer–supplier chains' in schools acceptable?
• Do students have views of their organizational world, management practices, or improvements they would like to see in their school?
• Could students make a greater contribution to the design of school policies and practices?
• Do students have views about whether they learn more with some teachers, and which can contribute to teaching effectiveness generally?
• Do teachers and students endorse the explicit setting of performance standards?

We have found in our fieldwork and from studies of the international literature that by 1993 the applications of TQM to schools and colleges in Britain and North America have covered the following topic areas: defining who the customers are and relating quality objectives to supplier–customer chains; defining and setting service standards; empowering students; carrying out customer audits and surveys; defining and making explicit whole school procedures and modelling and matching the student experience; process mapping and measurement; setting 'Hoshin' goals; and deriving customer data on classroom processes. We now present case examples of each of these, which give answers to the questions we posed above. In some cases, we give the actual name of the establishment where the TQM innovation has taken place; in others, we use a pseudonym because the innovation owners either see their TQM journey as being at an early stage of development and wish the experience to be judged after a longer period of time, or because some of the data are sensitive.

Defining customers, customer–supplier chains and empowering students

North Area College, Stockport, England, is a tertiary level institution which provides a full range of academic and vocational post-16 education for its catchment area. The principal began by developing the college on a very student-centred basis, and a friend told him that his approach was essentially a TQM one, so he decided to investigate the concepts further and to apply them formally so that the institution now has an official TQM policy. 'Quality education through partnership is the motto', and the aim is to respond to students as customers. The college documents reveal the essence of their TQM policy:

> In North Area College TQM, we see the customer/supplier relationship as two-way. For example, the teacher is supplier to a student. What must the teacher do to deliver TQM? Equally the student is supplier to the teacher. What must the student do to deliver total quality to the teacher? The mutual commitment to quality leads to each becoming motivated to make the partnership work.
>
> The college mission statement is QUALITY EDUCATION THROUGH PARTNERSHIP. This partnership is with the student who is our central customer and with each parent and guardian. Our aim is to provide a framework in which every parent and guardian can give an appropriate level of support to the young person. The college recognizes that students in the age range 16–19 are becoming more independent and more capable of taking responsibility for their own futures. The college supports therefore an adult ethos in which the students can learn and develop. We believe that parents supportive of these young people have a key role in this development. For this reason we consult with parents from the beginning, so that through dialogue, parents are able to have a positive role which complements and supports the student's work. We believe that the ongoing interchange of ideas between the student, the tutor and the parent provides a coherent and supportive framework in which each young person can plan and achieve for the future.

Other key elements in the TQM policy applied at North Area College are: the college has one vice-principal with a 'customer care and quality' brief; every teacher has a senior management sponsor and they meet on a one-to-one basis. The sponsor role is conceived to be both directive in terms of a five-year business plan and supportive to the individual by way of energizing staff development; every teacher is in a work team and all work teams have budgets; student empowerment is central and effected via a one-to-one relationship with a personal tutor. The personal tutor is a key

Table 14 Example of a teacher and student service standards agreement

---

For the teacher
- The teacher is always present
- The teacher is never late
- The teacher is willing to go over work if not understood
- Homework is set regularly. It is carefully matched to learning targets, and it is marked within three days and returned to the student with comments relevant to the student
- The teacher is approachable between lessons
- Lessons are well prepared
- Clear learning targets are set in advance and feedback is given on those achieved and which subjects need further work

For the student
- The student is never absent
- The student arrives at lessons on time
- The student takes a real interest in the subject and is active in lessons
- The student goes to bed at a reasonable time if there is an early morning lesson

---

role-holder, and the tutor must teach the student at least part of the time and meet the student on a one-to-one basis each month. Tutors have received training and work to a common checklist and ring parents every six weeks. The college has a quality assurance team which monitors the quality and frequency of tutoring by regularly talking with students about how they perceive the way they receive their entitlement and the value they place on the tutoring they receive.

No problem has been found with the transferability of quality concepts, but as was indicated to have been the case in health care in Chapter 4, some problem has been found in the acceptance of the language. Nevertheless, the college has pursued a strong customer empowerment focus as we indicated above, and allied with this has been the statementing of service standards.

In Chapter 4, we defined a service standard as 'a customer-driven agreed level of performance appropriate to the population addressed, which is observable, achievable, measurable and desirable'. A statement of service standards at Stockport has been developed on a customer–supplier contract basis, which teachers and students agree to. For staff and students, the current agreed service standards are those set out in Table 14. We see the essential concept and format of this 'service contract' as having a generic validity across the public sectors. Its prime elements can easily be transferred to other public sector circumstances.

We visited North Area College and spoke to the students, who had come to the college from a wide variety of schools at sixteen years of age.

We asked them to write and submit anonymously their answer to the following question, which we had written on the board: 'What is different about being here from where you were studying before?' Their responses almost equally referred to aspects of: the curriculum or teaching arrangements; the social relations of teaching; and views about their own autonomy as student learners. There was clear awareness and appreciation of their own empowerment from the comments made. For example:

> There is more emphasis on self study which requires far more independence and self-motivation.
>
> There is a mutual partnership between students and staff, which helps in attaining the academic aims of the former.
>
> A feeling of independence; no longer a number and am not treated *en masse*. The college is geared towards the individual rather than the group.

We also asked these student interviewees to complete in writing the following statement: 'If I were the principal I would. . .'. We found these young adult customers quite able to give decided views about the overall management and working of the college. For example:

> Make sure that students are in the college to work hard.
>
> Senior management of the college through the nature of their college position are in danger of distancing themselves from the student body, particularly with their 'business speak' – the majority of students would not know what TQM meant.
>
> I would enforce rules more on those who are just here for an easy ride.
>
> Change the canteen menu.

Writers on the customer service transaction in professional provisions such as health or education, have proposed that the customer perspective revolves around factors which we can summarize as the three P's. There is the 'P' of Procedures or rules – to include also aspects of the physical environment in which the transaction takes place; there is the 'P' of the perceived Personal relationships to the transaction; and there is the 'P' of the Professional standards expected and experienced in the transactions. The comments we received from the students of North Area College, Stockport, bore on each of these P's and give proof of the importance of the customer input to quality whatever the age of the customer.

Focus on the customer perspective has seen in some educational establishments the development of the concept of *service guarantee*, which we discussed in Chapter 1. Fox Valley Technical College in Wisconsin, USA, has an explicit TQM policy and a Total Quality Leadership Council which was formed very early in the process. Their 'Guaranteed Placement Job Readiness Policy' is published as follows:

Guaranteed retraining policy

Fox Valley Technical College graduates of programs at least one year in length who do not obtain employment in their program or related area within six months of graduation are guaranteed up to *six free credits* of additional instruction PLUS other student services.

(Spanbauer 1992: 12)

The Fox Valley TQM initiators have paid a lot of attention to the defining of customers in the educational context. As Spanbauer has emphasized: 'the first step when launching a customer service approach in education is to recognise that schools have customers just as industry or business does . . . A total customer orientation puts a different focus on how students and co-workers are treated' (Spanbauer 1992: 38). In his book, Spanbauer discusses the ways of determining customer expectations apart from the obvious one of sitting down with them and talking about their expectations. He draws attention to 'competitive benchmarking' and defines this as 'the continuous process of measuring products, services, and practices against the toughest competitors or companies renowned as leaders', and suggests that schools can also use competitive benchmarking. Teams from his own college visit other establishments identified as 'benchmark colleges' in order to examine curriculum programmes, student services, the use of technology, etc., so as to match and exceed competitor benchmark standards.

Customer audits and surveys: matching customer and supplier perspectives

Lakeside (not the real name) is a large secondary school in Wales, UK, which in 1993 is in the early days of implementing a TQM policy. The school's executive team at Lakeside have decided to undertake a customer audit in order to provide initial data for identifying quality issues and assessing the viability of TQM for the school. We were invited to carry out this customer survey. The initial survey focus was to be the two 'customer groups' of staff and pupils, and a survey strategy was adopted:

- To 'trap' the perceptions of these two customer groups regarding some process practices and the school context generally, as well as derive views on directions for improvement.
- With the staff, to test the viability of the customer–supplier chain concept to Lakeside and scan for the linkages which may need modification.
- To discover where the pupils and staff had similar or differing perceptions of school reality or needs.

The data were obtained by interviewing using standard instruments, and samples of teachers and pupils derived by quota sample methods. A cardinal tenet of TQM is that it is, as we discussed in Chapter 1, data-driven,

Table 15   Customer audit: teacher and 'pupil-customer' perspectives at Lakeside School

Matters about which teachers and pupils agree need action	*Matters on which teachers and pupils have very different perceptions*
Uniform	Perceptions of bullying
The canteen	Homework
Discipline	Why some pupils learn better
	School presentation and strategy

and that the data are obtained on a systematic basis that ensures its representativeness. It is our experience that few schools and colleges have a staff and student database of sufficient sophistication, or someone with the survey expertise to enable such data to be obtained on a reliable, quick, cost-effective and regular basis. Here again is a generic point for all public sector contexts. Do the expertise and resources for the customer audit and process appraisal to be undertaken exist? If not, what training, materials and equipment are needed to put them in place?

In surveying the teachers first, we were concerned to assess the extent to which the concept of the customer and the customer–supplier chain were recognized and found to be acceptable. We found no rejection of the use of the word 'customer', and almost all respondents listed those who are their obvious customers. They were not, however, quite so sure about who constituted the supplier entities, so that there was clear evidence that this is a concept which requires greater discussion in the professional work context. The teachers were – as were the pupils – very articulate and decided in their views about such organizational matters as school rules, school management and ethos, behaviour, the canteen, homework, etc., matters on which we posed parallel questions to both customer groups.

In Chapter 4, we stressed the importance of the customer audit, in that it could disclose crucial differences between the provider's view of the experience and the user's view of the 'same' experience. We designed our questionnaires in this customer audit both to discover which aspects of school life the students and teachers held similar views, and those for which there were significantly differing perceptions (Table 15).

It should be noted that at the commencement of our interviews, we took measures of how happy both the teachers and pupils were at Lakeside School, and found that staff morale and the pupils' liking of the school were distinctly above average for this type of school when compared with data we had collected on a wide range of similar schools.

Interestingly, these two customer groups at Lakeside School were agreed that changes or improvements needed to be made with regard to the school uniform, the canteen and school discipline – all matters that are hidden from each other and in fact from senior management in the normal course of events. There were many more concerns, however, where the views of the staff and the pupils differed greatly. For example, a clear

Table 16   Customer audit: a school staff self-completion instrument as used at Lakeside School

To what extent do you agree with the following statements – please place tick in appropriate box

'When I feel I have achieved something worthwhile I receive recognition for it'

Strongly agree

Agree

Disagree

Strongly disagree

'Management strategies within the school are clearly communicated'

Strongly agree

Agree

Disagree

Strongly disagree

'I usually have a clear picture of what is expected of me professionally'

Strongly agree

Agree

Disagree

Strongly disagree

majority of the staff believed that there was none or only a small amount of bullying, whereas 41 per cent of the pupils said that they had experienced it and 50 per cent said that they had witnessed bullying. Also, the teachers thought that the homework system was working well, but not so the pupils. These were some of the quality issues which were identified by matching the responses of these two customer groups.

The teachers were also given a fixed response self-completion questionnaire in order to obtain some measures of their views of certain 'overall management' aspects (see Table 16). A summary of the responses obtained using this instrument are shown in Table 17, and the data reveal

Table 17   Lakeside School: percentage of teaching staff responses to certain self-completion questions on management aspects

	Feel-receive recognition	Management strategies clearly communicated	Clear picture of what is expected of me
Strongly agree	8	16	46
Agree	67	46	31
Disagree	25	31	23
Strongly disagree	0	7	0

issues regarding quality. The data suggest that there is considerable scope for the executive team to improve their communication of management strategies, as almost 40 per cent of the teachers interviewed did not agree that these were communicated clearly. Evidence of quality issues raised by the other two measures indicate the scope for even greater quality achievement in respect of teachers feeling they receive 'recognition' and a clear picture of what is expected of them.

Perhaps the greatest value of the kind of data obtained from a customer audit such as this at Lakeside School, is that they give the proper systematic basis to discussion for the determination of formal service standards. For Lakeside, the interviews and use of the instrument illustrated in Table 16, identified a whole range of quality issues (such as those listed in Table 15) for which the customer realities were different from the beliefs held prior to the survey. On many of the issues, there was not previously thought to have been a problem. Similarly, the executive team were somewhat taken aback at the levels of disagreement expressed by their 'customers' to the propositions contained in the self-completion questionnaire. Lakeside School has had, we can vouch, a very good reputation with its audience groups. What the survey has shown is that defining and asking the customers gives clear leads on the quality issues for further enhancing the school's reputation and the quality of performance.

Hoshin or outrageous goals

In Chapter 1, we listed and described the TQM construct of *Hoshin* or outrageous goals. The setting of such goals can constitute a major signal that the school or any other public sector institution is being challenged to achieve beyond its comfort zone – to reach for substantive and steep slope quality improvements over time. The goals are outrageous because at the time they are set, few in the school will know how they can be achieved, but will see the benefit and value of their achievement. Here are some outrageous goals which have actually been set in educational establishments:

- In Wayzata, Minnesota, a service guarantee is offered: all students will achieve the performance standards for each grade of schooling; if they do not, the school system will provide support and training until they do.
- In Fort McMurray, Alberta, one school has the goal of 100 per cent completions in Grades 11 and 12 – no drop-outs.
- In Dortman School (not its real name), Alberta in 1991, staff identified four outrageous goals: reduce paper use by 80 per cent; reduce discipline problems to zero; involve every Dortman family in a parenting course; increase the student population by a third, mainly through retention strategies. Each of these goals would have goal 'crusaders' – teacher, parent, student and community crusaders to champion a particular goal and take all steps for its achievement.

It is our experience that when given time to grasp and apply the concept of outrageous goals in the workshop situation, teachers are quite comfortable with the idea. The following are some examples of outrageous goals we saw teachers set for their schools in a workshop in Alberta in 1992:

- 100 per cent of pupils to express perceptions of success;
- zero vandalism;
- marks not a criterion of success;
- 100 per cent Grade 12 graduation within 5 years;
- meet learning needs of every child;
- 50 per cent of learning to take place outside of school.

Of course, there are those who object to the whole idea of outrageous goals. They ask: What evidence is there that performance at certain benchmarks can be significantly enhanced? Take, for example, the external examinations of the GCE/GCSE, which sixteen-year-olds take in the UK. Over recent years, the percentage of the total examinees who achieve five subjects at grade C or above has gradually improved by some 5–7 per cent, and is now at a level which some would have doubted could be achieved a decade or so ago. Given the advance which has taken place in these results, the sceptics of outrageous goals might ask what possible hope could there be for another 5 per cent improvement? The TQM response would be that unless such an apparent outrageous goal is set, you will never know whether it can be achieved. The plain fact is, regarding the setting of outrageous goals in the public sector, that we do not yet have any empirical evidence available of Hoshin achievements in the way that we do for manufacturing or the commercial service sector.

Defining key whole-school procedures, process mapping and measurement

In initiating TQM in public sector contexts, it makes sense to focus on aspects of customers' experience which are frequent features and for which it is *a priori* difficult to really know what the customer is experiencing. Heathland School in England is one which has taken this approach. The school development plan for 1991–92 contained the commitment: 'Introduce the concept of Total Quality Management to senior staff and, progressively, to all teaching and non-teaching staff so that it permeates the institution'. The head has described how the school has:

> set up a task force with two 'quality circles' to review and improve procedures in two key areas which affect pupils. The first has asked: 'what do pupils experience when their timetabled teacher is absent?' The second is investigating homework. We have a homework policy – most schools do. Is it well conceived? Does it actually happen. Pupil questionnaires are part of this research.
>
> (Samuels 1991)

Data drawn from customer audit can therefore be matched with what was intended to happen with a particular procedure or process. Of course, the collection of such data may expose the intended procedure as being defective in the first place, in that it is not explicit, or that it has not been successfully modelled for the specific outcomes, or, if it has, the model is not known or not adopted by everyone. In Chapter 4 on health and TQM, we indicated that process modelling and measurement of what actually happens in the customer experience are seen to be a prime approach, and we think this is also to be commended in education, whether for important 'professional' student experiences such as those chosen at Heathland, or for the more common administrative and organizational processes.

In 1993, Heathland School, having been convinced of the benefits to be derived from a TQM approach, had given major emphasis to the defining and making explicit of key whole-school procedures. In common with all large and complex organizations, Heathland had found that important procedures had grown up over time. In 1993, there were no procedures consistently applied to all important policy matters. The internal customers (i.e. the teachers) had not been fully involved in their determination and, more particularly, where specific departmental curriculum requirements needed to have a distinct expression. With the adoption of a quality strategy, all stakeholders were empowered and resourced to determine the key procedures, and at the time of writing these had been completed for 13 areas: career planning; setting; delivery of curriculum; lesson planning; homework; timetabling; equipment; material requirements; financial planning; health and safety; assessment and examinations; inspection; and complaints. These key procedures are now explicit and known to school governors, parents, teachers and pupils alike.

Heathland has also made a start on mapping and measuring a key process (i.e. pupil attendance) by which their (and other schools') performance will be judged under government plans for inspection and evaluation to be applied in the coming years. Measures of attendance and punctuality of all pupils by group and year is to be carefully recorded on weekly data-sheets and entered onto a spread-sheet so that opportunities for enhancing attendance can be assessed.

This kind of data collection has in the past been made by schools and colleges in order to satisfy some external demand for record-keeping. This early example of a 'process control' approach by Heathland represents the wholly different TQM focus of data collection. This is not in the first place for the meeting of certain regulations imposed from outside, but is intended for actual process measurement in order to achieve internal quality enhancements.

Most schools and colleges (and other public sector establishments) do not carry out any data collection regarding their key administrative processes, yet the refinement of all processes is a central focus of TQM. Over time, administrative processes become 'taken for granted' and 'hidden' from consideration of their effectiveness and efficiency unless there happens to be some *cause célèbre* which exposes the nature of the problems. Studying processes and making them visible by collecting data on the processes themselves is as equally an important focus to any quality management approach as are data collected directly from customers. It is the need for data on processes which draws on the classical TQM tools, such as Pareto charts and scatter diagrams, for which we have already illustrated applications to health in Chapter 4.

Delaware College has reported an interesting study concerned with the administrative process responding to customer requests in their research office (Heverly 1991). One long-standing problem in the research office had been that various and sundry requests for information continually streamed into the office, interrupting ongoing work and scheduled projects. No data existed on the volume or pattern of these sundry *ad hoc* requests. As a result, there was no way to plan other projects around the unknown volume these *ad hoc* demands represented; hence staff began collecting data on each *ad hoc* request, noting the source and type of the request, and tracking progress in responding to the request. The data obtained showed a fairly consistent pattern from year to year (with peaks in October and January/February), identified exactly who the customers were, and the topics of this *ad hoc* information.

Several clear benefits derived from analysis of the data. It served first as an unobtrusive assessment of internal customer needs, and then allowed a range of responses. In response to the nature of some of the requests, new persons were added to the distribution lists of research office reports. In other instances, reports were modified to provide new information on the sort of topics customers were requesting. Following these responses, the volume of requests from 1988 to 1989 dropped 30 per cent. The changes appear, therefore, to have helped the research office better understand customer needs by meeting some of them before customers were driven to call for the information. Requests 'dealt with on the day they were received' constituted the sub category experiencing the greatest reduction (75 per cent of the total), suggesting that previously the information was readily available in the office but had not been distributed to everyone who needed it.

The data also facilitated planning and scheduling. For example:

> ... the relatively high volume of requests received in January was not anticipated. Before the data became available January had been assumed to be a relatively quiet month and an appropriate time to schedule the completion of pending projects. The request handling system has also reduced rework, because [as a result of the data obtained] operational definitions now describe how requests are handled ... [so] ... customers learn about the different varieties of data that are available, and they begin to better understand their information needs and communicate them more clearly.
>
> (Heverly 1991)

Subsequent to the collection of this body of data and the responses to it, the research office looked at the value of their key processes by having research staff and internal customers rate the importance of all office processes. Key processes were defined as those processes most critical to the college's core professional job of teaching and learning. The results were revealing. The process rated most highly by internal customers was 'providing information, research, and statistical support', that is, the very '*ad hoc* requests' which had been viewed by the office as interrupting the office's 'real work'. The data showed that this is a key service that should be monitored to anticipate the information needs of college staff. The view of the college is that 'implementation of Total Quality Management has changed the character of the work done in the Research Office'.

Deriving customer data on classroom processes

In Chapter 4 on health, we showed that there have already been some TQM applications to core professional processes despite many people believing that TQM is really only appropriate to organizational procedures or perceptions of the interpersonal relations of the service received. As we ourselves have elsewhere pointed out (Murgatroyd and Morgan 1993), if you want to improve the product of education, namely learning, attention must also be given to the processes whereby the product is made. For the classroom this principle, as Tribus has put it, 'translates to: If you want to improve the students' achievements, put your attention on the teaching/ learning process and not on the achievements in examinations' (Tribus 1992).

In early 1993, it appears to us that there is the beginning of interest in the educational world to apply quality approaches to classroom teaching–learning processes. Indeed, in some educational systems, influential sponsors are beginning to call for this to happen.

In the UK, in its published advice to the Secretary of State for Education in January 1993, the National Curriculum Council wrote about 'Developing more efficient approaches to the use of teachers' time', and cited research evidence that:

Key Stage 1 teachers in the sample were spending only 18 hours teaching out of an average working week of 52 hours. Their remaining time was spent with preparation, professional development and administration, the latter time accounting for some 13.6 hours ... Leaving aside the issue of whether the 18 hours spent teaching are used effectively, the question which needs to be asked concerns the extent to which the activities listed above, while important, could be done by non-teaching assistants and thus free more professional time for teaching and teaching related duties such as preparation.

(National Curriculum Council 1993: 11)

While the matter of how core professional time is used in classroom processes appears to be on the agenda for future studies in process mapping and refinement in the UK at least, there is still the central question of whether the customer can contribute to the enhancement of teaching–learning processes.

On this latter matter of quality and core professional activity in education, two pieces of customer-focused research have been carried out: the first by the US Army School of Engineering and Logistics' Engineering Department (Higgins *et al.* 1991), and the other by ourselves. Both studies strongly suggest that the student customer can help define good teaching and learning.

The US Army School of Engineering and Logistics' Engineering Department has an ongoing instructor improvement programme, part of which is concerned with defining good instruction using input from all engineering students and staff, or faculty as they are usually referred to in North America. The students were asked how they defined good teaching and their responses were compared with those of their instructors (Table 18). From the answers given by both respondent groups, six construct categories were evident in the thinking of both groups, though the teachers also used a seventh category. Table 18 shows both groups' views of the top ten characteristics of good instruction.

Close examination of the differences between the responses of the 'suppliers' and 'customers' shows clearly the nature of what forms the core of good teaching in the 'student customer' perspective. The four items in the students' 'top ten' which were not in their teachers' list in this American study were: 'simple straightforward teaching with complete examples'; 'open to questions during and after class'; 'lots of examples'; and 'logical order, avoids tangents'. 'Good teaching' as defined by these student customers is therefore very concerned with the expository aspects of teaching methods and the disposition of the teacher to explain and give examples. In contrast, the teachers' definitions of good teaching did not give particular emphasis to the methods of the teaching–learning transaction, but emphasized instead the technical expertise content and the affective relations aspect of the teaching transaction.

We conducted a parallel investigation in our 'quality survey' at Lakeside

Table 18   Matching student and teacher views of 'good teaching': US Army School of Logistics and Engineering

Student definitions of good teaching	Instructors' definitions of good teaching
1. Organized and prepared	1. Organized and prepared
2. Simple straightforward teaching with complete examples[a]	2. Sound knowledge of subject matter
3. Good communication/ pronunciation	3. Fair and consistent in grading[b]
4. Real-life applications/analogies	4. Enthusiastic[b]
5. Sound knowledge of subject matter	5. Concern for all students[b]
6. Open to questions during and after class[a]	6. Goals clearly stated at beginning
7. Goals clearly stated at beginning	7. Real life examples/analogies
8. Interested in subject	8. Flexible
9. Lots of examples[a]	9. Good communication/pronunciation
10. Logical order, avoids tangents[a]	10. Interested in subject

[a] Items in the students' list which were not in the instructors' top ten.
[b] Items in the instructors' list which were not in the students' top ten.

Table 19   Reasons why some pupils learn better than others at Lakeside School

Category	Teachers' response (%)	Pupils' response (%)
To do with teaching methods	15	55
To do with motivation, interest, concentration, ability, attitude, background, effort, etc.	85	45

School in Wales, when we asked teachers and pupils separately about what makes some pupils learn better than others (Table 19). We had asked the teachers, 'Do some pupils learn better than others?', and if they answered in the affirmative which was almost always the case, we further asked them for the reasons why this was so. We asked the pupils, 'Do you learn better in some lessons than in others?', and if they answered in the affirmative which was almost always the case, we further asked them for the reasons why this was so. We categorized the reasons into those which were essentially to do with teaching methods and those which attributed differential learning to a range of other causes. The summary position is displayed in Table 17 and there is a clear parallel between this Welsh study, which was of school children's view of classroom processes, and the American study, which had obtained the responses from young adults in a military learning context. Clearly, then, there is for education as there was for health, evidence that the customer voice can bear on issues of enhancement in relation to core professional processes.

Conclusion

In Britain, Canada and North America, the context of public sector education is changing fast in response to a crisis of funding and the need for greater 'performance' in the eyes of government. The context is now one in which competition between education providers is being encouraged, where control is being pushed more and more down to community level, and where the individual institution must be more and more financially self-managing, judged and funded on criteria of performance.

In response to this new context, some educational managers are increasingly coming to redefine their clients as customers by adopting and adapting TQM. The evidence of the case studies we have presented above and our other field contacts have shown that:

- Teachers are able and willing to accept some of the central concepts of TQM, if adapted to their world.
- Teachers readily recognize they have customers and that there are 'customer–supplier' chains, but need time and training to work these out fully.
- Students of all ages have definite views on their organizational world, management practices and improvements they would like to see in their school and can clearly make a greater contribution to the design of school policies and practices.
- Students have views about classroom practices and why they learn more with some teachers.
- Teachers and students find the explicit setting out of performance standards helpful.

For our part, we think there are good philosophical reasons why TQM should be more widely adopted in education, even without the 'quasi-market' developments now taking place:

- TQM is empowering and democratizing and so fits well with the ethos of the educational world, with its traditional focus on the person having both entitlement and unique learning needs.
- TQM can enhance the professional identity of the teacher. While TQM moves from the traditional altruistic relationship between professional and client towards client empowerment, the participation of the student as an equal partner in the securing of his or her own learning achievements can be seen to be one of enhancing the professional identity of the

teacher, an identity that rests on *reflective practice*, where the expert does not always hold to be right and can learn from the customers;

- TQM places detailed evaluation in the hands of the professionals. Education, like other areas in the public sector, has an external national inspectorate. TQM, with its focus on the internal appraisal of all processes, brings evaluation back from external inspection for quality assurance, into the hands of those most closely concerned with the professional provision, the teachers themselves.

Having said this, it must be acknowledged that TQM is a very demanding management regime to apply properly and comprehensively throughout schools and colleges, and it is, as yet, very early days for TQM in education. The number of case studies and range of data available are limited, and the whole question of whether TQM can bring about in education the degree of quality increases it has secured in manufacturing and some commercial services remains to be answered. There are not even as yet case examples of the cost–benefits of some TQM applications like those seen in health care. Were these to be demonstrated as they may well be in the near future, the jury is still likely to be out regarding the ultimate challenge for TQM in education – to demonstrate that by the application of its precepts to classroom processes TQM can bring about 'steep slope' improvements in learning achievements.

CHAPTER

6

TQM and social services

Introduction

Social services is not only a broad territory of work, but also a major area of social expenditure. Along with other key sectors – defence and foreign relations, local government, health, schools and universities – it constitutes a key sector of public policy and social practice. In this chapter, we look at the current developments in the management of social services and the extent to which these can be seen to be linked to TQM. Although much is happening in social services in 1993, there are few developments which can be seen to be directly focused on what we would regard as TQM. Later in the chapter we examine four possible explanations for this phenomenon. We also offer some suggestions as to how current developments in social services could be adapted to provide the basis for TQM initiatives.

The policy context of social services

During the last twenty-five years, social services in Canada, the USA and Britain have undergone major changes. For example, in the USA since the early 1980s, the real value of social service expenditure (i.e. inflation-adjusted expenditure per person) has fallen. In addition:

1. The legislated minimum wage has been frozen for nine years.
2. The percentage of jobless workers holding unemployment insurance (equivalent to a right of access to unemployment pay in the UK) has

fallen dramatically; in 1989, only four million of the 8.9 million unemployed carried unemployment insurance.
3. The development of new subsidized housing virtually ended and some subsidized housing was sold.
4. Federal job training funds fell to less than 35 per cent of 1970 levels.
5. Financial aid for college or university in the form of grants fell dramatically and was replaced by loans.
6. Basic inflation-adjusted real income for single-parent families on welfare has fallen dramatically (Orfield 1991).

Despite this decline in the real value of social service expenditure, the actual number of dollars expended has grown by 30 per cent in the USA in the last five years. In 1993, social service expenditure will exceed $304 billion and will, for the first time, exceed defence dollar expenditure (see Rubenstein 1993).

In Canada, unemployment has risen to an average of around 10 per cent and welfare payments and minimum wages have not been fully adjusted for inflation. In addition, schemes for national child care promised by government and support for community-based services, the handicapped, the disabled and battered women have been reduced. Changes are being made to support systems for the unemployed to inhibit payment for those who voluntarily leave employment or are dismissed for non-performance. Some provinces in Canada have ended student grants and moved to a loans-only scheme (e.g. Ontario), while others have changed the mix of grants and loans available to students. Despite growing levels of poverty, especially among young people, and homelessness, social service budgets have also been reduced in real terms.

Some dramatic changes have taken place in the provision of social services in Britain, with significant changes being made to the conditions under which unemployment benefits are paid; a greater range of providers entering certain fields, notably care for the elderly, child care, support of the mentally handicapped, psychological and social work services; an almost complete end to subsidized municipal housing, with council houses being sold and the housing stock not being replenished. While the British Government invests heavily in housing associations and housing cooperatives, these subsidy strategies are an implicit device for securing the privatization of former 'public' housing.

Indeed, it would be fair to say that social services have become a focus for policy concerns in the public sector. President Clinton, as Governor of Arkansas, adopted a strategy for welfare recipients which he has pledged to make the federal strategy for welfare. Known as 'workfare', this strategy involves seeking to 'reinvent' welfare payments as a temporary measure intended to enable individuals to recover from job loss, changed circumstance or some other disabling event just long enough so that they can return to the workplace, seek training or undertake some active community service. Building on the significant gap between the value of welfare payments versus the value of wages from employment (i.e. welfare payments are considerably less than wages for most types of work), the 'workfare' recipient receives welfare payments for a two-year period; all subsequent payments are conditional on the person undertaking training or education, or obtaining a job (where welfare is used to subsidize wages so as to enable the worker to receive the state-legislated minimum wage) or undertaking community service. Welfare recipients are interviewed regularly and at random to see what steps they have taken to meet their obligations until one of these conditions is met.

Clinton's policy strategy is based on the commitment of directing the energies of the able person to meeting the economic needs of society (employment) or the social needs of society (community service), recognizing that doing so may require some training. It is also based on the belief that welfare is 'too easy' and that the system of ongoing welfare support creates a welfare mentality and reduces individual initiative, drive and commitment to social well-being. How effective this strategy will be on a scale broader than Arkansas remains to be seen (see Reich 1991). It may not be sufficient to overcome the growing problem of America's 'underclass' – those on welfare who have developed a lifestyle that does not involve job-seeking, training or community service and who do not wish to be 'controlled' in the way Clinton envisages by the state.

The British Government's strategy for social services is, in part, based on these same concerns. In addition, the strategy is based on assumptions about the relative efficiency of social service agencies. By requiring strategy planning and fiscal accountability and by creating complaints procedures (supported by a 'Citizen's Charter') and Inspection Units, the British Government hopes to reduce duplication, minimize 'redundancy' in the system and secure cost efficiency. With a high level of unemployment (some three million in December 1992) and an economy in decline, 'workfare' is seen as a risky strategy by those responsible for social services policy in interviews conducted in preparation for this chapter. Indeed, one senior strategist in the DSS suggested that 'workfare, while attractive on the surface, carries political consequences for Britain which could be damaging to the whole of the fabric of social services' – referring specifically to the policing role of social services in such schemes and to the need to recognize and organize community work projects for workfare recipients. Similar comments were made by Sir Rhodes Boyson and others in a series of press articles concerning welfare. In addition, it should be recognized that 'policing' workfare may also involve new costs.

Total Quality Management and the management of social services

In a search of the available literature on social services, social work and social welfare and in interviews with social services directors and managers in Canada, Britain, Ireland and the USA conducted in preparation for this

book, TQM was not seen as a major force in early 1993 in the management and development of social service provision. Quality assurance, programme evaluation and the auditing of services are, however, widely
practised (Fricke 1992). While some see these practices as equivalent to
the practice of TQM – 'all these different approaches mesh in TQM'
(Fricke 1993) – few have written or examined TQM as a strategic force
for the management of their services.

There is a growing concern to balance the four E's of social service:
economy, effectiveness, equity of access and response, and environmental
process. But there are a vast array of responses to the challenge implied by
the attempt to balance these forces. Some, such as Rino Patti (1987) in
Seattle, have championed the need to drive the management of social
service organizations by the principles and practice of effective service
management, which he characterizes as follows:

1. Infuse the agency with a value-oriented mission that gives meaning to
   service effectiveness.
2. Select appropriate service technologies.
3. Develop service outcome indicators and measurement techniques.
4. Assess standards and determine whether performance meets expectations.
5. Determine the organizational arrangements and management practices
   needed to motivate and support workers in their efforts to achieve
   performance goals.
6. Mobilize constituencies around effective performance criteria to maintain the autonomy necessary to meet the participants' needs.

These principles of service effectiveness have some links with 'good
practice' models of social welfare management developed by others (see,
e.g. Neugeboren 1985), but are more strongly tied to notions of internal
management and professionally directed management than to customer-
focused and customer-driven quality. Though involving some of the
key features of TQM (e.g. vision/mission driven, strategically focused),
Patti's management requirements are not driven by the needs of primary
stakeholders, are not focused on team development and do not require
empowerment.

Others have examined the potential contribution of consumers and
workers to decision-making in social service agencies. Joseph Katan and
Edward Prager (1986), for example, have considered the extent to which
the principle of consumer involvement is practised in community mental
health organizations. They observe that, while strong support is given in
principle to consumer involvement, actual practice demonstrates that consumer involvement is declining over time, representing no more than 'partial
palliative measures'. What appears to happen is that, as professionals become
more involved in the management of their own services, they tend to
exclude their clients from decision-making. Their findings are supported by
the empirical work of Evers (1982) and Spilerman and Litwak (1982),

who studied the extent to which the elderly in care were able to make decisions about their own care and found that professionals tend to restrict significantly the ability of customers to manage their own affairs, despite their ability to do so. Consumer-driven quality is talk not reality in social services, at least according to these researchers.

These findings carry significant implications for empowerment – a key process within TQM. If empowerment is not customer-focused and based on the need to empower customers to make more of the decisions and take more of the actions of which they are capable, then empowering professionals may not be desirable from a TQM point of view. The issue is not empowerment here, but the values and vision which inform the process of empowerment.

When quality is defined by those delivering the service in terms of some quality assurance standards set by the profession, then some aspects of quality may in fact run counter to the needs of the 'customers' of the services. For example, information systems developed for social services (for some examples, see Turem 1986) for the management of case loads may work extremely well for the 'system', but may impair the ability of 'customers' to move between agencies and to receive direct help from a multiple agency system. While an information system may meet quality standards, it cannot necessarily be assumed that these standards meet the needs of customers.

Given that TQM is yet to have a role on the social services 'stage', whereas this has happened in education and health, we must now examine the developments which are taking place in social service agencies in Canada, Britain, Ireland and the USA in terms of the potential that they hold for TQM. Throughout, we will examine practice developments as well as developments in thinking about service provision.

It should be clear from the introduction to this chapter that a major preoccupation of government will be with ensuring service delivery to those 'most in need' at the lowest cost, while at the same time redefining social need to exclude non-essential or 'marginal' cases. Throughout the sections which follow, we will examine the extent to which TQM could be used to create opportunities for service improvement while at the same time contributing to cost reduction. Our task is to describe current developments and their rationale and to show how these developments could be refined so as to embrace TQM.

Quality tactics for social services

In a review of the tactics employed by six US states in their pursuit of effective social service provision at the lowest cost, Ezell and Patti (1990) looked at the key tactics used by Minnesota, South Carolina, Utah, Florida, Oregon and Delaware to improve quality while lowering costs. The primary tactics were: (a) becoming more responsive to local needs; (b) ensuring, through the systematic allocation of resources on an equal basis by geography, race and gender, equity in the provision of services and resource distribution; (c) easy client access to multiple programmes (one-stop shopping); (d) co-ordination and integration of client services; (e) accountability for performance to a central authority; (f) maximized efficiency when compared to similar services elsewhere and against set performance standards; and (g) inter- and intra-departmental co-ordination. In addition, user fees were also used as part of the efficiency tactic, with the intention of reducing 'frivolous demands', increasing the sense of commitment on the part of social service users and creating a climate of service within the organization through a more explicit financial transaction between user and provider. We will use these categories to look at some recent developments in social service provision across the developed world and to show the link between these developments and TQM.

Responsiveness to local needs

Various governments, including American state governments, Canadian provincial governments and the British Government, have decentralized some aspects of policy, management and decision-making to either regional or more local levels, thus accepting that there can be regional variation in practice. In part, this results from a key principle of TQM that those nearest to the customer are most likely to make effective decisions for meeting customer needs. But it is also due to the realization that effective provision must differ at a local level, since the combination of circumstances which lead to the need for social services is locally determined. For example, poverty and unemployment are linked but strategies for responding to these conditions may differ in mid-Wales or the Yukon or Harlem as compared to Cardiff, Vancouver or Houston. Decentralization permits professional workers locally to make informed choices and decisions which best reflect local needs.

Quality can be assured by reference to locally determined goals, rather than standards set by some central authority. In addition, service quality needs to be measured against services sought and provided, rather than against some centrally determined set of standards which may apply to some locations and not others.

On the other hand, some attempts at decentralization have been 'rolled back', since they gave rise to such varying practices that it became politically difficult to claim equity of access to programmes and resources. Furthermore, decentralization reveals inefficiencies in the central organization in responding to developing local circumstances and creates redundancy of activity or is non-value-adding (see Chapter 1), a point we explore in detail below. Gaster (1991) has reviewed the development of decentralized agencies with respect to quality development issues. She concludes that a focus on consumer-driven quality requires social welfare agencies to ask:

'Which services – or parts of services – would be improved by going local?' What is important, she argues, is that decentralization should lead to measurable gains in quality as determined by service users, not just professionals. To make these developments more TQM-like, there is a need to engage regional service users, not just professionals, in the response to Gaster's two questions.

Equity in provision and resource distribution

So as to ensure that everyone has equal access to programmes and that everyone receives equal resource entitlements, governments have traditionally used centralized control mechanisms to specify both service standards and agreed purchase prices for services. While local variations are permitted within tolerable limits (as measured by some form of statistical process control), these variations require a higher level of authority (e.g. decision by justified exception) than 'routine' transactions. Agreed prices (or costs incurred) may vary from location to location (e.g. sheltered accommodation in one location may be more expensive to operate than in another), but these variations are 'controlled for' – at the level of central policy and procedures, rather than through some local action.

Equity of service provision and accessibility does not mean that all clients must be treated in exactly the same way. There is a saying, used widely in TQM training activities, that 'if we treat everyone the same, the only thing that differs is satisfaction'. One distinctive feature of service quality is the ability to treat people both *equitably* and *uniquely*, thereby taking full account of individual circumstances and the more broad entitlement needs. In the concern with equity, some social service staff see this as a reason to minimize the differences which people bring to their situation. This is not at all the intention, nor is it good practice from a TQM point of view. There is a need to focus on ensuring equitable responses to similar circumstances balanced with individualized service for the customer – this is the TQM expectation here.

Quality is examined here through the use of performance indicators for accessibility and through the use of quality assurance mechanisms aimed at looking at the level of conformance between local action and central policy guidelines. In Canada and Britain, the definitions of access and the indicators used to measure performance have often been politically motivated. Indeed, a Select Committee of the House of Commons in Canada is currently seeking to redefine 'poverty' so as to show, at least in the eyes of the official opposition, that 'poverty is not as widespread in Canada as people seem to think it is'. In the 1980s, the British Government redefined unemployment so as to show a lower level of unemployment. A TQM perspective for these definitions would require that the measures be developed in association with the customers of the services and that the definitions not be subject to political interference. We explore the problems of performance indicators in more detail below in the section on accountability to a central agency.

Client accessibility to multiple programmes

A significant development during the last two decades in social services has focused on the integration of services at the point of delivery – what is known as collocation of service or, more commonly, 'one-stop social service shopping'. This came from the realization that an individual who has multiple needs (e.g. welfare support, child care, housing and training) could be supported by a 'customer service worker', part of whose function would be to facilitate and make arrangements between agencies on behalf of their customer. What is more, by a single case worker taking responsibility for linking service to the needs of the individual customer ('tailored' service), a higher level of customer satisfaction with service could be developed.

Typical objectives of collocation include: (a) to increase labour workforce participation of social service recipients; (b) to decrease turnaround time for re-entry into employment; (c) to increase the quality of advice and assistance to clients; (d) to better match available social service resources with the needs of clients at a local level in the most efficient way.

In practice, collocation has proven difficult to sustain. There are several reasons for this. They include:

1. The complexity of the rules and regulations governing provision and support in different areas of social service have become so complex that few individuals are able to master their way around the systems, so more often than not the individual case worker becomes a 'referral hub' rather than the one person who will ensure service provision.
2. The workloads of individual case workers become high because transaction time (time taken to liaise with other service providers) eats into case time and this has been seen as inefficient.
3. The volume of need is greater than the capacity of the system to respond in some locations.

Despite these concerns, a growing number of social service organizations are looking to collocation as a way of better meeting customer needs and increasing customer satisfaction. Rather than seeing these three concerns as barriers, they see them as issues to be overcome. If the systems can be streamlined, made more readily accessible (using expert systems and information technologies, for example) and training investments are made in case worker education and development, collocation could in the medium to longer term produce gains in efficiency and customer satisfaction, none of which would constitute, in and of themselves, key measures of quality and performance.

The development of collocation as a strategy of government to meet the needs of clients has generally been embarked upon with few data to support the development or few data to assess the outcomes of the work. It is regarded as a contemporary innovation. While some studies are now being undertaken on the impact and effectiveness of collocation (for example, the Department of Social Services of the Government of Alberta has recently commissioned a study of its collocation experiments in Athabasca-Lac la Biche), many of the investments made in this development are being done from a theory-pragmatism position rather than as a result of clear data from customers and front-line staff that such developments are desirable. Indeed, in one study of collocation involving ninety-eight clients who had experience of social services before collocation, 61 per cent noticed no difference as a result of collocation. The question arises, then: In whose interest were these changes being made?

Co-ordination and integration

One step short of collocation is the closer integration and co-ordination of services, using inter-agency case teams, inter-agency liaison mechanisms and resource sharing. The new vocabulary for this work is that of 'partnering' – a term borrowed from the service sector and which refers to the systematic linkages between customer-suppliers in the delivery of a service to the end-user. For example, Proctor and Gamble 'partner' with Wal-Mart (one of the largest retail operations in the world) and use electronic data interchange (EDI) to continuously supply products and services to Wal-Mart on an 'as-needs' basis. Once they see the inventory of a particular product or range of products decline, deliveries are made automatically without Wal-Mart having to place an order. This is possible because Wal-Mart uses bar-codes to track sales against their inventory – as each Proctor and Gamble item is purchased, the computer system adjusts its inventory database and automatically flags low stocks to both Proctor and Gamble and Wal-Mart's purchasing staff and appropriate action, as previously agreed, is taken. In a social service context, as a client enters into the system, the client's needs will be recorded in a database and the various agencies responsible for service delivery will immediately become aware of a need and of the resources required to meet that need. They will, within pre-set standards and limits (time, money, policy), allocate the needed resources and make this known to the client. The development of expert systems and information technologies are just now making such partnering between different social service agencies possible (Hudson 1991).

More commonly, the mechanisms now being used to secure gains in integration and co-ordination in social services involve the following components:

1. *Integrating services*: for example, family and child services used to be separate in many locations and are now merged; drug and alcohol treatments used to be separate in terms of management and resources but are now frequently merged in addiction units.

2. *De-layering the organization*: removing levels of management which are seen to add little value to the quality of client experiences or to secure efficiency.
3. *Regionalization of services*: grouping social services within a region for inter-departmental case work and co-ordination with regionally managed resources (staff, capital and budget).
4. *Outcome or mission budgeting* around performance expectations specified annually on a regional basis.

A key quality measure being used here is performance indicators, comparing one region with another in terms of outcomes, unit costs and customer satisfaction. These are often adjusted, at least in Canada and the USA, for local variations in poverty levels, homelessness and economic conditions. Also, quality is examined in terms of the link between outcomes and planning. The most common indicators suffer the problems we identify in the next section, especially the absence of customer-driven quality measures. Once again, there is little evidence that the changes referred to here are driven by the results of any systematic data gathered from front-line staff or customers or that the developments are being evaluated in terms of the experience of the customers. They appear to be internally driven rather than customer-driven changes.

Accountability to a central agency

All of the social services systems in Britain, Canada and the USA have a degree of accountability to a central agency. What differs from state to state, province to province and country to country (in the case of Scotland, England and Wales in Britain) is the extent and nature of this accountability and the way in which accountability policies are framed, interpreted and administered. In Britain, for example, the development of Inspection Units and monitoring procedures are intended as mechanisms for exercising control. In Canada, evaluation of local provision, through the practice of programme evaluation, is more often than not regarded as developmental or formative, as opposed to summative.

The primary 'control' devices here are performance indicators. These are increasingly seen as important in social services, especially in Britain (Social Services Inspectorate 1990, 1991; Hoyes 1990). Many see the existence of performance indicators as a sign of their commitment to TQM. Indeed, three of our interviewees in the USA, as well as two in Canada who manage social service budgets for their governments, suggested that the development of these indicators was their total TQM effort. Yet it was also clear that the existence of performance indicators may not be connected with quality efforts. The problems which the excessive or obsessive use of performance indicators have given rise to in social services, as well as in other government departments, carry cautions which are worth noting, and which argue for policy provision to be driven more by TQM. They include the following common problems (Radical Statistics 1991):

1. *Performance indicators for a specific service can change as a result of circumstances which have little or nothing to do with the provision of that service.* For example, in social services, if the stock of low-cost accommodation usually used by social services is exhausted, then the unit costs of accommodation will rise as the service moves to the next tier of available accommodation – the step costs of volume demand are the 'cause' of this, not some inefficiency in the service provision. It is a basic proposition of systems theory that changes in one part of the system will have an impact and show consequences in other parts of the system.

2. *Setting national targets tends to encourage work towards the mean, not excellence.* Setting targets for costs of service, for example, which are based upon the mean costs from a spread which has a high standard deviation, as is the case with many social service provisions, has actually been seen to do two things: (a) increase overall costs, as least-cost providers now spend more and above-the-mean providers seek exemption; and (b) focus attention on the performance indicator rather than meeting the needs of clients exceptionally well at the most appropriate cost. As Edwards Deming is fond of noting, setting such targets discourages the search for continuous improvement.

3. *Performance indicators may not indicate performance, since key variables are outside the control of the service provider.* To give one obvious example, when Florida and Miami were hit by natural disaster in 1992, the volume demand on all social service agencies was huge – far higher than could be predicted or measured in any strategic plan (other than the state disaster plan). These disasters would make performance indicators difficult to interpret. A less obvious example, but equally true, would be to look at performance indicators for social service systems in, say, Northumbria, Glasgow and Belfast in the UK versus the same measures for Surrey. Because levels of poverty, job vacancies, housing stocks and the age structure of the population differ between these areas, so will the performance of the social service on key indicators.

4. *Performance indicators do not 'speak for themselves', they have to be interpreted.* Imagine a situation in which the costs per child of day care differ significantly between one location and another in the same city. What are the implications of this? Is the least cost always desirable, or does the higher cost also produce added value and higher quality service? Least cost is not the only criterion against which performance in human services can be measured. It is important, therefore, that the 'data' trigger enquiry and further exploration, not 'quick' solutions.

5. *Many performance indicators are overly simplistic.* Most of the indicators now in use in social services (and also in health and education) are cross-sectional and short-term. What are actually needed, for each element and location of service, are longitudinal and comprehensive indicators which take full account of local conditions (i.e. are locally adjusted) and service mix.

6. *Few of the available indicators focus on customer satisfaction.* Almost all of the measures assume that receipt of the service as measured by the service provider constitutes satisfactory service delivery. Few performance indicators actually examine performance from the customer's point of view. Part of the reason for this is a continuing distrust of social service customers as valid arbiters of service quality. Until these indicators are included in the range of indicators available, the use of performance indicators will tend to lead to efficiency concerns as opposed to service quality concerns. This issue has been well explored by Pollitt (1988).

What is interesting is the way in which performance indicators are frequently seen as a key component of the response to quality concerns, when in fact they often act as a proxy for analytic understanding of service quality and do not necessarily speak to the development of a process for continuous improvement. A TQM approach to social services would attach importance to quality indicators which are owned by the customers of the service and those who work directly with clients. The six problems of performance indicators presented above (see also Carter 1989) strongly argue the need for a developed understanding of TQM to inform the systematic use of performance indicators in social services.

Under the heading of accountability to a central authority, typical tactics involve: (a) the development of a large volume of formalized policy and procedures; (b) performance indicators; and (c) the creation of inspection, audit and evaluation systems. The irony about centralized accountability systems of this sort is that they create redundancy of effort, are highly bureaucratic and tend to increase costs rather than lead to their curtailment. In the guise of control, centralized systems tend to create cost and do not necessarily lead to the kind of flexibility needed to respond to local need. From a TQM perspective, process control systems are essential. What are required are 'vision-related', 'process-specific' and continuous improvement rather than inspection-based systems. This would involve: (a) developing customer-based procedures which are simple, reliable, effective, least cost and equitable and which are constantly being improved; (b) customer-driven performance indicators; and (c) self-monitoring systems rather than systems based on audit and inspection. Many of the developments that have recently taken place with respect to accountability are not TQM developments.

Maximizing efficiency

So as to reduce the costs of supporting key social services (e.g. supply purchasing, personnel management and general administration), a tactic frequently pursued is the regionalization of service. This is seen as a means of both increasing service quality by localizing effort and reducing costs through gaining economies of scale. It is also seen as a means of avoiding the over-bureaucratization of service resulting from excessive centralization.

It is interesting to note, in the context of health systems development in the UK, that local purchasers of health services (fund-holding GPs) have started to form regional units to support their purchasing activities.

The underlying assumption of this general tactic is that there is some redundancy of effort (duplication of effort, wasted effort, too many steps in processes which require more effort than the task demands, etc.) in the delivery of social services and that, while some degree of flexibility needs to be retained, there is a need to minimize redundancy of effort and maximize the level of service and, in so doing, reduce unit cost. To make sense of this assumption, we need to look carefully at the whole idea of redundancy of effort (Streeter 1992).

Redundancy of effort is a concept very similar to that of 'non-value-adding activity', which we introduced in Chapter 1. It refers to ongoing activity in the organization which does not lead to the direct meeting of client needs and which *may* incur costs without adding value to the service as a whole. Four specific examples arise from Streeter's work. These are:

1. *The time spent developing contingency plans for emergencies and disasters.* While this time has some value, especially if the probability of the plans being called upon is moderate or high, there is also a lot of redundancy built into the process – usually referred to as transaction costs, the costs associated with plan development and 'transacting' with all of the players in the process (e.g. Red Cross, ambulance services, police, etc.).

2. *Underused talents and skills.* Many managers in social services have excellent field skills and casework skills which are underused in their managerial roles. While some or a high proportion of their managerial work is to be valued, they could also be valued for their work in coaching juniors in casework and field skills or by working with clients. Managers are valued to the extent that their work makes a direct contribution to either customer experience or the ability of fieldworkers to deliver customer satisfaction. Not all of the activities of managers are valued in these terms.

3. *Built-in redundancy.* The calculation of staffing levels usually takes into account rates of sickness, assumptions about casework loads, holiday arrangements, etc. While these are sometimes accurate calculations, there is a built-in level of redundancy here. What appears to happen, according to Streeter, is that the extra capacity contingency becomes harnessed for non-customer-related activity.

4. *Auxiliary and ancillary services.* There is a growth in the number and salaries of inspectors, programme evaluators, managers, information systems staff and managers, researchers, etc., who provide no direct customer support at all. While these developments may be of benefit to a social service, they are also a cost. The question is what is the value of these services relative to cost. This is usually examined in terms of the proportion of the budget spent on direct services versus auxiliary

and ancillary services. The questions here are: As the proportion of the costs allocated to auxiliary services increases, does the value to the customer increase in the same proportion? If not, what are the implications of this for the quality system?

The critical question, from an efficiency maximization point of view, is which of these four areas of potential for reducing costs and increasing performance (i.e. redundancy) should efficiencies be gained from, i.e. which has the least value-added? The response to this will vary from location to location, from service to service and from country to country. From a practitioner point of view, core services – the so-called service–customer interfaces – do not feature on this map of potential redundancy, yet it is the most frequently cut in drives towards efficiency. Further, it would appear that some efficiency efforts have led to a growth in some of these features (e.g. auxiliary services, such as inspection and programme evaluation) at the direct expense of customer service, with the result that staff at the customer interface carry higher caseloads, have fewer opportunities for training and development and find overall resources for service delivery scarce.

From a TQM standpoint, the concept of redundancy of effort is central. It leads those who practise TQM to remove waste and redundancy by focusing on:

1. De-layering of the organization: reducing the number of levels through which decisions are passed before an action can be taken.
2. Speed as a tactic: reducing the time taken to complete all tasks in the organization.
3. Labour content reduction: reducing the number of person hours required before a task can be completed.
4. Process simplification: simply reducing the number of steps associated with any given task.
5. Reducing or eliminating rework: minimizing or removing the duplication of effort involved in redoing case reports, tasks or processes over and over again.
6. Ending outdated and unnecessary practices.
7. Ending inspection and creating effective systems for continuous improvement which meet the needs of customers and the organization.

Significant gains in both service quality and cost reduction can be made by focusing quality efforts on meeting customer needs while eliminating redundancy of effort. Each of these focal points for a TQM strategy involves a fundamental rethink of the way in which social services are managed.

Reducing resources in areas seen to have redundant capacity is one tactic within this framework of maximizing efficiency. Another is the use of user fees. The thinking here is that the clients of services do not value resources like 'real' customers, since there is no direct exchange of service for money at the point of delivery. If such an exchange could be created, through user fees, then (the thinking continues) a stronger customer focus would exist both in the service itself and in the mind of the customer.

In some locations, users have certain resources allocated and paid for by the state, and resources used over and above these require some form of payment. For example, in the care of the elderly, the handicapped and in some aspects of community housing, some user fees are generally applied. Indeed, in the UK in 1987–88, seventeen different user fees were applied in social services and housing, producing a total income to the government of £1.594 billion. In the case of housing, the £893 million represented 12.2 per cent of the Department of Housing net budget, while in the case of social services, the £701 million was less than 2 per cent. As more governments look to 'pay as you go' services, some key questions need to be asked about the development of user fee policies. Rose (1990) suggests that there are nine key questions to ask. These are:

1. Who should pay the fee?
2. What exemptions should apply?
3. How much should the fee be?
4. To whom should the fee be paid?
5. For exactly what service is the fee meant to relate to?
6. What is the actual cost of delivering this service?
7. When should the fee be collected?
8. What statutory conditions should be associated with this fee?
9. What scope should be built into the user fee scheme for change and adjustment?

A tenth question needs also to be added: What is the cost of collecting and administering the user fee?

User fees for some social services (e.g. a fee for a housing assessment or a career assessment as a prelude to welfare payments) may seem strange, but there are a growing number of areas where fees are being charged. Part of the rationale for this appears to be reducing the 'frivolous' use of services. The other key rationale is to increase the resources available for service provision.

The underlying assumption that user fees create a clearer customer–supplier relationship has not been fully tested or evaluated. Indeed, there is little evidence available to support the contention that the collection of user fees promotes a more systematic service orientation in the service itself. There are also some clear examples of user fees costing organizations more money in collection, accounting, refunding and discounting and being a negative revenue source. From a TQM perspective, being a customer of a social service is something that many customers already pay for directly through taxation: most customers view their tax payments as creating a customer–supply relationship to social service agencies. The more obvious rationale for user fees concerns revenue generation.

From a TQM perspective, there is a need to be very cautious about suggesting that customers can only be defined in terms of those who pay a direct fee for a direct service. The customer's value proposition is calculated by the customer in terms of the perceived benefits they receive minus the perceived price they have paid for obtaining those benefits; price is more than mere cash – it also includes time, energy expended in obtaining services, as well as the 'hassle' associated with obtaining the service. Social service customers already perceive themselves as having paid a price – the fact that they are seeking the service in the first place, the hassle associated with obtaining the service, the travel and time taken in securing interviews for the service. Adding a user fee is an additional cost which the user will add to their already long list of perceived prices, and new costs are usually associated in the customer's mind with new benefits. What is in fact happening is that no new benefits are being added, only new costs. Customers are not easily duped. Since social service customers have little market choice (Hambleton 1988), there is a need to become very explicit about the value proposition and for a value contract with the customer to be developed, which both documents benefits to be obtained and the price expected, with price being interpreted in this broad sense to include all aspects of 'costs' (time, commitment, money) and for this individualized contract to become the basis of service. In this context, user fees may become appropriate.

Inter- and intra-department co-ordination

The third tactic being pursued under the heading of 'maximizing efficiency' is that of improving the extent and quality of internal linkages within social service systems by ensuring that those within a given department are fully aware of what is taking place within that department and that links to other departments are being maintained at a level of effectiveness which improves the quality of client service. This is presented here as a distinctive option, since collocation may not be involved, but exhortation to achieve closer co-ordination is.

Once again, the primary strategy for achieving this objective has been that of regionalization, local networks of teams and technological investment (see Hudson 1991). In North America at least, effective computer networks for information exchange, electronic mail and bulletin boards for information and services are also used. In Britain, the use of information technology in the provision of support services to communities and individuals is in its infancy.

The quality focus here is on improving the customer–supplier chains throughout the local network and increasing the speed at which 'network' linkages occur. In addition, the intention is to minimize errors – wrong information, inappropriate advice, incorrect entitlement calculations, etc., – and to minimize rework through the more systematic use of information technology.

Central to this tactic is a concern with speed, the speed at which information flows around the social service system. If speed can be increased and delays reduced, then services can be offered to the customer faster and with fewer errors and less rework, then customer satisfaction can be increased while costs are lowered – or at least this is the thinking. With new information technologies and more effective information systems, more work on behalf of a client can be undertaken as overlapping activities rather than activities conducted as separate and distinct phases, each of which needs to be completed before the next step can be taken. This has led some social service departments to design information systems in which: (a) less information is required from customers; (b) the information is networked so that all relevant agencies have direct access to it on-line; (c) less information is used in phases of work (e.g. assessment, notification, delivery, reassessment, reassignment, notification, etc.) and more can be used in concatenating services (rather than pushing, the system is one which pulls at the information so as to provide a range of services faster); and (d) the information system itself generates monitoring devices which permit quick and effective examination of activity levels and possible problem areas.

The quasi-market for social services

The final tactic pursued under the heading of 'maximizing efficiency' is that of creating a quasi-market for social service provision by extending the range of accredited providers to the private or voluntary sector. This has occurred in most countries with respect to housing, care for the elderly, care for the mentally and physically handicapped, those in need of psychological and counselling services, and child care. Regulation of these services is achieved through either professional regulatory bodies or through state regulations, or some combination of both. These developments represent a strategy shift on the strategy map provided in Chapter 3 (Table 8) from monopoly provider to multiple provider.

One example of this has occurred in Britain with respect to children ordered into care by the courts. It used to be the case that the majority of these children were sent to residential child care facilities (known as 'children's homes') which were managed exclusively by the public sector agencies under the umbrella of local municipalities. In 1992, approximately 11 250 children were in care in about 1300 residential facilities managed by local municipalities, voluntary organizations and private sector organizations throughout Britain. This number is significantly lower than was the case in 1960 – it is actually some 67 per cent lower. The change has occurred because more of the children found to be in need of such care are being placed in foster homes, thereby reducing unit costs to the authorities and increasing the personalization of service. In addition, voluntary child care organizations (responsible for 18 per cent of children in care) and the private sector (responsible for 14 per cent of children in care) have taken over some child care places from government (responsible for 68 per cent of children in care) by establishing their own residential homes. Increasingly, however, homes are needed to provide support and care for the highly disturbed children which foster care is not equipped to deal with.

But this is an interesting example of an unintended consequence of both the development of a quasi-market and a focus on cost reduction. By altering the balance of those in residential care to being just those who are most disturbed, the weaknesses of the residential care system have been exposed. It is the case that: (1) 80 per cent of all staff in residential care management and service delivery in the UK do not possess the appropriate qualifications for their positions; (2) 40 per cent of the heads of homes (site managers) have no qualifications for the positions they hold; (3) selection of staff is usually based on one 20–30 minute interview; (4) most municipalities with a responsibility for this service have no formal appraisal system for either the staff of the institution or its programmes; and (5) there are no requirements for ongoing training for staff, and few staff have attended in-service training (*Guardian* 8 December 1992). In addition, municipalities seeking to reduce costs by using agency workers (private sector employees hired out to local municipalities on an 'as-needs' basis) so as to lower overall overheads have actually ended up paying a premium for these workers, who cost an average 30 per cent more than staff fully employed by the local municipality (*Guardian* 8 December 1992).

Seeking to reduce costs by transferring children to foster care reveals quality weaknesses in the remaining provisions, weaknesses which were seen to be at the centre of scandals concerning drug abuse, staff sexual misconduct and inappropriate staff behaviour at a number of residential care facilities in the UK. The resultant enquiry, headed by Norman Warner, looked critically at the link between effectiveness on the one hand and quality of provision on the other and found these not to be balanced. Quality care was seen to be needed and government was required to act to provide quality commitments to a concerned public.

A strategy for maximizing efficiency that is also being pursued in the UK is that of inspection, i.e. examining social service provision through accredited and qualified inspectors who use predetermined standards to evaluate social service operations. The underlying quality model here is that of quality assurance and programme audit – inspection against pre-determined criteria – rather than Total Quality Management. The critical difference between the two is that the traditional model of quality assurance looks at outcomes in terms of predetermined standards for performance, whereas TQM requires a focus on the processes established within an organization for securing quality of outcome. A typical TQM self-evaluation process would ask the organization to focus on: (a) leadership; (b) information and analysis systems for ongoing evaluation and continuous improvement; (c) strategic quality planning within an institution; (d) the utilization of people's skills and talents; (e) the methods for specifying and achieving quality within the organization; (e) the results of the work of the organization expressed in terms of ongoing measures of quality performance; and (f) the extent to which customers are satisfied with their experiences of the systems and processes of the organization. The critical difference is the emphasis on process specification and development, as opposed to inspection on the basis of outcome.

Social services and the development of TQM

This review of the developments in social services over the last decade gives some emphasis to the varied responses to the challenge of a rapidly growing service demand with escalating costs which needs to focus on quality, cost-effectiveness and fast response. What is surprising is the marked absence of TQM strategies, vocabulary and practice in social welfare provision. This is even more surprising when contrasted with the significant development of TQM in the health sector (Grayson 1992; Lumsdon 1992).

Four explanations can be offered for the lack of development of TQM in social services. First, the services themselves are more varied and diffuse than in health in terms of the areas of social policy involved (housing, unemployment, child care, elderly care, mentally handicapped in the community, career development, community development, etc.), the range of professionals involved, and the range of demands placed on the system. Because of its diffuse management in separate units and structures with different traditions, cultures, funding arrangements and levels of professional engagement, social services is not as integrated and as focused on management concerns as health.

Second, social work practice and social service provision has a history of scepticism when it comes to adopting management practices from business (Staubbernasconi 1991). In part this is because the starting point for social work and social service practice is individual need as opposed to the management of illness, irrespective of the person who is ill. As Wilding (1982) has observed, the traditions of professional development in social work and health are different and the epistemology of their professional politics are different. Social work and social welfare workers view client-centred responsiveness as a core feature of their work, whereas historically health care has been more concerned with the management of illness than with meeting the needs of patients (Illich 1975). Further, a strong tradition in social work has been that of advocacy on behalf of the client – TQM, while striving to see that this advocacy is driven much more by clients themselves, is sometimes seen, according to our interviewees, as an unnecessary step for social services, since they are 'already client advocates and client-focused'.

The third explanation is that social services in the USA, at least, are not facing the same degree of financial crisis as health care. Indeed, the social services trust funds in the USA are actually in surplus, not in debt. Why would we wish to change and invest in quality when these developments are not driven by some fiscal imperatives? This explanation applies only to the USA – the same is not true of social welfare and social service provision in Canada, Britain and most of the EEC, where costs are rising faster than 'income' as demand grows. In our interviews with British and Irish managers, it became clear that they felt that managerial innovations like TQM 'come from the USA and migrate to Europe . . .' and they offer this as an explanation of why TQM has not yet developed in social services. This is a very narrow understanding of the situation, especially given the developments in health care in the UK, yet it was offered by eleven of forty interviewees.

The fourth explanation concerns understanding and leadership. A surprising number of interviewees saw TQM in the social services as equivalent to quality assurance and the systematic measurement of performance using performance indicators. There has not been the same determined emphasis and leadership from social service and social work departments concerning TQM that has taken place in health. In addition, the tradition of quality assurance and programme audit is strong in these services and few see the need to develop TQM from these beginnings. Without leadership and direction, TQM is seen as a 'fad' that will pass by many of those we spoke to in preparation for this book. One said, 'TQM . . . nothing more than another way of saying quality assurance . . .', and another said, 'I cannot see how something that is essentially all about manufacturing can produce anything of value for our work in the care of people . . .'. While these attitudes and assumptions persist, TQM will be slow to develop in social services.

As the social welfare system faces greater strains, it is likely that some leaders in the field of social services and social work will begin to look to TQM as a starting point for action. Until this occurs, TQM will develop at a grass-roots level (bottom-fed rather than top-led) as more and more fieldworkers develop their understanding of TQM and experience empowerment.

Conclusion

This chapter has examined some key developments in social service provision in the UK, Canada and the USA. Several approaches are being taken to control escalating costs and to ensure quality improvement at the same time. While some changes are taking place in the fundamental practices of welfare provision – for example, 'workfare' – the substantive changes in the early 1990s are more concerned with structural arrangements for the management of services and with the quality and speed of information processing and use within social service systems. Change is being internally driven rather than customer-driven. TQM is yet to find a significant voice in many social service agencies, though quality assurance (often seen as the rationale for the development of inspection systems) has developed and grown during the last twenty years. The core problem of social services is that they are demand-driven and linked to socio-economic issues beyond the control of social service managers – many see these as an inhibitor to the effective development of TQM in this area of public service.

By focusing on the following items, social service departments could link current developments to TQM more directly:

- The customer's value proposition and the development of customer service contracts.
- The speed of service and the integration of services so that customers can reduce any 'hassle' and get more service in less time.
- Reducing rework and error rates, so that customers get the right service at the right time at a lower per unit cost.
- Minimizing redundancy of effort and non-value-adding activities in the organization.
- Developing customer-driven performance measures and indicators.
- Process simplification – seeking to reduce the need for duplication of information, language problems in information collection (plain language) and reducing overall the need for so many steps and procedures to be gone through before services can be offered.
- Reducing the labour content of service delivery.
- Promoting self-help and self-managing systems.

Taken together, these eight points require a systematic approach to quality leadership, better and customer-friendly information and analysis systems, vision-based strategic quality planning, better human resource utilization, firm processes for continuous improvement and quality assurance, a focus on process outcomes and a commitment to higher levels of customer satisfaction. These demanding developments may or may not require structural change and decentralization: they *do* require social service departments to rethink the meaning of quality.

CHAPTER

7

TQM developments
in government service

In this chapter, we wish to look at developments in other sectors of government provision. Rather than provide detailed cases for particular occupational areas, the chapter looks at the trends in the adoption of TQM across areas of the public service and at the issues associated with the introduction of TQM. Our intention is not to provide an omnibus account of TQM throughout the public sector – this would be a mammoth undertaking – but to demonstrate some of the underlying features of the growth of TQM and some barriers to this growth.

The rationale for the development of TQM in other areas of the public sector – trade and industry, treasury and finance, environment, agriculture, intergovernmental affairs, the police, etc. – is the same as for the three areas already examined. That is: (a) government needs to rethink its strategic position for each of its service areas in the light of changing circumstances, especially in relation to the growing demand for services and the limited financing available for these services; (b) the need for internal economy measures across the public sector so as to assist in the reduction of GNP debt; and (c) as social, economic and political conditions change, so must the provision of services – a point being realized especially powerfully in relation to defence, the environment and agriculture.

As we have already noted, there are different responses in different public services to the combination of these three forces. This has led some to suggest that we are in the process of 'reinventing government' (Osborne and Gaebler 1992), seeking to find new ways of ensuring that services are provided and social needs being met by managing the public sector in a different way than has historically been the case. TQM informs many of the choices that many departments of government are making.

Developments in the USA

Kravchuk (1992), in an important and detailed survey of developments in the USA, looked at the extent to which TQM has been adopted by the fifty US states as a key governmental strategy. Thirty-one states report that they were embarked upon a systematic approach to TQM, with Arkansas and North Dakota being the clear leaders in terms of the extent of implementation. A further group of states are in 1993 beginning to implement TQM, while another fourteen are yet to start or declare any interest in TQM.

The methodologies used to develop TQM have varied widely from one state to another, as might be expected. Only four states have adopted the distinctive TQM emphasis of a particular guru (see Chapter 2), with the Deming method being adopted by three (Arkansas, Iowa and Massachusetts). Start-up and development strategies have varied between centralization and decentralization, with the states split evenly as to which one of these two choices they make. Almost all the states have a piecemeal approach to implementation, with Colorado being the only state with a mandate for agency or system-wide implementation of TQM according to an agreed schedule. In terms of the range of implementation models posed in Table 9, it is the 'parable of the sower' which has largely ruled.

Perhaps the most valuable findings from Kravchuk's systematic and detailed study concern leadership. His findings suggest that the key to TQM development is not so much leadership by elected politicians, but leadership by the executives of the departments (especially the civil service head) and agencies. That is, while commitment from politicians is clearly an asset, it is not a requirement for the development of TQM strategies and practices across the organization.

When it comes to resources, some interesting differences emerge between the states in their implementation of TQM. Almost none had appropriated large sums of money for their TQM efforts – the largest being $200 000 in Arizona. The obvious strategy being employed in most states is that of redeployment of existing resources and the reallocation of staff time. While some are using external consultants, others are using in-house training resources to meet training needs.

It is too early to examine detailed and specific outcomes from TQM developments in the USA, though Arkansas, Delaware, Texas and Maryland believe that their efforts have been highly successful. Subsequent work will be needed to examine the nature of these successes and the extent to which they have led to increased customer satisfaction, improved effectiveness and lower costs.

Getting TQM going in government: the Alberta experience

Alberta is one of ten provinces in Canada which is seeking to develop TQM as a part of its response to the challenges it faces in terms of a growing demand for services, a significant level of provincial debt, the need to rethink some aspects of government service in the light of changing circumstances and the decline of traditional sources of funding (i.e. federal government transfer payments, taxation from oil exploration and from the labour force).

The population of Alberta is approximately 2.6 million, some of whom are native Indians who are exempt from taxation because of treaty agreements. It is a large area, over twice the size of Britain, with over 65 per cent of its population in two major cities, Calgary and Edmonton. Its traditional industries are agriculture (grain, beef, pork), oil and gas, pulp and paper. Its growth industries are telecommunications, biotechnology and tourism. The province has accumulated debts of some $27 billion (approximately £15.6 billion) and has an annual operating debt of approximately $4 billion. It also has an ageing population which is making increasing demands on health care, and a mini baby boom which is leading to new demands on education and social services. It is seeking to downsize government by reducing the number of departments and agencies through mergers and closures, encouraging and enabling voluntary redundancy and early retirement, reducing programme expenditure and ending programmes which are under-used or seen to be redundant.

Getting started

In 1991, under the leadership of the Public Service Commission's Personnel Administration Office (PAO), a major TQM conference was held for agency heads and key managers with some 450 attending. The aim was to promote an understanding of TQM and to engender some interest in exploring TQM further. Speakers from both the public and private sectors in Canada and the USA were paraded to encourage understanding and interest. The PAO was very careful to make clear that it was not actively promoting TQM and requiring it of departments (i.e. it was not a directive), but was simply encouraging its most careful consideration. That is, the PAO was saying, 'TQM may help' – the exhortation/demonstration model of start-up and development (Table 9).

TQM organization

Subsequent to the conference, the TQM co-ordinator within the PAO was made responsible for the design of a six-module training programme which was commissioned from both within government and the private sector to create learning resources on both a general and 'just-in-time' basis for departments wishing to invest in TQM. These training modules ranged from a general awareness module (offered by Joseph Sensenbrenner), team development and basic quality tools modules, to work on quality function deployment. Individual departments were able to call on these resources to meet their needs or to use other resources as appropriate. The departments were left to their own devices for initiating TQM and training staff. Some Divisions, such as the Land Information Services, chose not to use the resources available through the PAO but to use other resources from the private sector for consulting and training. A Quality Management Co-ordinators forum was established in May 1992 with representatives from all department, so as to better create a co-ordinated effort.

Political support

Initially, there were no formal pronouncements by the Premier or cabinet ministers with respect to TQM though the new Premier has strongly endorsed TQM. The leadership role is taken by deputy ministers (the most senior civil servants in the department) and their executive colleagues. However, it is also the case that politicians have not blocked any efforts to develop TQM and are generally supportive.

Implementation schedule

Because the development of TQM within the Government of Alberta is decentralized and not co-ordinated, each department has to develop its own schedules for implementation. Some who have embarked upon this path have done so, while others are taking a more relaxed approach to timetabling. Key developments are taking place in the Department of Labour concerning teamwork and team skills, in the Department of Land Information Services concerning customer satisfaction and process improvement, in Federal and Intergovernmental Affairs concerning policy deployment and strategically focused human resource management, in Mental Health concerning strategic quality planning, and in Agriculture concerning customer-driven strategic management. It is, however, early days. A second TQM conference was to be held in 1993 to further encourage development and to review progress.

TQM methodology

The Personnel Administration Office in Alberta has adopted a strong focus on the Sensenbrenner model, which is itself linked to the work of Deming. It sees the Plan–Do–Check–Act cycle for improvement, when linked with a clear vision and strategic intent, to be central to the TQM strategy it recommends to its departments. However, departments are free to choose their focus and strategy and to call upon available resources from the PAO or elsewhere to support their TQM developments according to their own definition of need. There is no co-ordination and no single methodology adopted across departments. By its efforts, however, the PAO is able to bring some commonality to the presentations it makes to managers and executives and is in fact achieving a Sensenbrenner/Deming focus by doing so.

TQM resources

The PAO has itself commanded some resources to support its TQM initiatives, mainly through recouping its costs from user departments or by interest-free loan allocations from the Treasury which permit rapid resource development, with costs to be recouped at a later date. The departments pay the PAO directly for some of its services (training, consulting, etc.). The departments can also use their own budget allocations to pay for the services of TQM consultants from other agencies and the private sector.

Administrative culture

In parallel with its launch of TQM initiatives, the PAO also commissioned a study of how it would need to alter the reward and recognition strategies of the government if it wanted to 'tweak' the culture of government to encourage risk-taking, innovation, team work, empowerment and TQM. This study was followed a year later by a review of best practices in other Canadian jurisdictions and is being seen as a key component in rethinking human resource management practices in the government. To bring the customer's voice into the work of government more directly, many deputy ministers are undertaking programme reviews and customer audits, with the Department of Agriculture seeking to systematically and thoroughly consult some 2000 primary customers in 1992–93 and to rethink its strategy and processes in the light of these consultations. The province is also engaging a large number of interest groups and taxpayers in the rethinking of the economic strategy of the province. Unlike past practices, at least in the case of agriculture, consultation is leading to a rethinking of government activity at a fundamental level.

The culture is, however, resistant to change for other reasons: TQM development coincides with a period of downsizing of government, programme reductions, departmental mergers and the threat of job losses. The staff are concerned that working in a team which takes risks to rethink processes so as to reduce complexity and costs will ultimately lead some members of the team to suggest steps which will lead to their own subsequent unemployment. This is a culture problem.

A second problem is also not untypical – most training is designed for and taken by managers: Who is designing and delivering training to support field staff in the departments which adopt TQM? While some departments have started to work with their support staff on these issues (the PAO modelled this in a full day conference for support and administrative staff), others see TQM training as management training and hope that it will cascade down the organization.

The third cultural problem concerns priorities. The main priority is to provide a valued service while at the same time making a significant impact on the operating debt of the province – approximately $4 billion annually. TQM is known to be time-consuming and to be a medium- to long-term strategy: How can we deliver what is expected now, while at the same time maintaining TQM momentum? In early 1993, this is seen by many as a cultural issue.

Finally, it is widely recognized that TQM breakthroughs often involve risk-taking. During 1993 there will be a provincial election; many seem reluctant to take risks in such circumstances.

Overall experience

The experience in Alberta is little different from that in many other Canadian provinces or US states. It is just beginning, and there are some solid beginnings in the development of empowered work teams (Labour), customer-focused strategic planning and visioning (Agriculture and Mental Health), process redesign based on customer requirements (Land Information Services), vision linked to policy deployment (Treasury, Federal and Intergovernmental Affairs) and some large-scale attempts to make TQM a cornerstone strategy (Northern Alberta Institute of Technology). Few resources are dedicated to this, departments are free to opt in and opt out, there is no centralized strategy or timetable and no systematic way of evaluating consequences. We provide this detailed example to make clear what is involved in the implementation of TQM in one government. Kravchuk uses these same headings to describe developments in the USA and other developments can easily be examined on a case-by-case basis in this way.

In the sections which follow, we seek to examine developments more globally in terms of key areas for TQM. These are: (a) empowerment; (b) the design and management of TQM initiatives; (c) performance indicators; (d) benchmarking; and (e) self-assessment and evaluation. These areas warrant detailed attention, since many in the public sector who have begun their TQM journey appear to find these topics problematic or critical to their work. As we examine each of these topics, we will also make reference to case vignettes of success and failure so that the relevance of the key ideas are translated into action.

Empowerment as a key feature of TQM in government

The US Department of Defence has made major gains in performance through the empowerment of its staff. By asking staff to arrange for the design, building, inspection and development of their own physical facilities at defence bases around the world and to ensure that provisions are made for recreation, health, social well-being and the duties of that base rather than requiring each base to conform to a very long list of centrally determined base construction and development rules, the department has provided more services at the same or lower costs for its staff than was hitherto the case. The Revenue Division of the Ministry of Finance and Corporate Relations of the Government of British Columbia, Canada, has made savings of approximately $500 000 every year as a result of changes in work procedures for real property tax payments suggested by employees working in quality improvement teams. The Utilities Collection Service for the City of Edmonton in Alberta, Canada, has reduced bad debt on utility bills from $1.46 per $100 billed to 53 cents per $100 dollars billed through the imaginative work of bill collection teams, saving the city some several millions each year. In the Corporate Registry of the Finance Ministry in British Columbia, a team solved the problem of bar-coding all 245 000 active files for corporations registered in that province. All staff in the registry at all levels (top-to-bottom team) were asked to work for just one day to bar-code the files; something it would have taken two people many months to complete was completed in just 52 person days. In this same ministry, the cheque management system was so complex that enquiries concerning the status of a cheque took six days (on average) to respond to – there was also an enquiry backlog. By rethinking the information flow and the system associated with this, staff in all ministries are now able to provide a direct response to a query at the time the query is made. There is now no backlog and the number of manual cheque enquiries is down by 11 per cent from when the new system was introduced.

The Internal Revenue Service (IRS), responsible for the collection of taxes in the USA, has trained some 10 000 of its staff in basic quality principles and skills and formed some 500 teams with the intention of making specific gains in cycle time and the reduction of errors. In a single year, the IRS were able to: (a) reduce the number of Federal Tax Deposit errors from approximately 35 000 per week to 4000 per week, and (b) in one district office (San Francisco), response times for taxpayer enquiries for certain categories of work have been reduced from an average of 45 days to an average of 9 days.

The Equal Opportunities Commission (EOC) in the USA has been engaged in a quality journey since 1984. In 1988, through empowerment and the systematic use of statistical process control methods, the EOC was able to increase its case throughput by 17 per cent, reduce year-end inventory of cases pending by 12.8 per cent and won more awards for its customers – a 79 per cent growth in customer awards on 1987.

In each of these cases, public sector employees working in an empowered team have been able to produce economies in the operation of service, while increasing service quality to their customers. In doing so, they are following the definition of TQM advanced by the US Federal Quality Institute (an institute for TQM in the federal public service in the USA), namely 'a strategic, integrated management system for achieving customer satisfaction which *involves all managers and employees* and uses quantitative methods to continually improve an organization's process' (our emphasis).

Achieving the empowerment of intact work teams and valued results is not an easy process: both take a lot longer than many expect. For example,

T.O. Edick of the US Federal Highway Administration in a paper to the Canadian Institute on Governance in 1992 noted that, for their own quality initiatives, they had originally set 'about 3 years for ourselves to adopt and institutionalise the new philosophy', but experience taught him that 'we missed the mark by a wide margin . . . after some initial training, we re-focused and set a more realistic schedule of seven years' (Edick 1992). He also found, as have others, that the process of empowerment can be counter-productive unless it is informed by strategy and planning. Rather than just creating a large number of employee teams, training them in the use of quality tools and hoping that something will come out of the process at the end, teams need to be challenged to produce specific measurable results which are themselves desired as part of an overall departmental strategy.

The process of empowerment of intact work teams within a public service organization also involves changes in the nature of management within that department, as several who have embarked upon their quality journey have discovered. It is no longer a top-down, 'command and control' kind of management style that is needed, but one that more readily supports teamwork and 'bottom-up' initiatives. Rather than controlling, managers need to develop coaching, guiding, counselling and mentoring skills as well as the skills to recognize and support change teams and to end the work of unproductive teams as quickly as possible. We can call this 'top-led, bottom-fed'.

Stages of empowerment

From observation and research, there are four stages to the development of empowered intact work teams within the public sector, each stage having different implications for management and the work of team members. We are grateful to the Conference Board of Canada and the staff of Northern Telecom (wireless) in Calgary for their assistance in the development of this framework, the four stages of which are:

1. *The hmmm . . . stage*: when managers and leaders recognize the need to act, but are not sure what action to take.
2. *Awareness*: when the team becomes aware of the possibilities of their work and of the changes being made in the organization.
3. *Involvement*: when teams really become involved in the management of their own work processes and secure gains in the way in which these processes are undertaken.
4. *Ownership*: when teams take complete control of the management of their own work, including the recruitment and rewarding of staff, the definition of tasks and work process flows within their sphere of control, and set themselves challenging goals for the future.

Stage 1: hmmm . . .

At the hmmm . . . stage, the management of the department seek out op-tions, ideas and ways of working that will lead them to a framework for resolving their quality and performance problems. They may try a number of things – management by objectives, policy deployment, etc. – all in a 'milling about with intent' kind of way before settling on empowered teams as a basis for action.

Stage 2: awareness

At the awareness stage, the management of the department generally concerns:

1. Increasing the quantity and quality of information shared with all members of the organization. Everyone is encouraged to know in detail the financial position of the department, its operational and procedural targets for improvement, the staffing implications of decisions being made and the implications of current discussions regarding the future of the department. These are communicated effectively and efficiently, frequently and openly. It is frequently the case in the public sector that information is used as a basis for power, status and control. In the development of quality-focused teamwork, information is the basis for development and improvement of all, not just some.
2. Showing a strong link between individual goals and the goals of the department. Many have recognized the need to develop what is known as policy deployment, where a systematic and specific link is made between the goals of staff at one level and the goals of staff at all other levels, showing how the achievement of these goals will lead to the achievement of the measurable outcomes being sought within the department.
3. Challenging staff to go beyond their normative performance – to achieve at a higher level – and reward them for doing so. This has been seen to involve changing the performance management systems most generally used in the public sector as well as encouraging risk-taking and rule transformation.
4. Investing in the training and development of all staff in the team, especially in terms of the principles and practice of TQM.

These steps involve some difficult challenges for public sector managers, some of whom do not want to give up the situational power they have achieved by rising through the bureaucratic hierarchy of the organization. Three features of this appear especially difficult in the public sector: (a) the encouragement of risk-taking in the public service, with the consequence of risking public disavowal of actions taken; (b) the linking of personal and organizational goals through a clear and effective policy deployment system; and (c) the changing of reward and recognition strategies in the public sector, especially in terms of union-negotiated contracts that, in general, give emphasis to seniority over performance and discourage team-based performance management systems in favour of individualized reward.

At this same awareness stage, the team members themselves can be seen to take some actions to become more empowered. These include:

1. Systematically working to understand the changing nature of the public service, i.e. developing their knowledge and understanding of the challenges of government in the 1990s. They also often begin to recognize the problems as business problems rather than challenges to power, authority or job security.
2. They start to look more critically at the organization of the workplace and determine the real and imagined boundaries between teams. One thing that is quickly realized in the public sector is the interconnectedness of teams. What becomes important is that teams recognize the work they have in common and the work that makes each team unique.
3. Teams recognize and embrace learning and training as key characteristics of their future: without a persistent investment in their own learning, team members find the challenges they see ahead very difficult. They usually make clear their training needs as they see them at this stage.
4. The team starts to analyse and systematically examine just what it needs to provide to guarantee performance at levels that meet the expectations of customers. Many departments have not conducted a competency audit of their work and find it difficult to define just what it takes to produce success in their work.
5. They recognize that management needs help in developing their new role as coach, guide, mentor, counsellor and educator and help them perform well in this role.

Not all of these tasks appear easy for team members in the public sector. For example, in Public Works Canada (Architecture and Engineering Services, Pacific Western Region), which recently established a number of teams aimed at changing the way in which the organization does business in the 1990s, real understanding of the fiscal, political and competitive climate in which they now work and of the nature of the challenges they now face as an organization is slow in coming, as also is the acceptance that all staff need to change. Coaching is not a behaviour that comes naturally to many managers in the organization and they find the need to coach, rather than 'show and tell', difficult to accept. Team members have just begun (after almost a year) to learn that they can show their managers what it is that they need from them.

One device sometimes used to help both managers and team members at this stage is the empowerment contract – a formal document developed and signed off by all team members and all managers associated with their work, which makes clear what the expectations are of the team and what the team requires for support of its work. Empowerment contracts have been used by the Bath Mental Health Trust (UK) in the start-up of their 'Teams for Change' and by Public Works Canada (Architecture and Engineering Services, Pacific Western Region) and have been found to be valuable in creating a team culture and understanding commensurate with the needs of the organization. While teams are sometimes concerned about the extent of negotiation such contracts require and about the performance specificity of such contracts, they prove invaluable to the initial stages of teamwork. In the Bath Mental Health Trust, the contracts required teams to outline their responses to the questions set out in Table 3.

Each team developed its response to the 'empowerment contract' questions for negotiation with the Chief Executive Officer (and, in some cases, the Management Board) and made absolutely clear its needs and expectations. The teams report that not only were the outcomes of doing this empowering, but so also was the process of developing and negotiating these contracts.

Stage 3: involvement

The third stage, involvement, builds on the work that has been completed in Stage 2 and introduces new implications for management. These are often seen to be:

1. Reducing the number of levels through which ideas, suggestions and decisions have to pass before they can be acted upon. Some departments have been successful in doing this; for example, the Department of Agriculture of the Government of Alberta has reduced decision points from thirteen to three. Others find this difficult to do, since it involves a loss of managerial control.
2. Shifting power to make key decisions about workloads, priorities and work-flow from management to the team itself, e.g. the Ministry of Finance in British Colombia example given earlier (see page 148).
3. Further developing the competencies of managers regarding future thinking, the delegation of decision-making, coaching and teamwork.
4. Providing systematic education to everyone in the organization regarding data-based decision-making, problem-finding and -solving skills and imagineering.

To some extent, these measures are natural outflows from the work undertaken in Stage 2 (awareness). The difference is that managers have to relinquish their authority and control formally, whereas at Stage 2 they simply indicate this to be their intention. What is also critical at this stage is that managers do start to behave as coaches, counsellors, mentors, guides and educators. They generally need a lot of help to do this, since it involves not simply changes in attitude but changes in behaviour.

At this same stage, team members can also be seen to develop. Typical developments include:

1. Defining very clearly the responsibilities of each individual within the team by rewriting job descriptions and specifying performance in terms of both required competencies and outcomes.

2. Developing one-to-one coaching skills within the team, so that each member is able to provide support, assistance and coaching to others – every team member is both a learner and a coach.
3. Regularly reviewing how the team is functioning as a team and looking critically at what needs to be done to improve team quality.
4. Undertaking systematic training in the use of quality tools and beginning to use these as part of the daily discourse of the team.

As can be seen, the team takes responsibility here for the definition of its own work (through the rewriting of job descriptions) and for the work that is needed to improve team quality. The team is also beginning to focus on the 'how' of teamwork rather than the 'why' – the team members are looking to the mechanisms that will produce performance, not just the ideas.

In the public sector, there are a great many union-related issues in moving from Stage 2 to Stage 3. For example, the rewards given to staff are often based on a job evaluation task-points system where points are given for various components of a job, based on the job description. If individuals, through their own team, are able to rewrite the job description, then many consequences follow. It is therefore important that the unions are fully involved in the creation and development of an empowerment strategy within a public service department. Further, the development of self-managing work teams within the public sector carries many implications for some positions, most notably that of supervisor. In the Department of Labour of the Government of Alberta, which is now in its second full year of team development, a key issue in the transition from 'old-style' to team-based management has been 'what happens to the role of supervisor?'. A third issue in this transition concerns progress reporting. To whom does the team report: is it up a line or up the line and across to other teams? The answer given, for example by the UK Department of Trade and Industry and by the US Defense Department, is the latter. The reporting line changes from a linear one to a multidimensional one, with all 'connected' teams being kept informed of developments in 'sister' teams.

Stage 4: ownership

At the ownership stage, which few in the public sector have reached at this time, management has developed a variety of tasks. These include:

1. Being futures-focused and able to connect ideas and skills that are developing within a team or group of teams to the future needs of the department. This also can be seen to involve managers developing their business knowledge and competencies to a high level.
2. Improving and working on communication quality within and between teams.
3. Encouraging and enabling team decision-making.
4. Conducting systematic evaluations of teams based on learning and personal development of team members, as well as team outcomes.
5. Constantly monitoring the learning needs of the organization.

It will be noted that this stage involves a significant emphasis on learning and communication. In fact, what is implied here is that this stage involves the manager as the agent for learning and evaluation in the team – a very different role to that played by managers in the public service at this time. The thrust of Joseph Sensenbrenner's TQM initiatives during his term as Mayor of Madison, Wisconsin, was very much about getting key parts of the municipality to this stage of empowerment (see Sensenbrenner 1991).

As managers are seeking to develop learning at this stage of the empowerment process, team members begin to invest in some key developments. These have included:

1. Taking responsibility for all work processes within the sphere of work of the team.
2. As a team, assuming ownership of all work issues, especially recruitment, pay, rewards and recognition issues, grievances, etc., and managing the team's activities in the light of this ownership.
3. Undertaking all the planning and forecasting needed by the team to complete its work, using the manager as a resource if necessary.
4. Participating in team and individual goal-setting in alignment with the policy deployment work of the manager.
5. Accepting full responsibility for team performance.

There are few examples of empowerment at this level in the public sector, though several are already evident in the private sector (for details, see Johnston and Farquahar 1992). This is not because these features are impossible to achieve, but few have arrived at this stage of development. One of the organizations that is fast approaching this stage of empowerment is the Experimental Police District in Madison, Wisconsin. This district, which has a staff of 38 and is responsible for policing a population of some 30 000 persons, has used empowerment to develop a different kind of police organization. They have:

- elected their own captain and lieutenants and determined with them their roles relative to that of other team members;
- developed their own staff rosters, work schedules, performance management systems and agreements concerning staff disputes;
- designed, contracted out for, and built their own police station at a location they themselves determined to be the most appropriate;
- following customer survey work, the district adopted community policing methods, integrated the work of traffic wardens (meter monitors) and began to develop a high preventive and community profile.

So successful have the results of this work been that all of the policing in the city, as of 1991, was moving from traditional management approaches to policing to the decentralized and empowered model outlined here.

There are two kinds of empowered work teams: (1) cross-functional teams of workers from different parts of the organization coming together to work on a specific problem; and (2) intact or natural work teams working in the same organizational unit on a regular basis and having ongoing and daily responsibility for the work they are seeking to improve, such as those of the Madison Police. Significant developments can arise from each. The most significant and sustainable come from ongoing teams of either kind who build into their philosophy the work of continuous improvement.

One obvious question that arises about these developments in the public sector concerns the role of politicians in the process of empowerment. What is it and when is it most evident? While many have sought to interfere with empowerment developments, most have appeared to have taken a 'hands off' view of the work of teams. If the work is presented as focused on key policy objectives (increasing customer satisfaction and service effectiveness while lowering costs), many have had few problems with the work undertaken, especially if the teams are rigorous in their use of data and the quality tools. Indeed, in the case of the Madison Police Department, an attempt by politicians to take issue with the police unit over the location of the new police station was thwarted by the very rigour with which the team had collected and analysed the data and by the fact that the decision was made solely on the basis of data and had nothing to do with politics whatsoever.

Managing quality initiatives in the public sector

In describing some developments in relation to empowerment, the importance of the strategic management of quality initiatives in the public sector was briefly mentioned. In reviewing the developments that have taken place across a variety of public service agencies, it is sometimes the case that special structures were created to focus quality efforts and to ensure that quality is 'managed' as part of a strategy for change within the department or group of departments seeking to secure significant improvement. By and large, however, states, provinces and councils have chosen not to use such structures so as to avoid a new bureaucracy or a parallel tier of management. In this section, we will describe the kinds of structures which have been adopted.

Joseph Sensenbrenner's (1991) work has had a significant impact here, as also has the work of Coopers and Lybrand (see Carr and Littleman 1989). Both suggest that structural arrangements should be made to manage quality. These arrangements usually involve the creation within a department of: (1) a *quality council*, which has the task of co-ordinating the quality efforts of the organization as a whole, creating specific quality initiatives and supporting training; (2) a *steering group*, which has the responsibility for making sure that a particular project has the authority and resources it requires to complete a task; and (3) a *project team*, which undertakes the work necessary to complete the quality improvement desired. Two quite different things have happened with these structural arrangements.

In the City of Edmonton, for example, the quality council (which has as members a cross-section of key managers in the city) has outlined seven projects which it sees as essential for the future development of the city and for service quality improvement (SQI) and has created appropriate steering groups to oversee these SQI developments.

These structural arrangements are intended to link quality initiatives with critical policy deployment issues faced by a government agency, reduce the potential for teams 'hitting a brick wall' when they are seeking to make changes in the way a process works within an organization, and to ensure that the task team has the appropriate mandate and resources to complete the task set. This is very different from the empowerment strategy just outlined. Some task teams will be short-term, skunk-works (Peters 1989) with a specific period job to do in a specific period of time. Others may have more medium- to long-term activities to undertake, but are usually cross-functional teams covering more than one branch within a department. The description of empowerment provided above relates to intact or natural work teams and the management of continuing functions; these structural arrangements relate to the control of specific, planned initiatives aimed at making sustainable gains in performance.

One example of these arrangements at work can be taken from the City of New York's Sanitation Department. In the motor equipment bureau of this department, some 1300 persons are employed to maintain and support the fleet of 6500 garbage collection trucks and street-cleaning vehicles. In 1978, just over half of these vehicles were able to operate on any given day. Using a series of project teams, each of which has a steering group reporting to a quality council, some 85.4 per cent of the vehicles are now able to operate daily, customer satisfaction has improved and the city is saving $16 million in its operations in this area alone. Ronald Contino, who was the head of this unit, says of the structural arrangements for managing these initiatives:

> This was possible because an environment had been created where each individual knew that he was being represented in the decision-making process, and that he had a direct pipeline to the top to voice his very own concerns and desires. Changes in procedures were no longer viewed as orders generated by a distant elite, but rather as a product of teamwork and a universal desire to see the job improve.
>
> (Contino 1985)

Similar developments have taken place under Joseph Sensenbrenner's management in Madison. The Motor Equipment Division has saved some $700 000 each year by creating preventive maintenance programmes, which reduces average vehicle downtime from nine days to three.

There is a danger in creating such structural arrangements for the management of quality initiatives in the public sector that the structures become a new bureaucracy and actually inhibit rather than enable change. There is a need to avoid this by being very clear about what each of the three levels of this quality management organization have to do. Sensenbrenner has observed that the use of this structure in a variety of settings suggests the following roles for the respective levels of management of the quality process.

The *quality council* generally adopts three functions:

1. Promoting awareness throughout the departments that quality is a key component of the strategy the government is pursuing.
2. Ensuring that key quality issues are being tackled in a systematic way.
3. Encouraging the development of quality initiatives throughout the organization by giving its 'seal of approval' to quality projects suggested by staff.

For example, in the Ministry of Education and the Ministry Responsible for Multiculturalism and Human Rights in the Government of British Columbia, their service quality council has the following eleven roles:

- to develop a service quality framework to assist branches and provide focus;
- to serve as a 'sounding board' for service quality ideas;
- to assist in the development of service quality courses;
- to help branches assess service quality needs and priorities;
- to identify in-house facilitators;
- to liaise and communicate service quality information at branch level;
- to model new ways of working;
- to facilitate access to resources to respond to the service quality needs of branches;
- to serve as a link between branches and the executive;
- to act as a catalyst for change and encourage participation;
- to sponsor service quality events.

As sponsor, encourager and model, this council seeks to provide leadership, support and encouragement to branches within the department.

In some models of the structural arrangements for quality, the department of the central agency will create a *steering group* for each individual *cross-functional* project team. These have been seen to take on the following tasks:

1. Give a project team permission to innovate by formally signing-off on an empowerment contract.
2. Provide technical assistance to the project team on as-needs basis, including training and information resources.
3. Ensure that managers are responsive to the needs of the project team; it facilitates listening by managers and removes management blocks to action.
4. Afford protection to the project team when it is challenged or when its improvements meet resistance.

One way of looking at the steering group is as a buffer for the project team which will undertake the work. In fact, one member of a very controversial project team referred to the team's project steering committee as the team's 'immune system'. This can be especially important in cross-functional work where 'turf wars' frequently inhibit innovation.

The individual *project team* working on tasks will vary its work according to the problem, whether or not it has a clear empowerment contract and whether it is an intact team or a cross-functional team. By and large, project teams can be seen to:

1. Be very clear about the measurable outcomes it is seeking to achieve.
2. Be innovative in its approach to process improvement.
3. Test ideas before seeking wide-scale implementation.
4. Persist.

These distinctive roles for different levels of the quality initiative structure, require different kinds of players. The project team needs to have as members those most familiar with the actual processes requiring improvement – the people nearest the process and the customers for that process. The steering group needs to have as members those who are able to ensure that the obstacles to improvement which may be placed in the way of the project can be removed – they need to be executive managers or persons with sufficient authority to overcome practical and political barriers to action within the organization. The quality council needs to comprise all those who have a strategic responsibility and fiscal responsibility for the operation of the department or organization – a departmental executive team.

As more public sector organizations move to TQM, these structural arrangements are increasingly being used to effect quality improvement. Many variations of this basic model are emerging, one of which is worth mentioning here. In some cases, the steering group has been replaced by a *process owner*, a single person of very senior rank who acts both as a champion for the project team and also as a mentor and guide to the team, advising them on the politics and appropriate practices needed to secure change. Ontario Hydro, a Crown Corporation in Ontario, Canada, and also the largest power-generating company in North America, is using process owners instead of a steering group on the grounds that an individual can work faster than a group to secure necessary resources and approvals if they are senior enough to do so.

Whatever the structural arrangements made, our point here is simple: when we review the way in which TQM is being enacted within the public sector, such structural arrangements may be found. While the specific detail of the arrangements may differ between one location or function and another, they have in common the idea of focusing quality efforts through management choice and ensuring that teams are resourced, enabled and supported in their efforts to make a difference. The absence of such arrangements may be one reason for the failure of TQM in some public sector organizations and for its slow rate of growth in others. Further, there is a danger that these arrangements become overly mechanistic and bureaucratic: this danger needs to be countered by a focus on performance rather than control and through clarity over the respective roles of each level of decision-making in the quality process.

The creation of new structures does not imply that existing structures cannot be used to drive TQM initiatives. Indeed, the study of developments across the USA by Kravchuk shows that the most common arrangements are built on existing structures. In British Columbia, Ministerial quality councils report to the executive of their Ministries, where quality initiatives are being pursued. What is implied by the growth of structural arrangements relates more to the need to focus efforts rather than just 'trust' that they will occur. Each Ministry or Department which embraces TQM needs to have some systematic way of ensuring that progress is focused and measured: the structural arrangements outlined here provide just one of the basic ways of doing this.

Performance indicators

As with many of the other aspects of public service already examined in the chapters on health, education and social services, many government and public sector organizations are making use of performance indicators to look at service quality and to examine relative efficiencies of performance between different organizations working in the same area of provision or the same organization's different regions or units providing similar services in different locations. For example, housing agencies look at the unit costs of housing, inventory turns (number of times a house has new tenants), cycle times (time taken to let a property), and so on.

Performance indicators are seen as part of the movement towards focusing on the 'outcomes' of public investment, of the consequences of the relationship between the purchasers (the taxpayers) and their agents. However, many of the performance indicators examined so far are actually concerned with process, not outcome. We will return to this theme in the concluding chapter of this book. The point to be stressed here is that performance indicators do not necessarily speak to issues of quality unless they have been designed to do so, for reasons we have already explained in Chapter 6.

Benchmarking

Another development in the public sector has been the increasing use of benchmarking as a way of looking at service quality. Benchmarking is the process of 'measuring an organization's operations, products and services against those of its competitors in a ruthless fashion' (Oakland 1989). In the public sector, the word 'competitor' is replaced by 'best equivalent provider' where appropriate.

Table 20 Benchmarking for a purchasing agency

Key area benchmarks	This department	World class
Supplier per purchasing agent	34	5
Agents per £100 million purchased	5.4	2.2
Purchasing costs as % of purchases made	3.3%	0.8%
Supplier evaluations (weeks)	3	0.4
Supplier lead times (weeks)	150	8
Time spent placing an order (hours)	6	0
Late orders	33%	2%
Rejected supplies	1.5%	0.0001%
Materials shortages (instances per annum)	400	4

Public Works Canada's (Architecture and Engineering Services, Pacific Western Region) are just beginning their benchmarking journey. Their intention is to compare their architectural processes and engineering outcomes with the best in the architecture and engineering business in terms of some key dimensions. By doing so, they hope to highlight areas in which they already achieve 'best practice' when compared with the best in the private sector and to locate areas where they need to improve their performance significantly. To some extent, benchmarking in an area of public service where there are obvious private sector counterparts, as in most areas of public works, is not difficult. What is being looked for are the gains that can result from a systematic, objective and detailed perform-ance comparison – gains which can be significant, as Table 20 shows for just one area of service common to all public sector organizations, i.e. purchasing.

Increasing use is being made of the International Benchmarking Clearing-house in Houston, Texas, a key part of the American Productivity and Quality Centre housed there. This use, which is paid for on a graduated scale, provides data in exchange for equivalent deposits of data. In addi-tion, the data provided reduce the cost of benchmarking within a single organization while providing a basis for looking at quality both at an organizational level and across a functional area of government or indus-try. Only a small number of public service agencies and government de-partments are using this clearing-house at the present time, though its use is increasing. To make the point, Table 20 is a benchmarking table devel-oped by the purchasing agency of one UK government department which compares its performance against that of purchasing agents ranked as the best in the world on the basis of data gleaned from the database in Houston. The UK department concerned is now focusing its efforts on improvement across the key areas listed in Table 20.

As was seen in relation to both education and health care, benchmarking is growing. One way in which performance indicators in both of these sectors are beginning to be used is in comparing the performance of similar institutions on similar tasks. While there are dangers in taking simple performance indicators and comparing them, their value in focusing energies around quality is increasingly being realized.

In the private sector, there is a growing realization that benchmarking is not for everyone. Ernst & Young's 'Best Practices Report' (1992), which looks at the impact certain key quality practices have on the performance of the organization, found that low-performance organizations may actually be harmed by investing in benchmarking. This study suggests two reasons for this. First, low-performance organizations in comparing themselves with the best in the world are comparing themselves with the wrong role models – the gap between current performance and world-class performance is too great to be bridged by the efforts of the low-performance organization. Second, low-performance organizations need to focus on the basic aspects of quality before they can consider investing in the more advanced features, such as benchmarking.

The definition of low-, medium- and high-performance organizations used in Ernst & Young's study relates entirely to return on assets (after-tax company income divided by total assets) and value-added per employee. Neither of these are easy calculations in the public sector. What is more, since many public sector organizations do not have good data on which to base reasonable comparisons between themselves and other government departments or private sector organizations undertaking similar functions, the data collection and analysis process required for benchmarking may in itself be costly, time-consuming and of limited value. Any public sector organization undertaking benchmarking needs to have a very good reason for doing so. This is not to say that it shouldn't be done, only that doing so requires those responsible to have a very clear answer to the questions 'so that we can . . .'.

Self-assessment and evaluation

While some are attempting to use benchmarking as a means for identifying key areas for improvement in their department or branch, others are using systematic self-assessment – the Malcolm Baldrige National Quality Award, the Canadian Awards for Business Excellence, the European Quality Award or IS09000 (or its equivalent in Britain, BS5750) – as the basis for this work. Each of these provide different starting points for the evaluation of the organization, its readiness for quality initiatives and the focal point for quality work that is needed.

The most widely used is the Malcolm Baldrige National Quality Award, simply because it has been in existence longest (since 20 August 1987), has systematic guidelines for assessment which are freely available (see Evans and Lindsay 1992) and various training opportunities exist for managers and others to develop competencies as evaluators. More recently, software has been developed to help organizations conduct speedy self-assessment.

The assessment involves the systematic analysis of the practices of the organization in seven categories and a total of thirty-two sub-categories. The analysis involves the awarding of points by category. The following listing shows these categories and the points to be awarded.

The Malcolm Baldrige award criteria

*Leadership (100 points)   *Points*
Senior executive leadership   40
Quality values   15
Management for quality   25
Public responsibility   20

*Information and analysis (70 points)
Scope and management of quality data and information   20
Competitive comparisons and benchmarks   30
Analysis of quality data and information   20

*Strategic quality planning (60 points)
Strategic quality planning process   35
Quality goals and plans   25

*Human resource utilization (150 points)
Human resource management   20
Employee involvement   40
Quality education and training   40
Employee recognition and performance management   25
Employee well-being and morale   25

*Quality assurance of products and services (140 points)
Design and introduction of quality products and services   35
Process quality control   20
Continuous improvement of processes   20
Quality assessment   15
Documentation   10
Business process and support service quality   20
Supplier quality   20

*Quality results (180 points)
Product and service quality results   90
Business process, operational and support service results   50
Supplier quality results   40

*Customer satisfaction (300 points)
Determining customer requirements and expectations   30
Customer relationship management   50
Customer service standards   20
Commitment to customers   15
Complaint resolution for quality improvement   25

Determining customer satisfaction	20
Customer satisfaction results	70
Customer satisfaction comparison	70
Total score available	**1000**

The aim of the assessment process is to use the very detailed criteria under each of these headings and sub-headings to complete a comprehensive analysis of where you are and where you need to get to. In two public sector organizations which completed the tasks, they found themselves to be in the 350–400 points range, much lower than they hoped they would be. What they found was that the process of assessment helped them recognize key areas for improvement while at the same time encouraged them to become more realistic about where they are and what they need to do in the short, medium and long term to make a difference.

Such self-assessments are demanding on the organization. For example, Hermann Sahmann and Ray Menard of 3M Canada have told us that thirty-two key areas of the worldwide business were assessed by thirty-two assessment teams, each of between twelve and twenty-two persons (approximately 475 persons were involved for an average of two days per person – the equivalent of 1139 person days). Though the 'up-front' investment in assessment looks considerable, the thirty-two team evaluations produced a total of 18 000 improvement opportunities. After prioritizing and amalgamating areas of common interest, 179 quality improvement teams were established and are now working to improve 3M's overall quality position.

The Department of Federal and Intergovernmental Affairs (FIGA), Canadian Intergovernmental Division of the Government of Alberta, has been engaged in its own self-evaluation since October 1992. Rather than use the elaborate criteria, its Assistant Deputy Minister, Francie Harle, chose a very direct way of assessing the division, and we are grateful to her, Randy Fischer, Amy Gerlock and Shelley Tobo Gaudreau for their assistance with the material in the section which follows. Francie Harle asked the following questions, which we think have a generic utility for all public sector managers:

• Why are we here – what is our mission?
• Who do we serve – who are our customers?
• Who are we – what are our characteristics?
• What do we provide – what business are we in?
• What is the basis for our service?
• What is our competitive advantage?
• What financial objectives must we meet?
• What do we value?
• What does success look like – what outcomes do we seek?
• How do we measure success?

The responses to these questions, developed by the senior management team and refined through discussion with all staff members, were as follows:

Why are we here – what is our mission?
To provide leadership and co-ordination in the conduct of intergovernmental relations relating to economic, resource, fiscal and social issues within Canada so as to protect provincial interests and advance Alberta's objectives as an equal partner within a strong, united Canada and to promote and adopt results-oriented intergovernmental cooperation leading to improved effectiveness and efficiency in government.

Who do we serve – who are our customers?
Internal clients: the premier, our minister, deputy minister and other divisions within this department.
External clients: other ministers and deputies, other departments of government and their agencies, the people of Alberta.

Who are we – what are our characteristics?
A group of highly qualified and motivated people committed to individual and collective excellence.

What do we provide – what business are we in?
• Quality advice and assistance.
• Superior intergovernmental analysis.
• Sound recommendations.

What is the basis for our service?
• Intergovernmental policy – development and deployment.
• Intergovernmental intelligence.
• Credibility.

What is our competitive advantage?
Relevant, reliable, useful and timely information provided in a form that satisfies client needs.

What financial objectives must be met?
We must ensure: (a) prudent use of taxpayer funds; (b) responsible budgeting; and (c) creative allocation of available resources to activities and tasks that support our mission.

What do we value?
• Respect and understanding for: (a) the taxpayer; (b) all staff members; and (c) our clients.
• Recognition of the value of everyone's contribution.
• Individual and personal responsibility for all that we do.
• Initiative and innovation.
• Self-development.
• A commitment to continuous improvement.

What does success look like – what outcomes do we seek?
- All departments will be aware of broad operational intergovernmental policy.
- All departments will understand the implications of intergovernmental agreements and activities.
- All departments will be fully aware of trends in intergovernmental affairs and their implications for policy and action.
- There is an ongoing and effective liaison with other divisions within this department.
- Client needs are accurately assessed and service is provided in accordance with need.
- Intergovernmental products and services are directed to the appropriate level within a department.
- Alberta's needs, concerns and priorities are effectively communicated to the federal government and other jurisdictions.
- Intergovernmental positions that are reflective of needs of client departments.
- The department makes effective use of intergovernmental processes.
- The Alberta position is seen to be consistent in the intergovernmental arena.

How do we measure success?
- Departments regularly seek advice and assistance.
- Analysis of intergovernmental trends is done regularly.
- No surprises.
- Divisions within the department are aware of and involved in any departmental activity that affects them. (The department sings from the same song book.)
- There exists an updated and up-to-date intergovernmental policy document.
- The division is involved at an early stage in any intergovernmental agreement.
- Division receives and reviews client feedback.
- Federal policies and legislation are sensitive to Alberta's interests.
- Alberta has effective, cooperative alliances with other jurisdictions.
- Intergovernmental irritants are being addressed.
- Alberta issues are placed on intergovernmental agendas.
- Other jurisdictions are not confused about Alberta's priorities and positions.

Some further work was undertaken on this last question to convert these general statements to specific outcome measures which could be reviewed frequently by all staff in the division. Work is also in progress in revising all job descriptions and evaluation procedures to fully reflect these descriptions of the task of the division and its measures. In future, all staff in this division will be evaluated against criteria directly derived from this analysis of core functions and tasks.

The questions and the responses may look somewhat obvious, yet the construction of this document and its use as a basis for policy deployment, performance management and planning within the division were new. As with many other departments, such basic self-evaluation and description had not been undertaken in such a way before. We include this example here because it indicates the potential for a simple activity – self-assessment – to begin a process of policy deployment within the division. In this division of FIGA, this self-evaluation activity focused all staff on the need to develop accountable measures in terms of mission, strategy and client needs.

Conclusion

This chapter has looked at key developments in the pursuit of quality across a number of government departments and public agencies. In particular, the focus on empowerment, the structural arrangements for managing quality, performance indicators, benchmarking and self-evaluation appear to encompass many of the developments now taking place. Though some governments have adopted TQM as a focus for the development of public service – this has happened in Canada (through Public Service 2000 policy) and the USA – there is yet to be widespread adoption of a radical quality agenda in government.

Much depends on executive leadership of the quality efforts of a public sector department. Indeed, the evidence seems to suggest that the clearer the leadership in the department is about its vision, values, strategy and goals, the more likely it is that TQM will develop as an effective response to the problems which governments face. The Madison Police Department realized this when it outlined the twelve Principles of Quality Leadership and gave emphasis to some key words in these principles. We end this chapter with these principles, since for us they summarize the key 'drivers' for TQM across government:

1. Believe in, foster and support *teamwork*.
2. Be committed to the *problem-solving* process; use it and let *data* drive decisions.
3. Seek employee *input* before you make decisions.
4. Believe that the best way to improve the quality of work or service is to *ask* and to *listen to employees who are doing the work*.
5. Strive to develop *respect and trust* among employees.
6. Have a *customer* orientation and focus towards employees and citizens.
7. Manage on the *behaviour of 95 per cent* of the employees, not the 5 per cent who cause problems.
8. *Improve systems* and examine processes before blaming people.
9. Avoid top-down, *power-oriented* decision-making whenever possible.
10. Encourage *creativity* through *risk-taking* and be tolerant of honest *mistakes*.

11. Be a *facilitator and coach*. Develop an *open atmosphere* that encourages the provision and acceptance of feedback.
12. With teamwork, develop with employees agreed *goals* and a *plan* to achieve them.

Stating these twelve principles is a relatively easy exercise. Asking that you be judged as a leader on them, using a complete staff survey as part of a comprehensive evaluation (as required by a full Baldrige assessment), is another matter altogether. Yet in those organizations where TQM is flourishing, the leadership of the organization is striving to behave in a way which conforms to these twelve statements.

CHAPTER

8

Issues and problems in adopting TQM in the public sector

Introduction

So far in this text, we have examined the nature of TQM and the appropriateness of its application to the public sector (Chapters 1 and 3), the development of quality practices in the public sector and illustrated these developments with short case vignettes wherever this has been possible. In addition, we have drawn attention to some basic themes of development and some key practices, especially in relation to the structuring of quality efforts and the development of empowerment. Throughout we have offered a critical perspective, highlighting both the strengths and potential weaknesses of the initiatives being taken. In some previous chapters, we have noted some further problems with the application of TQM in the public sector. We have also recorded some significant successes.

We now turn our attention to the problems encountered in the development of quality initiatives in the public sector and document both the findings of others and our own observations, based on a significant level of involvement with government departments from agriculture to youth affairs in Canada, Britain and the USA. Our intention in this chapter is to show the dilemmas faced in applying TQM in the public sector and respond to some criticisms of TQM, other than those already examined in Chapters 1 and 3. We will end the chapter with an analysis of these dilemmas, which makes use of the distinction developed in Chapter 3 between core, adaptive and problematic concepts of TQM, and document these.

Central to our analysis here will be the concept of *contrapreneurship*. This concept, developed and refined for the first time in this text, develops from our observation of effective resistance and resentment to TQM among public sector employees. Contrapreneurship, as you will see, is not to be confused with plain resistance. The essential feature of contrapreneurship is that those who display these features seek to become entrepreneurial in their attempts to inhibit, delay or prevent TQM from developing in their department. They are not just opposed to TQM, but are active resisters who use creative methods to exercise their contrary views.

Resistance to TQM change: contrapreneurship

A key barrier to the effective introduction of TQM in the public sector is contrapreneurship; that is, the active resistance to change experienced in all organizations. We define contrapreneurship as *the effective and creative use of skills and competencies to prevent significant change from occurring*, and much of what follows is based on the work of Stephen Murgatroyd and Donald Skilling of Lee–Skilling Associates (Calgary) who are developing a text on this phenomenon. In contrapreneurship, the kinds of resistance encountered are active, rather than passive, creative rather than blunt rejection, and powerfully effective rather than being just a nuisance.

The public sector is not affected, in many areas, by significant and fluctuating market pressures. Further, the public sector is highly professionalized and has adopted procedures for working which are highly formalized and, in some cases, regulated. Control and command structures are hierarchical and again formalized; in some government departments we have examined, there are between eight and eleven layers of decision-making. While this description is changing, as governments move to more market-driven solutions to their value and cost problems, there are many areas of government in the developed world as yet untouched by the new *perestroika* of TQM.

As with many private sector employees, public sector employees are not especially enthusiastic about change. While some embrace change and development as a key feature of organizational life, others resist and reject change and seek to actively maintain the *status quo*. Others do not express a view, but by their behaviour and inaction, can be seen as uncommitted. In fact, consultants often talk about the 30–30–30 rule: 30 per cent of any group favour the change being proposed, 30 per cent resist the change, and the remaining 30 per cent wait to see which of the other two groups obtain the dominant position in the organization (the 'missing' 10 per cent commissioned the consultants in the first place!).

What lies behind contrapreneurship is complex, but essentially involves three categories of response: resistance to the social and personal consequences of change; resentment about the nature of the changes being made;

and technical objections to the change process. Let us examine each of these in turn, since they provide insights into why TQM sometimes fails in its introduction in an organization.

Contrapreneurship: the resistance components

The most common points of resistance to TQM we have encountered are as follows:

- *A fear that the widespread adoption of TQM will reduce the number of jobs available or the opportunities for promotion.* When employees look at terms like 'labour content reduction', 'cycle time reduction' or 'process elimination', they see their own work being described as vulnerable. The emotion felt here may be personal (fear of losing their own job or opportunities for development) or general (fear on behalf of their peers as well as themselves).
- *A fear that their own sphere of influence and control may be affected as empowerment develops.* As self-managing work teams develop in the department, managers, supervisors and influence holders recognize that power, influence and control have shifted from individuals to groups and from themselves to others. This is a source of discomfort and fear.
- *A fear that the work they undertake will become more complex.* Effective TQM implementation leads teams of employees, and therefore the individuals within teams, to accept significantly increased responsibility for their own work and the work of their section or division. With responsibility comes risk, and perceptions of risk can appear threatening, and some are unwilling to accept this.
- *A fear that the risks of TQM will not be compensated for through the reward and recognition structure.* As employees accept more responsibility, and therefore risk and uncertainty, there is often a concern that the reward and recognition system of the organization will not be adjusted to reflect this. Indeed, Juran has suggested that any change in the organization's commitment to quality must be reflected in the way in which rewards and recognition are managed and performed. A failure to adjust the rewards and recognition system will lead some to take significant risks and not to feel compensated or recognized for having done so. The other side of the coin, if the system is not adjusted, is that individuals will be compensated whether or not they adopt the new working methods of TQM.
- *A fear of skill inadequacy.* A common experience when faced with TQM initiatives is that individuals look at the technical skills and competencies they see they are going to need – skills in communication, project management, technical tools of TQM, etc. – and judge themselves inadequate. Since training investments in the public sector are, in general, meagre (especially for support and administrative staff), this fear eventuates the other fears listed here.
- *Concerns about teamwork.* Because of the role culture (Handy 1989)

developed in most public sector organizations, individuals have assigned duties and tasks and perform them with a degree of independence from others. Systems of position evaluation tend also to promote an understanding of work in terms of specific and individual roles. TQM, in its full form, as exemplified by self-managing work teams, involves a significant change in the nature of work. Work is something distributed through and within teams. A key competence required from everyone is the development of collective work skills and shared responsibility for task achievement. This is a major change to the culture of the workplace and to the relationship of the individual to the work that they are asked to perform. Many resist this change in terms of either (a) a feeling that this depersonalizes their work or (b) a feeling that they are unable to accept shared responsibility for their own work and that of others. While teams can be organized in many different ways, this fear exists.

- *The fear of data-based decision-making.* There is a common fear that the systematic analysis of work processes by any method will result in embarrassment, revelations of inefficiency or accusations about performance and that these will all be personalized. One employee of a major government department said: 'Once we actually start looking systematically at the work we do, the stuff will really hit the fan . . . I'm not sure I want to be around for that!'
- *The reluctance to accept full accountability for action.* With process responsibility being devolved to the lowest possible level of the organization (the 'subsidiarity' of TQM) comes accountability. Also, as the organization moves from an awareness stage of empowerment to an ownership stage, accountability becomes a key component of performance-based task management within teams. Some are reluctant to accept the level of accountability implied by this.

There are other fears that exist that will lead to individuals or groups resisting TQM. Whether these fears are real or imagined is not important; if they exist, they are real and may provide the basis for contrapreneurial actions within the organization.

Contrapreneurship: the resentment components

Resistance forms one significant category of contrapreneurship; a second is *resentment*. Here are some of the common forms of resentment found in the public sector when TQM is being introduced:

- *TQM is another 'management fad' and we are the victims of management in this latest experiment.* There is a phrase we encountered in our work with IBM which many staff members there use to describe management initiatives: the phrase is BOHICA. It means 'Bend Over, Here It Comes Again!' It implies the idea that if we ignore all this, it will just go away, like the last initiatives introduced by management. In one city administration in the last decade, the staff had been introduced to all

172 Total Quality Management in the public sector

of the following as 'major changes which will radically improve all that
we do': management by objectives, project management, quality circles,
strategic planning, zero-based budgeting, stream analysis and several
other management ideas. For these staff, TQM was 'just another fad'.
They resent being used as guinea-pigs in the experiments of managers.

- *It's a fine mess you got us into.* This is the phrase used by one team of
employees in describing their initial reaction to TQM in the City of
Edmonton. They suggest that the problems they are now grappling with
in their teams are problems created by the very same managers who are
now promoting empowerment and team-based problem-solving. As one
member of this team said: 'They [the managers] got us into this mess
and they now ask us to solve it!' A part of the resentment here is the
feeling that managers cannot be trusted to see the process through.
Closely associated with this resentment is:

- *TQM is a cover for me being asked to solve the problems created by
others – the big burden problem.* Some staff, for example in the treasury
or finance ministries of governments, feel that the burden of making
significant and substantial quality and performance gains has fallen on
their shoulders and that it is too great a burden for them to carry. One
treasury official in a government in Canada suggested that 'low level
staff are being asked to make significant savings through quality efforts,
yet the Government itself continues to spend in excess of its resources
. . . we are being asked to solve the debt problem created by someone
else'. Some feel resentment for this reason.

- *Quality management tasks are not my job: This is not what I was hired
to do.* Some clinical staff at the Bath Mental Health Trust who were
asked to participate in TQM teams felt resentment that this work would
further reduce the time they could spend with patients in need, despite
the fact that the long-term intention of the teams to be established was
to increase resources for patient care while at the same time improving
the effectiveness and efficiency of such care. This is a common reaction
to the creation of teams. One employee of the US Department of Defence said: 'This place is teeming with teams . . . I have no time now to
do my work!'

- *Just as I get to the time when I can apply for promotion, we get into
teams . . . THANKS A LOT!* As the organization reorganizes itself around
teams and self-managing work groups, some individuals get 'caught'
between eras. In the 'old era', an individual would be ready for promotion into a more senior position. In the 'new era', the more senior
position is replaced by a team and the team shares the rewards. This
significant cultural change can lead some to feel 'caught' and 'left out'
of the promotion stakes, especially if the organization also changes its
rewards and recognition strategy. Feeling 'caught' in this way can lead
to resentment.

These roots of resentment can act as triggers to contrapreneurial activity.

Contrapreneurship: the technical objections

The third basis to contrapreneurship activities relates to a systematic or technical assessment of TQM. Some of the common technical objections we encounter in the public sector include those listed below. We express them in the form of the arguments used by public sector employees we have encountered, usually at the middle and senior management levels:

- *Scepticism about the scope and work of teams: Teams are not needed for some of the tasks envisaged.* The view that teams are needed to do everything in TQM is promoted by some TQM consultants and is rejected by some managers. They suggest that: (1) teams are not always the most effective way of reaching decisions about change; (2) teams can extend the time taken to complete a task rather than speed it up; and (3) teams need training and development time, which is expensive. While accepting that teams can be useful in some circumstances, they reject the universality of teamwork and therefore the idea of self-management. They recommend retention of existing decision-making mechanisms for certain (usually critical and significant) work activities.
- *TQM requires me to give up some professional independence to the team.* Some medical consultants, professional architects, social workers and others can perceive that working in teams leads to the loss of personal autonomy. In fact, TQM works to improve and increase the opportunity to provide professional advice and assistance better based in data and collaboration.
- *We cannot start until everyone in the organization starts: We don't want to be left out on a limb.* In fact, not a single jurisdiction in Canada, the USA or Britain is working on TQM across all departments simultaneously and at the same pace, though some have co-ordinated strategies (see Chapter 7). Most initiatives are departmental and local rather than centralized and top-down.
- *Only senior managers can determine strategy: Management knows best.* Because of their role in the organization, managers can see and better assess the strategic value and tactical importance of tasks and work activities than can front-line workers. In the move towards empowerment, there may be a loss of strategic focus and an over-emphasis on processes which are secondary to the strategic thrusts of the department. Making explicit strategy and the basic assumptions on which it is based may be politically sensitive and not in the interest of the department.
- *TQM is too slow to produce results.* It is well established that TQM does not produce 'quick fixes' or immediate results. It takes time for teams to develop, for data to be collected and for improvements to take effect. It also takes time to standardize improvements across the organization and to secure departmental or organizational gains. For some of the problems which need to be tackled, TQM is not seen as an appropriate strategy.
- *TQM only works for management procedures (finance, payroll, HR*

functions, etc.) and has nothing to do with the core functions of our service (teaching in classrooms, treating patients, caring for the elderly and so on). As we have seen in the chapters on health, education, social services and government developments, TQM often begins in non-core functions and moves to core functions. For example, getting the right prescriptions to the right patients at the right time is a core health treatment task. Improving delivery of the curriculum by developing better learning contracts with students and pupils or offering service guarantees, as at Fox Valley Technical, leads to changes not just in auxiliary and support services but also in core functions.

- *The specific tools available through TQM training are not best suited to our needs.* The most common tools – the seven quality tools, statistical process control, process mapping and the House of Quality – may not meet the needs of the organization. Rather than see this as a starting point for the search for new tools and resources, this problem is seen to be an inhibitor and stumbling block.
- *Our problems are not amenable to TQM processes.* Some managers and others take the view that not all problems are amenable to a 'TQM approach' and that the distinctiveness of their services limits the applicability of TQM. We discussed this earlier (see Chapter 3), but this is seen as a technical objection by those who raise it.

Sometimes, individuals will use technical objections as a 'cover' for safely voicing resentment or resistance.

Effective contrapreneurs use the arguments outlined in all three sections above – resistance, resentment and technical – to prevent, slow or inhibit the development of TQM within the organization. They do not always do so obviously or directly; they will often use subtle methods to achieve these aims. Among these methods are: (1) agreeing to lead or support a team and then in reality not doing so; (2) systematically inhibiting the work of a team by either disrupting its dynamic or challenging the process; (3) being passive players in the process and active players *behind* the process – using informal communication (rumour, whispers, casual conversation) to achieve their objectives; and (4) going along with the work of a team until it comes to implementation and then raising a series of detailed objections which could better be dealt with earlier in the process.

These are just some of the tactics of contrapreneurs. No-one seeking to introduce TQM in the public sector should be surprised that these methods of resistance will occur. It is also important to recognize that not all of these resistance, resentment or technical objections will be overcome easily or quickly. What is important is that the champions of TQM work with those who really wish to see TQM be successful and that, in the light of some initial success, seek to work through the concerns of those who are less convinced but are likely to respond to reasoned argument based on sound achievements and success.

This description of contrapreneurship provides a basis for looking at some of the issues faced by those charged with the responsibility for launching and developing TQM in the public sector. We now turn our attention to other matters which affect the adoption of TQM in these organizations.

Trade union concerns and TQM

The role of trade unions in the development of TQM in the public sector is critical. Often, managers introduce TQM in a government department or a public sector agency without the full support of unions and their local shop-stewards. Using 'management rights' as the basis for introducing TQM is not a substitute for effective dialogue and joint approaches for what will be, after all, a significant cultural change for the public sector.

Public sector unions are concerned that TQM will result in one or more of the following:

- Job losses resulting from increased efficiency.
- Significant and substantive change in the structural arrangements of the organization which affect union–management relations.
- Even if job losses do not occur, the fear is that workers will be asked to undertake more work with a higher level of responsibility (because of empowerment) with no adjustments in pay.
- Significant changes in the rewards and recognition system which will reduce equity across departments as well as increase the number of equity issues within departments.

These concerns are not helped by the fact that, in many cases, the introduction of TQM is associated with or closely linked in time to downsizing government and public sector organizations, de-layering management and cost-cutting of programmes. Some unions see TQM as a part of a package which fundamentally challenges the basis of their bargaining position.

In some cases, unions jointly launch a TQM programme with management. For example, this was the case with Ontario Hydro (the largest power generation company in North America and a Crown Corporation). Sustaining this joint venture in the light of changing circumstances can prove very difficult. Nonetheless, joint work is preferable to opposition.

One key problem from the union point of view concerns the impact of empowerment and self-managing work teams on the role of shop-stewards or local organizers. As teams move into the involvement and ownership stages of empowerment (see Chapter 1), the role of managers and union officials in the determination of work roles and performance declines relative to the level of empowerment within the team. As the power of union officials declines at this level, so union objections to TQM arise. As they do, tension between the top-team of the union (who are often more open to TQM) and the front-line of union officials grows. So as to minimize this tension, some unions seek to look again at their stance on TQM and begin to make it more conditional.

Management and unions need to work together if TQM is to be successfully introduced in the public sector. This requires management to:

1. Systematically work to understand the concerns of the union about TQM and to see this as a necessary part of the work of launching TQM.
2. Encourage the union to work out their own position on TQM and to do so on the basis of the fullest possible information about the actual intentions of management.
3. Develop an understanding about the 'rules of engagement' – the conditions under which the union will work with management and management will work with the union on the development of TQM, paying particular attention to any 'no go' areas.
4. Draw a clear distinction between TQM development activities and collective bargaining.
5. Involve the union formally in any quality structure (e.g. quality council, etc.) created to manage quality initiatives.
6. Engage them in active learning about TQM.

At the same time, the union should:

1. Do all it can to learn about TQM and educate its members.
2. Be clear about the roles it wishes to play and does not wish to play in relation to TQM.
3. Engage all members in understanding TQM developments in the organization.
4. Develop a clear and unequivocal policy about TQM.
5. Focus union concerns on the collective bargaining consequences of TQM, especially in relation to job design, job security and the rewards and recognition strategy.

These are not easy issues for either side to deal with, but equally they cannot be ignored. Union support and cooperation in the launch and development of TQM could make the difference between success and failure.

We have examined the need for managers to look at inverting the traditional hierarchical pyramid within their organization. In relation to union–management relations, which have traditionally been based upon independence and negotiation, there is a need to look at other, more collaborative models of working. One model now being developed in some public sector organizations is that of *partnership*, whereby both parties to any agreement (union and management) enter into clear agreements and jointly sign-off the empowerment contracts for cross-functional teams and agree the framework for the development of intact or natural work teams. One model for the latter kind of framework is the joint agreements between management and unions on health and safety issues, which could be used as a template for TQM initiatives through partnership in all areas of an organization.

Problems in the design and launch of TQM initiatives

In a previous work (Murgatroyd and Morgan 1993), we documented some of the issues associated with the poor design and launch of TQM in education. Clemmer (1992) has done the same for the corporate sector. Surprisingly, there are few accounts of design and launch problems in the public sector. We therefore offer six key public sector design and implementation problems we have encountered, as a starting point for the further analysis of these problems.

Management commitment

Some managers in the public sector believe that stating a policy is the equivalent of enacting it. Others simply provide instructions to staff 'down the line' in the hope that doing so will produce results. The reality is that rhetoric is no substitute for behaviour. What employees look for is visible commitment from the leadership of their organization. They look for: (a) the use of quality tools at every level of decision-making within the organization; (b) vision-based and strategically focused decision-making; (c) effective rewards and recognition strategies which reinforce the quality initiatives of the department; and (d) effective and frequent communication within the department about strategy, performance and quality achievements. The absence of these behaviours suggests to employees that the managers are just paying lip-service to quality rather than dedicating themselves to continuous improvement and quality performance.

Further, as empowerment and self-management grows within the organization, managers need to accept significant role changes and a higher degree of risk. Public sector managers find these two challenges difficult to accept. For example, moving from a command and control management style to one which is based on guiding, mentoring, coaching and educating is a major transition. Pushing responsibility, accountability and risk further down the organization is also something that is difficult for public sector managers to undertake, given that responsibility to political masters is seen by politicians as hierarchical.

In almost every situation in which we have worked with public sector employees, the most common problem we have encountered is the feeling that management has launched TQM without a full understanding of its implications or without a realization that it involves a significant and substantial change in their own behaviour. Managers are often perceived at best to be ambivalent about TQM. As a quality co-ordinator in the UK Health sector put it: 'It is only when some of the present quality co-ordinators reach chief executive status that you will see the real breakthrough'.

The auditor problem

Public institutions are subject to both financial audits and, increasingly, value-for-money audits. Most audit procedures involves adding steps to processes so as to increase the control that can be exercised by either the politicians or the financial management system or both. A frequent complaint of employees working on project teams and quality improvement teams in the public sector is that their work and the potential for improvement is constrained by the actions of audit departments. The common complaint is that they 'add process steps without ever taking any away'. In one city government, they were seen as a part of the problem, rather than a part of the solution to quality problems within the city.

In fact, auditors are very insightful about the duplicity of process steps within the organization and the need for efficiency. As members, they can be a real asset to project teams. They have insights into the control of work process procedures and into the measurement of activity costs. They need to be involved in quality initiatives from the start. Further, they can be very valuable in persuading both senior management and political leaders that the revised work processes both save money while increasing customer satisfaction and overall performance.

Political support

It is seen as axiomatic, at least among public sector employees at all levels, that political support for TQM will last so long as nothing goes wrong. The minute risks are taken which do not pay off, politicians will abandon their commitments to TQM and look to control and audit processes to minimize risk in the future.

Further, it is felt that TQM will only be supported if it results in 'favourable news' for the politician. As one cynic expressed: 'TQM is good if it helps in the bid for re-election.' The problem is that most TQM outcomes will not be achieved within a single term of a mayor, alderman, minister or senior government official. The short-term focus of most government initiatives is a function of their period in office. Since many TQM initiatives will take two to three years to proceed from the planning stage to action, some politicians do not support TQM initiatives, seeing them as 'expensive and unproductive'.

As Osborne and Gaebler (1992) suggest, it is part of the reality of government that such political forces are at work. However, as one seven-year-old put it to one of the authors, it is increasingly the case that 'it doesn't matter who you vote for, the government always gets in'. The problems faced by all levels of government in the advanced democracies are such that short-term solutions will not work; what is needed is a commitment to re-invent government. When such a commitment is made, in terms of managing the deficits, reducing public expenditure, and increasing the perceived value of public services, there are not, however, many options between which governments can choose. By educating politicians about TQM and gaining their understanding, TQM can become part of a medium- to long-term strategy.

In our interviews with politicians, they frequently complain that TQM has been 'oversold' to them as a panacea for the problems of government. They have been sold TQM 'as a solution', though they are not fully clear just what problem TQM seeks to address. As one said: 'TQM sounds like the answer, now tell me what the question is!' Clearly, it is not a panacea. There are other strategic steps which need to be taken by governments in their attempt to cope with the competing demands and declining resources which they face; for example, the development of a vision, some sense of overall strategic intent, departmental strategy commitment, effective communication of issues to the people and an engagement of communities in the problems which face them. Nonetheless, politicians who are encouraged to understand TQM in a systematic way find it invaluable as one key component of their strategic thinking about what government can become (Sensenbrenner 1991).

Structures for action

Many attempts to create TQM initiatives in the public sector have resulted in the creation of new quality structures. These structures are intended to: (a) focus the energies of the organization on strategically important initiatives which are intended to have a major impact on the operation of the organization; (b) maintain the involvement of key players in the organization at the policy and deployment levels while ensuring that most of the teamwork is undertaken by those best able to understand core work processes; and (c) provide for a review and evaluation process within the organization. We describe a pattern of quality structures in Chapter 7.

In some cases, these structures are placed on top of existing structures and are seen to duplicate the efforts of extant organizational mechanisms. In other cases, these structures can become the 'new bureaucracy' of the organization and create new layers of decision-making and new forms of reporting. Finally, we have noted in some cases that the new structure has been poorly communicated throughout the organization, leading to confusion and uncertainty about who reports what to whom and when they should do so. Indeed, in one city organization, line managers and front-line staff were largely unaware of the developments in the field of service quality improvement.

These 'launch' problems can only be overcome by systematic pre-launch planning and effective analysis of whether or not the organization does need new structures to manage quality or whether it can adapt existing mechanisms to meet the focusing, co-ordination and evaluation needs of management with respect to quality. A failure to undertake this planning and assessment could lead to quality costs increasing rather than declining and to managers and others unnecessarily creating new processes rather than eliminating duplication and waste.

One particular problem encountered in one city was that the steering group was comprised of precisely those managers who were seen to have created 'the problems' in the first place. When faced with the results of the work of the project teams, they were reluctant to accept them on the grounds that they implied criticism of their past efforts. A linked problem here was the reluctance of the steering group to 'sign-off' the empowerment contracts (simply called 'mission statements' in this case), since they involved what one called 'over-empowerment'. This same steering group member wanted to sit in on every meeting of the project team to make sure that they 'kept on track'. The structures were used as leverage points to control and disempower project teams, and this may well be a danger.

'Turf wars'

A problem in many organizations, not just in the public sector, is the battle between one section and another within an organization for resources, power and influence. For example, there is an historical tension in the health professions between doctors and nursing staff over responsibilities, roles and relationships with respect to patient care. In most government departments, there is a tension between managers and auditors, between managers and purchasing departments, and between staff and human resource representatives. Everybody is 'just doing my job', but in doing so seeks to protect and retain 'territory' against erosion, interference and change. Karl Albrecht (1990: 63–4), a leading American writer on quality issues, defines 'turfism' as 'a jealous preoccupation with one's assigned area of responsibility, to the exclusion of common sense and compromise in the name of getting results'. This definition captures the essence of turfism as the basis for turf wars.

These 'wars' erupt both within departments and between them. For example, in one government with which we have worked, there is a constant battle between the purchasing agents working for 'central purchasing' and the managers of line departments. The latter argue, correctly, that they are able to find products and services which meet their needs at a lower cost with shorter delivery times and the same maintenance and service contracts than those recommended by purchasing, but are unable to avail themselves of these 'deals' because purchasing 'will not' approve them. The delays that such arguments create usually mean that opportunities are lost, costs are increased and lead time between request and delivery for purchased goods is inordinately long.

Empowerment relates not just to individuals, but also to units. So as to achieve effective service delivery and cost reduction, barriers between departments and within them need to be blurred and often removed. This does not mean that there is no need for separate functional units for purchasing, human resourcing and other cross-departmental activities, only that the way in which these functional requirements are met should be a matter for redesign and rethinking.

Outsourcing (the placing of work formerly done by an in-house department outside the organization to gain the competitive advantages of the marketplace) and *optionality* (giving departments the option of using in-house services or the services of a private sector company for equivalent work) will become more commonplace in government and the public sector, so that demands for increasing flexibility and creativity in meeting functional needs will become more urgent still. Turf protection is a real barrier to effective performance. In many organizations, including some of those in the public sector, the 'solution' to this problem has been significant restructuring associated with devolution of responsibility and optionality for service. This 'package' of measures has led some 'service departments' to redefine their functions in terms of customer needs and to focus on performance and outcomes more than protocol and procedure.

Milakovich (1990b) draws attention to the growth of specialization within the public sector as a potential barrier to the effective implementation of TQM. His argument is that the systematic hiring of specialists has lead to 'overspecialization, fragmentation, and compartmentalization', which makes it difficult to 'promote teamwork, manage across functions, and break down barriers to co-operation'. Hiring more specialized staff to undertake narrow functions may well constitute a further barrier to the effective implementation of TQM by establishing 'specialist turf' reinforced by professional qualifications. Hiring practices may also be worthy of careful rethinking.

Measurement in general and benchmarking in particular

Many TQM initiatives ultimately depend on the quality of information and data analysis which teams complete. The information base becomes critical in 'fact-based decision-making'. Many organizations, though inundated with data, find that they do not have the measures in place to take the decisions they really need to take and find it difficult to collect these data.

Further, key data needs in relation to cycle time, rework and error rates, customer satisfaction, labour content of work, etc., are generally estimated rather than calculated and generally based on managerial assumptions rather than a systematic examination of work actually performed. For example, in Ontario Hydro, it had been claimed for many years that the minimum cost of processing an expense claim (in terms of time and resources) was in excess of $50.00, based on a set of assumptions made by management. When a service quality improvement team looked at the actual process and costed it, the actual cost was a little over $12. A great many management decisions were to be made based on the $50 figure which were not appropriate when the actual costs of $12 per item were examined. Such examples are commonplace throughout the organizations with which we have worked. In the rush for certainty, uncertainty and unreliability of data become normative. This is not a healthy development. When TQM specialists call for decisions based on data, they do so with some assumptions about the validity, integrity and reliability of these data.

This is not a problem encountered just in the public sector, but it is made more complex in the public sector by the very size of some organizations. For example, the National Health Service in the UK is Europe's largest single employer. The Government of Alberta employs some 35 000 persons, as also does Ontario Hydro (a Crown Corporation). Collecting meaningful data which are representative of the work done for a particular process, group of processes or functions within the organization is therefore a complex and demanding task which takes time. In the pressure to get 'quick results', there is a tendency to cut data collection corners. This leads to what statisticians are fond of calling 'dirty data' and 'dirty data' lead to 'muddy solutions'.

This becomes compounded when the strategy for quality includes benchmarking – the comparison of one set of performance measures from one organization with parallel measures from another organization. Often, the data being compared are not in fact equivalent. Cycle time for 'order processing' may be defined differently between two organizations and the difference could add or reduce the time taken to complete the order cycle. Additionally, labour content definitions may differ not because the process differs, but because union agreements differ or the way in which labour content is priced and measured differ.

In our earlier discussion of performance indicators (see Chapter 6), we noted that indicators were problematic for a variety of reasons. Johnes and Taylor (1990), in looking at performance indicators used in the comparison of the 'outputs' of higher education institutions in the UK, note that a multiple regression model of these indicators, which takes account of the mix of programmes offered by the institution, its historic commitment to research, non-completion rates, subsequent careers of graduates and some other measures, indicates the very high level of sensitivity of these 'benchmarking' data to the inclusion of certain variables, thus begging the question: What kind of bench are we actually drawing our marks on? How the bench is being constructed (what is included in and what is not included in the regression model) and how it is being marked (just what is being determined by the measure and its subsequent use) will determine the kinds of data that result.

The bottom line here is simple: many of the outcomes of TQM initiatives in the public sector will depend on the quality of the data collected and the subsequent analysis of these data by quality improvement teams. They need to be mindful that data need interrogating and cannot be accepted at face value and that the way in which the data were obtained is often as important as the actual measures themselves. Poor data will lead to poor decisions.

The following six launch and implementation problems are encountered frequently in the public sector. The extent to which they create barriers to TQM is a function of the veracity of the TQM strategy being pursued within the organization.

Defining customers in the public sector

One particular problem that is encountered in the public sector, in a way that is different from the private sector, concerns the definition of the customer. To make clear the nature of this problem, we give five examples from our direct experience:

- A deputy minister of health in a provincial government in eastern Canada told us that his ultimate customer was 'his minister . . . if she is not satisfied, then all other customers are secondary'.
- A senior educational policy maker in Britain suggested that his customers were 'children yet unborn'.
- Staff at a health trust in the UK defined customers as 'fund-holding general practitioners, not patients', since it was these GPs who determined where patients would and would not go for treatment and who would then allocate appropriate resources and funds.
- A city manager in a large US city said that his three key customers were: (a) the mayor and the alderman of the city; (b) the state minister for municipal affairs; and (c) the auditor-general. If these three were happy, he could 'handle the press and, through them, the public'.
- A dean of faculty at a major university in Europe said, 'let us imagine for just one moment that students are "customers" – *a fact that I cannot personally accept* – then the implication is that we should really strive hard to meet their needs *as they understand them*, despite the fact that 'we know best' (her emphasis).

These sets of statements suggest that the focus on the customer can, however, be confused or too restricted in the public sector, though realistic in sociopolitical terms. In each case, what is being said is that income and continuance are not necessarily dependent on key stakeholder needs being met.

Just as in the private sector, public sector managers adopting the TQM perspective are recognizing that there are a variety of stakeholder needs that need to be met and these needs represent different focal points for evaluation and assessment of the performance of the organization. For example, the primary stakeholders for a private sector organization are the employees (sometimes represented by unions), the management, the board, auditors, shareholders and customers. In the public sector, the list is in fact similar but more elaborate – employees, management, politicians (equivalent to the board), regulatory authorities (auditors), electors (customers). While the list looks similar, given our connotations, what is different is the 'leverage' that can be exercised by these different constituencies of stakeholders. In the public sector, the city manager's analysis given above is probably right – if he can please his mayor and alderman and keep the press happy, then the service will survive. In the private sector, if customers simply stop buying, all other players are secondary.

In fact, the traditional monopoly position of the public sector has established the primacy of hierarchical priority over that of the ultimate customer – the citizen seeking support and service from the public agency. As strategies for ending monopoly and creating community- and service-oriented government emerge, so the definition of the 'customer' is changing and becoming more focused on end-users. Indeed, the whole notion of entrepreneurial government, as championed in a number of US states (see Osborne and Gaebler 1992: xix–xxii), is based on the idea of 'bringing the customer [end-user] back into the equation in the development of services and policies in the public domain'. Though this is recognised as difficult to do across the 83,000 different government agencies in the USA, at least it is being attempted.

Time

In this description and interpretation of the barriers and problems associated with the introduction of TQM into the public sector, a number of references have been made to the problems associated with both time and timing. It is worth drawing special attention to these problems, since they are often presented as key issues by those who become engaged in quality improvement work. Three problems are highlighted in the public sector, though they are not unique to it:

1. While TQM is seen as a valuable component of strategy, when is the best time to launch the work?
2. Where will we get the time to complete the work of teams on top of our other work?
3. The work of teams takes a long time, relative to our 'old ways' of doing things.

A feature of the public sector which does get in the way of responding to these three issues is the fact that a great deal of activity in the public sector is driven by annual budget cycles and line-by-line budgeting. Both of these significantly affect the way in which time is understood as measured within a particular cycle. This also affects the annual objective setting which some public agencies still engage in as a part of their management-by-objectives methods. Until these annual cycles for resourcing and performance management are changed, then time will be a barrier to the effective implementation of TQM.

The core, adaptive and problematic aspects of TQM

A key reason for describing these barriers and problems in the adoption of TQM in the public sector was to explore the question: What do these problems suggest to us about the usefulness and adaptability of TQM concepts and practices to the public sector? In Chapter 3, we introduced the idea that it is likely that there are certain aspects of TQM that should be regarded as core if TQM is to be understood as a coherent managerial strategy and process, but that there are also some aspects of TQM which need to be adapted to the context of their implementation. Equally, some aspects of TQM are problematic: they are unlikely to be of full value in the public sector or very difficult to implement; they may, in fact, be impossible to translate from their original starting points in manufacturing.

In conclusion, we now attempt to put flesh on this skeleton and to identify which components fit where in this scheme. Clearly, the resulting analysis, though informed by several years of experience and work in the public sector and a thorough-going analysis of the literature, represents a preliminary step in understanding the potential of TQM for the public sector. We present it as a basis for discussion and debate.

Core constructs and practices for the public sector

The following appear to us to be core components of TQM. Without these, while some quality efforts may be pursued, TQM cannot be seen to be being practised:

1. *Vision and strategy*: TQM is not a management strategy that can stand independently of the organization's vision and strategy. Even in the public sector, TQM is a function of the kind of vision and strategy being pursued by a public sector organization.
2. *Policy deployment*: the systematic deployment of policy down the organization, as demonstrated in our case example of the Government of Alberta's Federal and Intergovernmental Affairs Department, ensures that vision and strategy are translated into outcome-focused plans for all staff.
3. *Measurable goals*: for TQM and empowerment to be effective, individuals and teams need to have a sense of the goals they are trying to achieve and an agreed way of measuring whether or not these goals are being achieved. In the absence of clear, measurable goals, quality efforts may become disorganized and overly diffuse. What these goals are will need to be defined very carefully. The following appear to be core bases to the definition of these goals: customer satisfaction, reduced cycle time, reductions in labour content, reductions in rework and error rates, and on-time performance.
4. *Quality structure and support*: when practising TQM in most organizations, including the public sector, quality efforts need to be managed and co-ordinated. Just how this is done will vary from organization to organization. In Chapter 7, some suggestions are made for how this is typically done in the public sector, but there are many variants on this model. What is core is the need for some kind of co-ordination and management structures to the quality efforts.
5. *Empowered work teams*: in the framework of empowerment offered in this text, engaging front-line staff in the redesign of their own work

and enabling them to make continuous quality improvements are core requirements of TQM. How far the principle of self-management and empowerment is extended will vary from organization to organization. But unless teamwork is practised in the context of some degree of empowerment, TQM is not taking place.

6. *Data-based decision-making*: it is a core feature of TQM that improvement efforts are based on some systematic attempt to understand a process or a customer need and that these systematic efforts make use of data. This is core: what may vary is the tools most frequently used to ensure that data are being collected and interpreted. We may say here that Deming's P-D-C-A cycle appears common to most total quality management efforts.

7. *Managerial commitment and communication*: in any accounts of the failure of TQM, the lack of management commitment or the inability of management to communicate their commitment directly and in a meaningful way to all employees within a unit is regarded as a key cause of the failure. It follows, then, that a core feature of TQM is the ability of management to communicate effectively, by words and actions, their commitment to TQM and to demonstrate that their decisions are data-driven.

8. *Rewards and recognition system alignment*: at several points in the accounts of barriers and problems in this chapter, reference has been made to the need to realign the performance management system of the organization around the work of teams and the strategic goals of the organization. A failure to do this can lead to the failure of TQM to change the behaviour of the organization, even though the rhetoric may change. Just what these changes should be is a matter for discussion, but the need to align the performance management system with the goals and practices of TQM is core.

9. *Meeting the needs of primary stakeholders*: the need to understand the needs of primary customers and suppliers is critical. To do this requires a careful understanding of stakeholder value propositions and the need to address the key question: Who are our primary stakeholders and who do we regard as secondary?

10. *Training*: quality teams and the improvement process require an investment in the training of people in imagineering skills, problem identification and solving skills, teamwork and related skills. Training investments are core requirements of TQM.

Adaptive features of TQM for the public sector

These are the features of TQM that relate to most organizational settings *once* they have been adjusted to take account of the context. That is, they require modification to make them applicable to the organization or industry being examined. In the descriptions which follow, we will indicate the nature of the adaptation needed to make the construct, skill or practice 'fit' the public sector.

1. *Zero defects*: there are several possible interpretations of this construct. Here we use Crosby's (see Chapter 2) notion that a defect is a failure to meet a specification. For the public sector, as we noted in Chapter 3, the need is for services to be delivered in appropriately differentiated ways to meet the needs of individuals or groups of customers. What is 'appropriate' is defined either by statute or by guidelines defined by professionals and customers. A defect would occur if a service could have been provided within the statutes and guidelines, but was not because of some failure. To give an example from education, imagine that each individual student or pupil has a learning contract with their teachers for their programme of study. A defect would be that the programme could not be completed in the time allocated or that the student was not able, because of the demands of the programme, to complete it. In this case, it is not the student or the teacher who is 'defective', but the programme they designed together. This is a very particular meaning of the term 'zero defect'. In some public service contexts, however, the term can be applied in just the same way as it originated in manufacturing. For example, in medicine and defence, public works, payroll, taxation and other departments, there are specific outcomes (the right baby assigned to the right mother every time; the right target selected and fired at every time; the appropriate tax deducted from the right person or company; and so on) which are precisely measurable on a standardized basis across different locations, and which should be defect-free.

2. *Customer satisfaction*: because defining who the customer is and what their needs are can be difficult in some organizations, since there are competing customer or stakeholder interests, the very construct of 'customer satisfaction' needs to be reviewed and adapted on an organization-by-organization basis. In most public services, the end-user is one key customer, but there are others. Meeting the needs of primary stakeholders is core, but determining who these primary stakeholders are is a matter for adaptation.

3. *Self-managing work teams*: we outlined earlier in this text a three-stage model of empowerment for the development and creation of self-managing work teams. We have also suggested that empowered work teams are a core component of TQM. What needs to be adapted is the extent of empowerment. This will vary from one organization to another and from one department to another.

4. *Just-in-Time inventory management (JIT)*: many believe that JIT refers only to the management of warehouse and distribution functions within a manufacturing environment. In fact, the idea relates to all work in progress (see Kobayashi 1990) and to the elimination of non-value-adding activity. In illustrating the concept of 'value-added' in Chapter

1, we gave public sector examples of where value-added can be enhanced. Given the wider definition of Kobayashi, we see the status of
JIT as adaptive for the public sector.

5. *Partnering with suppliers*: the concept of 'partnering' for quality
between a supplier and a user so as to improve service to customers has
been developing over the past decade. Essentially, partnering involves
the closer integration of supplier–user interfaces and the development
of arrangements for delivering services which are 'seamless' from the
customer's viewpoint. The aim is to eliminate the gaps between a supplier and user which have an impact on the customer's experience. For
example, in a grocery store, because of the seamless data systems created
by the store and suppliers like Proctor and Gamble, customers should
not experience product shortages – just-in-time delivery will ensure
that.

Problematic features of TQM

When we look at TQM, there are some features which are problematic
when applied to the public sector. It should be noted that we are not
suggesting that these practices and constructs have no utility in the public
sector, only that they are problematic in the way defined in Chapter 3. We
include the following among our list of problematic features:

1. *Benchmarking*: this is problematic for two reasons. First, Ernst &
Young's (1992) study of 'best practices' suggests that benchmarking is
counterproductive for low- and medium-performing organizations: the
practice actually has a deleterious effect on organizational performance,
especially in low-performing organizations. For this reason alone, we
include benchmarking on our list of problems. Second, some of the
functions undertaken by public sector agencies are functions of unique
legislation which may make comparison with others difficult, though
not impossible.

2. *Zero defections*: a key idea from the service sector implementations of
TQM is that of 'zero defections', not losing a customer. For example,
credit card companies recognize that the value of a customer increases
significantly over time; by reducing the rate of defection, they can increase their profitability. In the public sector, this construct may need
adapting. Welfare workers, for example, seek to encourage their clients
to defect from their 'register' as soon as possible, because they have
found work, entered training or found other means of support. Clinical
psychologists working in mental health seek to 'cure' their clients in the
most effective and efficient way. Zero defections, therefore, needs to be
re-cast in terms of completing a course of treatment, having needs met
to a certain level, and so on. The re-casting of this construct is problematic for some public sector organizations.

3. *Daily management reporting*: GOAL/QPC, probably the leading TQM

organization in the English-speaking world, strongly supports the notion that progress towards the achievement of goals should be examined and measured and reported on a daily basis. The rationale for this is simple: if goals are measurable and data collection systems are efficient, then it should be possible to show employees how successful the organization has been in meeting its goals on a very regular basis, preferably daily. Doing so will help focus the energies of employees on continuous improvement and will also motivate staff to give constant attention to outcome-focused activity and reduce non-value-adding activity. However, many processes in public sector provisions have extended time-scales, and their outcomes take time to achieve a measurable state. Daily management reporting, therefore, appears to need a great deal of adaptation and to be very problematic in some kinds of organizations.

This analysis is intended to trigger debate within public sector organizations about how they can apply core constructs and practices, adapt others and solve any problematic elements. For some public sector organizations – defence, public works, clinical medicine – some of the adaptations and problematic features are easier to deal with than in other departments, like foreign affairs, education, etc. Each 'top team' within a public sector organization needs to examine each of the features of TQM described here and determine for themselves what place they have and what form they will take in their TQM implementation plan.

Conclusion

We have attempted in this chapter to outline some of the barriers to TQM implementation in the public sector and analyse the implications of these barriers for our understanding of TQM as a set of ideas and practice forms. The chapter is intended to be a realistic assessment of the issues faced by those in the public sector who are considering, or who have already embarked on, a TQM journey. We do not intend to suggest that the process of introducing TQM into public sector organizations is necessarily fraught with difficulties, nor that it is impossible. Our intention is to demonstrate that significant cultural change, which TQM represents, requires significant strategic analysis and planning *before* implementation for it to be successful.

If TQM is to be implemented on a wide scale within a particular government, municipality or agency, what are the consequences? As we write, it is early days for TQM in the public sector, and so far the consequences are not 'revolutionary', but they are important. They are leading public sector organizations to ask serious questions about their roles, relationships and performance, and seeking to create a new framework for achieving the outcomes which their customers want. In addition, workers within the public sector at all levels feel and are more engaged in the process of continuous improvement. Some achievements are significant, and we have documented some of these in the text.

This book has explored TQM in the public sector across several countries, and we see ten key principles underlying all that we have presented. They are that TQM for the public sector needs to be:

1. *Customer-driven*: the focus is on providing outstanding service at an appropriate cost to all primary customers.
2. *Strategically focused on outcomes and processes*: TQM is a focused practice that seeks to turn strategic intent into direct, practical achievements.
3. *Driven by goals and values, not regulations*: staff working in the public sector are able to make decisions on the basis of clear processes which are value-driven rather than regulatory and disabling.
4. *Empowering for communities, workers and customers*: the aim is to empower people to achieve that which they need and to achieve it by working cooperatively and creatively.
5. *Effective and efficient*: TQM is a set of management practices which aim to improve performance and increase customer satisfaction while lowering costs.
6. *Evaluated as successful by customers in comparison with comparative providers of services*: when customers compare the performance of a public service with that of others or with private sector provision, they will recognize value for money and quality performance in what they see.
7. *Valued by staff and customers alike*: there will be a respect for process and service quality among everybody associated with the service.
8. *Enterprising, not simply spending-oriented*: TQM encourages the public sector to both reduce costs and to gain income from being more enterprising about the potential resale of processes, technology, ideas, resources, etc. Teams should be encouraged to be entrepreneurial, not just spending-oriented.
9. *Proactive rather than reactive*: TQM encourages teams and management to anticipate and plan before they act – it seeks to encourage insightful forecasting, planning and the management of development.
10. *Benchmarked against the best in the world*: the aim of every public sector organization should be to lead the world in the provision of its core services in terms of customer satisfaction, efficiency and appropriate cost. Careful benchmarking will enable them to show the extent to which they can deliver to this promise.

If TQM in the public sector focuses on delivering to these ten principles, then it can be a key component of the process of reinventing government. If TQM simply focuses on cost reduction, it will not deliver the new kind of customer service citizens now appear to want from government. The promise of TQM exists and its performance can be demonstrated, what is needed is the determination to implement TQM as part of a strategy to enhance the commitment of public agencies to the service of the people.

Appendix

Deming's 14 points

1. *Create constancy of purpose* to improve product and service.
2. *Adopt new philosophy* for new economic age by management learning responsibilities and taking leadership for change.
3. *Cease dependence on inspection* to achieve quality; eliminate the need for mass inspection by building quality into the product.
4. *End awarding business on price,* instead minimize total cost and move towards single suppliers for items.
5. *Improve constantly and forever the system of production and service* to improve quality and productivity and to decrease costs.
6. *Institute training on the job.*
7. *Institute leadership*; supervision should be to help to do a better job; overhaul supervision of management and production workers.
8. *Drive out fear* so that all may work effectively for the organization.
9. *Break down barriers between departments*; research, design, sales and production must work together to foresee problems in production and use.
10. *Eliminate slogans, exhortations, and numerical targets* for the workforce, such as zero defects or new productivity levels. Such exhortations are diversory as the bulk of the problems belong to the system and are beyond the power of the workforce.
11. *Eliminate quotas or work standards, and management by objectives or numerical goals*; substitute leadership.

12. *Remove barriers that rob people of their right to pride of workmanship*; hourly workers, management and engineering; eliminate annual or merit ratings and management by objective.
13. *Institute a vigorous education and self improvement programme.*
14. *Put everyone in the company to work to accomplish the transformation.*

From Deming, W.E. (1988) *Out of Crisis*. Cambridge: Cambridge University Press.

Juran's 'quality planning road map'

1. Identify who are the customers.
2. Determine the needs of those customers.
3. Translate the needs into our language.
4. Develop a product which can respond to those needs.
5. Optimise the product features so as to meet our needs as well as customer needs.
6. Develop a process which is able to produce the product.
7. Optimise the process.
8. Prove that the process can produce the product under operating conditions.
9. Transfer the process to Operations.

From Juran, J.M. (1988) *Juran on Planning For Quality*. New York: Free Press.

Fiegenbaum's 10 benchmarks for total quality success

1. Quality is a companywide process.
2. Quality is what the customer says it is.
3. Quality and cost are a sum not a difference.
4. Quality requires both individual and team zealotry.
5. Quality is a way of managing.
6. Quality and innovation are mutually dependant.
7. Quality is an ethic.
8. Quality requires continuous improvement.
9. Quality is the most cost-effective, least capital-intensive route to productivity.
10. Quality is implemented with a total system connected with customers and suppliers.

From Fiegenbaum, A.V. (1983) *Total Quality Control*. New York: McGraw-Hill.

Crosby's 14 steps to quality improvement

1. Make it clear that *management is committed to quality*.
2. Form *quality improvement teams* with senior representatives from each department.

3. *Measure* processes to determine where current and potential quality problems lie.
4. Evaluate the *cost of quality* and explain its use as a management tool.
5. Raise the *quality awareness* and personal concern of all employees.
6. *Take actions to correct problems* identified through previous steps.
7. Establish *progress monitoring* for the improvement process.
8. *Train supervisors* to actively carry out their part of the quality improvement programme.
9. Hold a *Zero Defects Day* to let everyone realise that there has been a change and to reaffirm management commitment.
10. Encourage individuals to establish *improvement goals* for themselves and their groups.
11. Encourage individuals to communicate to management the *obstacles* they face in attaining their improvement goals.
12. *Recognise* and appreciate those who participate.
13. Establish *quality councils* to communicate on a regular basis.
14. *Do it all over again* to emphasise that the quality improvement programme never ends.

From Crosby, P.B. (1979) *Quality is Free*. New York: McGraw-Hill.

Peters' 12 attributes of a quality revolution

1. *Management obsession with quality* – this obsession to find expression in practical action to back up the emotional commitment.
2. *Passionate systems* – failure will occur if there is a system without passion or vice-versa and an ideology is important, though not one necessarily based on a particular guru.
3. *Measurement of quality* – this should be a feature from the start, enacted by everybody, and the results of it widely displayed.
4. *Quality is rewarded* – recognising quality achievement with tangible rewards provides the incentive to bring about breakthroughs in attitude.
5. *Everyone is trained for quality* – extensive training should apply to all in the company, and this should encompass instruction in cause and effect analysis, statistical process control, and group interaction.
6. *Multi-function teams* – teams which span the traditional organisational structures should be introduced: quality circles, or to be more recommended, cross functional teams such as Error Cause Removal or Corrective Action teams.
7. *Small is beautiful* – there is significance in every change and no such thing as a small improvement.
8. *Create endless 'Hawthorne' effects* – new events are the antidote to the doldrums or flagging interest in quality.
9. *Parallel organisational structure devoted to quality improvement* – this describes the creation of shadow quality teams and emphasises that it is a route through which hourly paid workers can progress.

10. *Everyone is involved* – the quality process is comprehensive embracing suppliers, distributors and customers.
11. *When quality goes up, costs go down* – quality improvement is the primary source of cost reduction. The elementary force at work is simplification – of design, process or procedures.
12. *Quality improvement is a never ending journey* – all quality is relative, it does not stand still.

From Peters, T. (1989) *Thriving on Chaos*. London: Macmillan.

References

Albrecht, K. (1990) *Service Within*. Homewood, IL: Dow-Jones, Irwin.

Arikan, V. (1991) Total quality management: Applications to nursing service. *Journal of Nursing Administration*, Vol. 21, No. 6, June.

Baron, G. (1975) Some aspects of the 'Headmaster Tradition'. In Houghton, V., McHugh, R. and Morgan, C. (eds), *Management in Education: The Management of Organisations and Individuals*. London: Ward Lock Educational.

Bendell, T. (1991) The quality gurus. In *Managing into the '90s*. Department of Trade and Industry booklet. London: HMSO.

Berry, L.L. and Parasuraman, A. (1991) *Marketing Services*. New York: Free Press.

Bull, N. (1992) *Quality For Those Who Care*. Bedford: IFS Publications.

Burwick, D.M. (1989) Continuous improvements as an ideal in health care. *New England Journal of Medicine*, Vol. 320, No. 1, pp. 53–6.

Cammel, J. (1992) *Just In Time*. Department of Trade and Industry booklet. London: HMSO.

Camp, R.C. (1989) Benchmarking – The Search for Industry Best Practices that Lead to Superior Performance. Milwaukee, WI: Quality Press.

Carr, D. and Littleman, I. (1989) *Excellence in Government*. Washington, DC: Coopers and Lybrand.

Carter, N. (1989) Performance indicators – back seat driving or 'hands off' control? *Policy and Politics*, Vol. 17, No. 2, pp. 131–8.

Clemmer, J. (1992) *Firing On all Cylinders*, 2nd edn. Toronto: Macmillan.

Collins, J.C. and Porras, J.T. (1991) Organisational vision and visioning organisations. *California Management Review*, Fall, pp. 30–52.

Contino, R. (1985) *Waging Revolution in the Public Sector: Operational Improvements Through Labour/Management Co-operation* (mimeo). Available from the author at Surface Transit, New York City Transit Authority.

Crosby, P. (1979) *Quality is Free*. New York: McGraw-Hill.

Donabedian, A. (1980) *Explorations in Quality Assessment and Monitoring, Vol. 1: The Definition of Quality and Approaches to its Assessment*. Ann Arbor, Mich.: Health Administration Press.

Drucker, P. (1980) The deadly sins in public administration. *Public Administration Review*, Vol. 40, No. 2, pp. 103–106.

Drucker, P. (1988) *Why Service Institutions Do Not Perform*, Oxford: Heinemann.

Drummond, H. (1992) *The Quality Movement: What Total Quality Management is Really All About*. London: Kogan Page.

Edick, T.O. (1992) *Getting Top Management on Side*. Paper presented to the Conference on Total Quality Management in the Public Sector, Ottawa, Canada (mimeo).

Evans, J.R. and Lindsay, W.M. (1992) *The Management and Control of Quality*. Minneapolis: West Publishing.

Ernst & Young and American Quality Foundation (1992) *Best Practices Report: An Analysis of Management Practices that Impact Performance*. Ernst & Young, 1600 Huntingdon Building, Cleveland, Ohio 44115, USA.

Evers, M. (1982) Professional practice and patient care. *Aging and Society*, Vol. 2, pp. 57–75.

Ezell, M. and Patti, R.J. (1990) State human service agencies: Structure and organization. *Social Service Review*, Vol. 64, No. 1, pp. 22–45.

Ferlie, E., Fitzgerald, L. and Ashburner, L. (1992) *Boards and the New Health Authorities: The Challenge of Purchasing*. Centre For Corporate Strategy, Warwick Business School. Paper delivered to the British Academy of Management Conference, Bradford, September.

Fricke, J.G. (1992) Quality assurance, program evaluation, and auditing: Different approaches to effective program management. *Canadian Public Administration*, Vol. 34, No. 3, pp. 435–52.

Fricke, J.G. (1993) From an interview with John Fricke conducted by Stephen Murgatroyd.

Gaster, L. (1991) Quality and decentralisation: Are they connected? *Policy and Politics*, Vol. 19, No. 4, pp. 257–68.

Gillem, T.R. (1988) Deming's 14 points and hospital quality: Responding to the consumer's demand for best value health care. *Journal of Nursing Quality Assurance*, Vol. 2, No. 3, pp. 70–77.

Grayson, M.A. (1992) Benchmark TQM survey tracks new management era in administration. *Hospitals*, Vol. 66, No. 11, pp. 26–7.

Hambleton, R. (1988) Consumerism, decentralization and local democracy. *Public Administration*, Vol. 66, pp. 125–47.

Handy, C. (1989) *The Age of Unreason*. London: Business Books/Arrow.

Haywood-Farmer, J. (1987) A conceptual model of service quality. *International Journal of Operations and Production Management*, Vol. 8, No. 6, pp. 19–29.

Heverly, M.A. (1991) *Total Quality Management: Institutional Research Applications*. Delaware Community College, PA. Paper presented at the 14th Annual Conference of The Eastern Evaluation Research Society, Princeton, NJ, May.

Higgins, R.C, Jenkins, D.L. and Lewis R.P. (1991) Total quality management in the classroom: Listen to your customers, *Engineering Education*, Jan./Feb., pp. 12–14.

Hill, F.M. and Taylor, W.A. (1991) Total quality management in higher education. *International Journal of Educational Management*, Vol. 5, No. 5, pp. 4–9.

Hill, S. (1991) Why quality circles failed but total quality might succeed. *British Journal of Industrial Relations*, Vol. 29, pp. 541–68.

Hofstede, G., Neuijen, B., Ohavy, D.D. and Sanders, G. (1990) Measuring organisational cultures: A qualitative and quantitative study across twenty cases. *Administrative Science Quarterly*, Vol. 35, pp. 286–316.

Hoyes, L. (1990) *Promoting an Ordinary Life: A Checklist for Assessing Residential Care for People with Learning Disabilities*. Bristol: School of Advanced Urban Studies, University of Bristol.

Hudson, W. (1991) Computer assisted social services. *Research on Social Work Practice*, Vol. 1, No. 3, pp. 319–21.

Hutchins, D. (1992) *Achieve Total Quality*. Cambridge: Director Books.

Illich, I. (1975) *Medical Nemesis: The Expropriation of Health*. London: Calder/Boyars.

Imai, M. (1989) *Kaizen: The Key to Japan's Competitive Success*. New York: McGraw-Hill.

Johnes, J. and Taylor, J. (1990) *Performance Indicators in Higher Education*. Buckingham: Open University Press/Society for Research in Higher Education.

Johnston, C. and Farquahar, C.R. (1992) *Empowered People Satisfy Customers: Strategies for Leaders*. Lessons from the Canada Award for Business Excellence Winners. Ottawa: Conference Board of Canada.

Katan, J. and Prager, E. (1986) Consumer and worker participation in agency-level decision making: Some considerations and their linkages. *Administration in Social Work*, Vol. 10, No. 1, pp. 79–88.

Kleefield, S., Churchill, W.W. and Laffel, G. (1991) Quality improvement in a hospital pharmacy department. *Quality Review Bulletin*, Vol. 17, pp. 138–43.

Kobayashi, I. (1990) *20 Keys to Workplace Improvement*. Cambridge, MA: Productivity Press.

Kogan, M., Henkel, M., Joss, R. and Spink, M. (1991) *Evaluation of Total Quality Management Projects in the National Health Service*. Centre for the Evaluation of Public Policy and Practice, Brunel University, November.

Kogan, M., Henkel, M. and Joss, R. (1992a) *A Comparison of Total Quality Management in the NHS and the Commercial Sector, and a Review of Other Approaches to Quality Improvement in the NHS*. Centre for the Evaluation of Public Policy and Practice, Brunel University, May.

Kogan, M., Henkel, M., Joss, R. and Balkwill, C. (1992b) *Developments at National Health Service Total Quality Management Demonstration Sites, Between July 1991 and July 1992*. Centre for the Evaluation of Public Policy and Practice, Brunel University, October.

Kravchuk, R.S. (1992) *Total Quality Management in the States: A 50 State Study*. Boston, MA: American Society for Public Administration (mimeo).

Kuhn, T. (1970) *The Structure of Scientific Revolutions*, 2nd edn. Chicago, IL: University of Chicago Press.

Lewis, B. (1987) Customer care in service organisation. *International Journal of Operations and Production Management*, Vol. 8, No. 3, pp. 67–75.

Liswood, I. (1990) *Serving Them Right: Innovation and Powerful Customer Retention Strategies*. New York: Harper and Row.

Lumsdon, K. (1992) TQM shifts hospital-vendor focus to total value productivity. *Hospitals*, Vol. 66, No. 13, p. 114.

Mastenbroek, W.F.G. (1991) *Managing for Quality in the Service Sector*, Oxford: Basil Blackwell.

Marzalek-Gaucher, E. and Coffey, R.J. (1990) *Transforming Healthcare Organisations: How to Achieve and Sustain Organisational Excellence.* San Francisco, CA: Jossey-Bass.

Masters, F. and Schmele, J.A. (1991) Total quality management: An idea whose time has come. *Journal of Nursing Quality Assurance*, Vol. 5, No. 4, pp. 7–16.

Merry, M.D. (1990) Total quality management for physicians: Translating the new paradigm. *Quality Review Bulletin*, Vol. 16, No. 3, pp. 101–105.

Milakovich, M.E. (1990a) Enhancing the quality and productivity of state and local government. *National Civic Review*, Vol. 79, No. 3, pp. 266–76.

Milakovich, M.E. (1990b) Total quality management for public sector productivity improvement. *Public Productivity and Management Review*, Vol. XIV, No. 1, Fall.

Milakovich, M.E. (1991) Total quality management in the public sector. *National Productivity Review*, Vol. 10, No. 2, Spring, pp. 195–215.

Mills, A.R. and Murgatroyd, S. (1991) *Organisational Rules: A Framework for Understanding Organisational Action.* Buckingham: Open University Press.

Morgan, J. and Everett, T. (1990) Introducing quality management in the NHS. *Journal of Health Care Quality Assurance*, Vol. 3, No. 5, pp. 22–35.

Morgan, J., Everett, T. and Hawley, A. (1992) *Local Strategies for Health: Developing Public Involvement. Guidance Notes.* Welsh Health Common Services Authority.

Morris, B. (1989) Aspects of quality in health care. *International Journal of Health Care Quality*, Vol. 2, No. 4, pp. 25–9.

Mortiboys, R. and Oakland, J. (1991) *Total Quality Management and Effective Leadership.* Department of Trade and Industry booklet. London: HMSO.

Murgatroyd, S. (1989) KAIZEN – school wide quality improvement. *School Organisation*, Vol. 4, No. 2, pp. 171–8.

Murgatroyd, S. (1991) Strategy, structure, and quality service: Developing school wide quality improvement. *School Organisation*, Vol. 9, No. 2, pp. 241–60.

Murgatroyd, S. and Earle, G. (1992) *Total Quality Management and the Public Utility.* London: British Academy of Management (mimeo).

Murgatroyd, S. and Morgan, C. (1993) *Total Quality Management and the School.* Buckingham: Open University Press.

Musfeldt, D.E. and Collier, T.A. (1991) Outlines for improvement of clinical care quality. *Journal of the Society for Health Systems*, Vol. 2, No. 3, pp. 25–43.

National Curriculum Council (1993) Report to the Secretary of State for Education, January.

Neugeboren, B. (1985) *Organization, Policy and Practice in Human Services.* New York: Longman.

Nicholls, B. (1993) *USA Today*, 22 January.

Oakland, J. (1989) *Total Quality Management.* London: Butterworth.

Oakland, J. and Followell, R. (1992) *Statistical Process Control.* Department of Trade and Industry booklet. London: HMSO.

Open University (1987) Course PMT605, Unit 6, *Achieving Quality*, p. 6. Milton Keynes: Open University Press.

Orfield, G. (1991) Cutback policies, declining opportunities and the role of the social service provider. *Social Service Review*, Vol. 65, No. 4, pp. 516–30.

Ormell, C. (1993) Why the NHS needs smooth operators. *Daily Telegraph*, 7 January.

Osborne, D. and Gaebler, T. (1992) *Reinventing Government*. Reading, MA: William Patrick.

Ott, J.S. (1989) *The Organisational Culture Perspective*. Pacific Grove, CA: Brooks-Cole.

Ovreteveit, J. (1990) What is quality in health services? *Health Services Management*, June, pp. 132–3.

Parasuraman, A., Zeithamsi, V.A. and Berry, L.L. (1985) A conceptual model of service quality and its implications for future research. *Journal of Marketing*, Fall, pp. 41–9.

Patti, R. (1987) Managing for service effectiveness in social welfare organizations. *Social Work (USA)*, September, pp. 377–81.

Peters, T. (1989) *Thriving on Chaos*. London: Macmillan.

Pollitt, C. (1988) Bringing consumers into performance measurement: Concepts, consequences and constraints. *Policy and Politics*, Vol. 16, No. 2, pp. 77–88.

Pollitt, C. (1990) Doing business in the temple? Managers and quality assurance in the public services. *Public Administration*, Vol. 68, pp. 77–88.

Porter, M.E. (1990) *The Competitive Advantage of Nations*. New York: Free Press.

Radical Statistics (1991) Vol. 5, pp. 30–33.

Reich, R. (1991) *The Work of Nations*. New York: Knopf.

Reynolds, D.R., Jones, D., St. Leger, S. and Murgatroyd, S. (1980) School factors and truancy. In Hersov, L. and Berg, I. (eds), *Out of School*. London: John Wiley.

Riggs, S.A. (1992) *Managing The Practice*. Nottingham Business School, Nottingham Polytechnic. Paper presented to the British Academy of Management Sixth Annual Conference, University of Bradford, September.

Rose, R. (1990) Charging for public services. *Public Administration*, Vol. 68, pp. 297–313.

Rubenstein, E. (1993) Behind the deficit. *National Review*, 15 February, p. 17.

Rutter, M., Maughan, M., Mortimore, P. and Ouston, J. (1979) *Fifteen Thousand Hours*. London: Open Books.

Samuels, G. (1991) The Q-word in action. *Education*, 22 November, p. 412.

SCANS (1991) *What Work Requires of Our Schools*. A SCANS Report for AMERICA 2000, The Secretary's Commission On Achieving Necessary Skills. Washington, DC: US Department of Labor.

Schmele, J.A. and Foss, S.J (1989) The quality management maturity grid: A diagnostic method. *Journal of Nursing Administration*, Vol. 19, No. 9, pp. 29–34.

Senge, P. (1990) *The Fifth Discipline: The Art and Practice of the Learning Organisation*. New York: Doubleday.

Sensenbrenner, J. (1991) Quality comes to city hall. *Harvard Business Review*, March/April, pp. 65–75.

Shingo, S. (1987) *The Sayings of Shigeo Shingo: Key Strategies for Plant Improvement*. Cambridge, MA: Productivity Press.

Shingo, S. (1989) *A Study of The Toyota Production System*. Cambridge, MA: Productivity Press.

Smith, D.J. and Tomlinson, S. (1989) *The School Effect: A Study of Multi-Racial Comprehensives*. London: Pinter.

Social Service Inspectorate (1990) *Homes for Living In*. Department of Health. London: HMSO.

Social Service Inspectorate (1991) *Inspecting for Quality*. Department of Health. London: HMSO.

Spanbauer, S.J. (1992) *A Quality System for Education*. Milwaukee: ASQC Quality Press.

Spilerman, S. and Litwak, E. (1982) Reward structure and organizational design. *Research on Aging*, Vol. 4, pp. 43–70.

Staubbernasconi, S. (1991) Social action, empowerment and social work: An integrative theoretical framework for social work and social work with groups. *Social Work with Groups*, Vol. 14, Nos 3/4, pp. 35–51.

Steffen, G.E. (1988) Quality medical care: A definition. *Journal of the American Medical Association*, Vol. 260, No. 1, pp. 56–61.

Stewart, R. (1992) Management in the public and private sectors. *Higher Education Quarterly*, Vol. 46, No. 2, pp. 157–65.

Streeter, C.L. (1992) Redundancy in organizational systems. *Social Service Review*, Vol. 66, No. 1, pp. 97–111.

Swiss, J.E. (1992) Adapting total quality managment (TQM) to government. *Public Administration Review*, Vol. 52, No. 4, pp. 356–62.

Taylor, A. and Hill, F.M. (1992) Implementing TQM in higher education. *International Journal of Educational Management*, Vol. 6, No. 4, pp. 4–10.

Taylor, W. (1947) *Scientific Management*. New York: Harper and Row.

Tribus, M. (1992) *Quality Management in Education*. Unpublished manuscript. Hayward, CA: Exergy Inc.

Turem, J.S. (1986) Social work administration and modern management technology. *Administration in Social Work*, Vol. 10, No. 3, pp. 15–25.

Van Der Hart, H.W.C. (1991) Government organisations and their customers in the Netherlands: Strategy, tactics and operations. In Willem, F.G. (ed.), *Managing for Quality in the Service Sector*. Mastenbroek: Blackwell.

Warner Report (1992) *Choosing with Care*. London: HMSO.

Warner, T. (1991) Implementing continuous quality improvement in a hospital. *Business Quarterly*, Autumn, pp. 42–5.

Weir, D. (1992) Organizations in the year 2000: Strategy, skill, pace and timing. Paper delivered to the *British Academy of Management 6th Annual Conference*, University of Bradford, September.

Welsh Office (1990) *A Quality Health Service for Wales*. Cardiff: NHS Directorate.

Welsh Office (1991) *NHS Wales: Agenda For Action 2, 1992–1994*. Cardiff: NHS Directorate.

Wilding, P. (1982) *Professional Power and Social Welfare*. London: Routledge and Kegan Paul.

Williamson, J. (1991) Providing quality care. *Health Services Management*, February, pp. 9–23.

Index